THE SHADOW PRESIDENT

THE SHADOW PRESIDENT

THE TRUTH ABOUT MIKE PENCE

MICHAEL D'ANTONIO
AND PETER EISNER

THOMAS DUNNE BOOKS
ST. MARTIN'S PRESS
NEW YORK

THOMAS DUNNE BOOKS
An imprint of St. Martin's Press

www.thomasdunnebooks.com
www.stmartins.com

Designed by Omar Chapa

The Library of Congress Cataloging-in-Publication Data
is available upon request.

ISBN 978-1-250-30119-2 (hardcover)
ISBN 978-1-250-30120-8 (ebook)

Our books may be purchased in bulk for promotional, educational, or business use. Please contact your local bookseller or the Macmillan Corporate and Premium Sales Department at 1-800-221-7945, extension 5442, or by email at MacmillanSpecialMarkets@macmillan.com.

First Edition: August 2018

10 9 8 7 6 5 4 3 2 1

For Toni and Musha

CONTENTS

ACKNOWLEDGMENTS

With the Trump administration pursuing the sources of news leaks as if they were espionage agents, officials in Washington were quite cautious about speaking to us on the record about events and personalities inside the White House. For that reason, we must offer our gratitude to several sources, including Pence confidants and members of Congress, without mentioning names. Those who shared their insights did so in the interest of establishing an accurate record in a time when even the existence of facts has been cast into doubt. Their efforts stand in contrast to the vice president's aides, who declined repeated requests for even the most basic information.

Among the reliable, on-the-record helpers in Washington we thank retired senator Richard Lugar, former members of Congress Phil Sharp and Baron Hill, Stephen Moore of the Heritage Foundation and former *Indianapolis Star* Washington correspondent George Stutteville.

Our reporting efforts were aided, quite heroically, by Indiana-based journalist Adam Wren and Brooklyn's Victoria DeSilverio, whose way with data is a wonder to behold. Brian Howey, the dean of Hoosier political reporters, was most generous with recollections, advice, and sources. Steven Porter, journalist, shared many sources and perspectives. Cheryl Owsley Jackson opened doors in Columbus, which led us to, among others, Rev. Mike Harris, a high school classmate of the vice president, as well as former Columbus mayors Fred Armstrong and Kristen Brown. Jan Carroll, Jeff Smolyen, and Ambassador Dan Kurtzer were generous with their time and insights.

Other Columbus-area insiders who aided our effort included Tracy Souza, Cummins executive and daughter of Lee Hamilton, who served Indiana as a member of Congress for thirty-four years, and Bob Hyatt of the Bartholomew County Democratic Party. Bud Herron, former publisher of the Columbus *Republic,* shared much of what he knows about his community and its characters. We recommend his writing, especially "Cat Bathing as a Martial Art," which can be read at http://blakjak.org /cat_bath.htm.

We received much valuable insight and advice from Chris Warren of Indy Pride, Mayor James Brainerd of Carmel, Indiana, and from Bill Oesterle, who is one of the state's leading businesspeople. Sherman Johnson, Jim Shella, Ann DeLaney, Ed Delaney, John Krull, and Mary Beth Schneider provided invaluable recollections and insights. Joshua Blachorsky, Orly Azoulay, and Tal Schneider demystified scriptural and political issues arising out of the vice president's activities in the Middle East. Thanks also to Calev Ben-David, anchor at TV i24 in Jerusalem, for his time in discussing Mike and Karen Pence's Israel trip. Just as thorny were the legal issues made understandable by attorneys Jay Jaffe and William Groth. Cole Varga of Exodus Refugee aided our understanding of Governor Pence's opposition to refugee resettlement in Indiana.

As with every book, this one is built upon the foundation of writing done by many others, especially newspaper journalists in Indiana, Washington, and New York, and authors including Jane Mayer, Jeff Sharlet, Julie Ingersoll, Katherine Stewart, Marie Griffith, Nancy MacLean, Frances FitzGerald, and many others.

Our editors of first resort, Musha Salinas Eisner and Toni Raiten-D'Antonio, contributed brilliantly to the cause of this book. At St. Martin's Press we were ably served, and sometimes saved, by publisher Thomas Dunne, editor Stephen S. Power, and assistant editors Janine Barlow and Samantha Zuckergood. A production team headed by John Morrone and Amelie Littell made a tight schedule comfortable, and Michael K. Cantwell proved, once again, to be the best friend authors could want.

Likewise, the publicity and marketing efforts of Tracey Guest, Kathryn Hough, and Laura Clark have assured that the most important people in the publishing world—readers—learn of our efforts.

Finally, we acknowledge our late friend and editor at *Newsday*, Les Payne, whose enthusiasm and encouragement energized our efforts. Les brought us together as a team thirty years ago, and inspired us ever since. In this book, we take to heart his rallying cry for all journalists: "tell the truth . . . and duck."

1

THE SYCOPHANT

Behold, I tell you a mystery.

—*1 Corinthians 15:51*

As noon approached on January 20, 2017, Associate Supreme Court Justice Clarence Thomas summoned Michael Richard Pence before him at the lectern on the West Front of the United States Capitol. Surrounding the two men were politicians, public officials, family, and assorted dignitaries arrayed to form a tableau of democratic tradition. Allies and adversaries, their conflicts and contests set aside for the moment, bore witness to the transition of power.

Pence had chosen one of the most conservative Supreme Court justices in U.S. history to administer his oath of office as vice president of the United States. The symbolism was complete when Thomas directed Pence to place his left hand on Ronald Reagan's Bible, which was held by Pence's wife, Karen. Reagan had been Pence's midwestern hero and role model, even before he had met him briefly twenty-eight years earlier.

"Mr. Vice President elect, would you raise your right hand," said Thomas, though Pence had already done so. The justice grimaced slightly. Known for rarely speaking from the bench or in public at all, Thomas appeared ill at ease. After a pause, he summoned a resonant baritone voice and said, "Repeat after me." The vice president elect did as instructed, swearing that he would "support and defend the Constitution of the United States against all enemies, foreign and domestic. . . . So help me God."

After he finished the oath, the vice president embraced his family, shook hands with some of the assembled luminaries, and then retreated from the center of attention. As he stood beside his wife, Pence struck his humility pose—brow furrowed, mouth downturned, eyes focused on some distant point—as he had on countless public occasions.

For decades, Pence had presented himself as a humble servant who could be entrusted with power because he was, at heart, a mild-mannered midwesterner. Friends and foes alike said his major character trait was extreme niceness. When given the opportunity, Pence described himself as a true "Hoosier" son of Indiana who was "a Christian, a conservative, and a Republican in that order." This is how he had introduced himself to the country at the Republican National Convention six months earlier. The list contrasted with the usual pledge politicians make to put country first. This is what President Obama did after the 2016 election when he said, "We are not Democrats first. We are not Republicans first. We are Americans first."[1]

The vice president's self-declared identity revealed both his priorities and the source of his power. For thirty years he had helped lead the Republican Party into a closer alliance with preachers who were turning evangelical Christianity from a religion into a political crusade that engaged in a culture war against nonbelievers. The aim of many was to destroy abortion rights, roll back the equality gained by gay citizens, and prepare the nation for the Second Coming of Christ.

Pence and others used martial metaphors and considered themselves warriors of the Christian Right, both besieged and called upon to fight. "Those who would have us ignore the battle being fought over life, marriage and religious liberty have forgotten the lessons of history," said Pence in 2010. "America's darkest moments have come when economic arguments trumped moral principles."[2]

Pence's allies in his war included hugely wealthy donors who, despite their vast wealth, accumulated at a time of historic inequality, also posed as victims. As libertarians in the mold of Ayn Rand's cardboard characters they felt inhibited in the pursuit of even greater riches by a government that imposed foolish regulations and would redistribute their wealth to the supposedly indolent poor. Starting with this perspective they denied the science behind environmental protection, demanded tax cuts for themselves, and insisted on massive reductions in programs serving anyone who wasn't rich.

The victimhood claimed by both the libertarians and the Christian Right permitted the construction of an alternate reality that denied their own power and masked their ambition to make politics and culture conform to an ideology that included white Christian supremacy and predatory capitalism. It also denied the progress they had made in their construction of their own political might. With his oath of office Vice President Pence became both the free-marketeers' hero and the most successful Christian supremacist in American history.

Most of Pence's life had been preparation for this moment, and possibly one more. His lifelong goal, set when he was a boy, was the Oval Office itself. Remarkably, he had reached this point by tying his fate to Donald J. Trump, a man whose immorality in the form of lying, cheating, and deceiving in every aspect of his life, from his marriage to his businesses, had made him a living exemplar of everything that Christianity and conservatism abhorred. However, this record also suggested that Pence was more likely to assume the highest office in the land than most vice presidents who had come before. To put it bluntly, Trump was vulnerable to impeachment. If this occurred, Pence would see the hand of God at work in his elevation to the presidency. In the meantime, he would wait, and watch.

On Inauguration Day, with Pence looking on, a slightly stooped Donald Trump stepped forward when it was his turn to face the chief justice of the United States Supreme Court, John Roberts. Beside Trump stood his wife, Melania, the former fashion model, who held two Bibles—Lincoln's and Trump's own. At the stroke of noon, the president-elect raised his right hand and placed his left on the Bibles. As he did this, Trump's family members and hundreds of political and government figures strained to view the moment.

Trump and Pence were a study in contrasts. At age fifty-eight, Pence appeared trim, perhaps even athletic, and could have passed for a man ten years younger. His jacket was neatly buttoned. His hands were clasped at his waist, and his smooth face was set in a half smile. In sum, he resembled a small-town pastor or even a funeral director. Mere feet away, a stern-faced, seventy-year-old Trump stood with his coat hanging open, like a kaftan, to reveal a long red necktie. Despite much cosmetic intervention, he looked old and tired.

At the conclusion of the presidential oath, which had been voiced by forty-four presidents before him, Trump said the words *"so help me God"* and accepted the congratulations of those closest to him with a thin-lipped, toothless grin. He then delivered a fifteen-minute speech replete with the distortions and falsehoods that were his hallmark. He declared that America was awash with crime and despair and under constant attack. "This American carnage stops right here and stops right now," said Trump. It was the most remembered phrase of the address.

"That was some weird shit," former president George W. Bush was heard to remark as he left the inaugural stand.

Weird was the mildest word one could attach to the forty-fifth president of the United States as he launched an administration that would be stained by scandal and corruption so broad it defied a citizen's effort to grasp. Cronyism, secrecy, and nepotism would flourish. Presidential lies, duly catalogued by *The Washington Post* and others, would come at the rate of more than 150 per month.

From the moment of his oath, Mike Pence, the vice president, faced the historic—some would say daunting—challenge of dealing with an erratic and undisciplined commander in chief. From the start, he would seek to be a stabilizing force in a government rocked by presidential whims and mood swings. Pence intended to do this while preserving his own image as a man of calm judgment and rectitude who would be ready to take over as commander in chief should Trump ever leave office.

Fourteen previous vice presidents had risen to the top office. In eight cases, a sitting president died in office. Five vice presidents were elected to the higher office after serving as number two. One, Gerald Ford, took office when Richard Nixon resigned to end the Watergate crisis. Given the strange reality of the Trump presidency, no one could put odds on the chance of a Pence presidency. However, among those who knew Pence, the refrain was "Mike will be ready."

To be ready to succeed the chief executive is a vice president's main duty and one of just three prescribed by the Constitution. The others include presiding over and breaking tie votes in the United State Senate and conducting the quadrennial meetings of the electoral college. Otherwise, vice presidents serve by handling duties assigned to them by the president and sometimes develop their own areas of interest that they pursue with the president's blessing. Al Gore was concerned with technology and environmental policy. Dick Cheney was deeply engaged in national security. The portfolio taken up by Pence would be more wide ranging and include functioning as a kind of minder for a notoriously undisciplined commander in chief.

Throughout his first year at Trump's side, Pence would be a constant, attentive presence who generally spoke only when the president requested it. For weeks at a time, he seemed to have just one major public assignment: admiring Donald Trump. He performed this duty consistently despite the fact that the bellicose and chaotic Trump—he of the infamous "grab 'em by the pussy" videotape—was so personally objectionable that Pence had considered trying to replace him at the top of the ticket as the 2016 election neared.[3] (A Pence aide denied that he had considered doing that.)

Inside the administration, amid the turmoil caused by a record number of dismissals and resignations, Pence proved to be as unflappable as a monument. Like a regent charged with humoring a temperamental boy king, Pence conducted himself in a way that he clearly felt was necessary to maintain the president's trust and preserve his own status. This was a difficult task as the scandal of Russian meddling in the 2016 election, which was being investigated by Congress and special counsel Robert Mueller, grew ever larger and raised obvious questions. What did Pence himself know of the Russian scandal and all the efforts made by the president to stop the investigations? Was he one of Mueller's targets? Could

Pence survive scrutiny if a scandal or crime forced Trump out? Within weeks of Mueller's appointment, Pence hired a criminal defense lawyer to represent him in the probe.[4]

As the year passed and Trump bellowed and brayed, Pence told Republican Party leaders, everyday Americans, and allies abroad that all was well. At the same time, he massaged Trump's ego in a way that was so undignified that it was at once comic and sad. This self-abasement reached a low point on December 20, 2017, when the president invited TV cameras to record the start of a cabinet meeting. The setting was the White House Cabinet Room, where the president's department heads and top advisors gathered around a huge table. The light pouring through the crystalline windows evoked a church in the countryside. After remarking on his own successes and how little credit he had received for them, President Trump sat back in his chair, folded his arms across his chest, and stared at the members of his cabinet like a less-eloquent Lear. Ben Carson, secretary of the Department of Housing and Urban Development, said a prayer that expressed his gratitude "for a president and for cabinet members who are courageous, who are willing to face the winds of controversy in order to provide a better future for those who come behind us."

When Carson finished, Trump looked across the table at Pence, unfolded his arms, and said, "Mike, would you like to say a few words?"

Pence offered about three minutes of impromptu praise in which *The Washington Post* discovered one expression of gratitude or admiration every twelve seconds. Among them were:

"I'm deeply humbled, as your vice president, to be able to be here."
"You've restored American credibility on the world stage."
"You've unleashed American energy."
"You've spurred an optimism in this country that's setting records."

When Pence concluded his praise, President Trump offered up a verbal pat on the head, saying, "Thank you, Mike. That's very nice. I appreciate that."

Pence replied, "Thank you, Mr. President, and God bless you."[5]

The vice president's cringeworthy display, broadcast live on television, prompted an avalanche of mockery. The nonpolitical website Dictionary.com used Pence's remarks in a tweet to illustrate the definition of the word *sycophant*. Late-night TV talk-show host Seth Meyers imagined Pence as a lovesick suitor and Trump telling him, "Dude, I'm married." Conservative pundit Matt Lewis confessed his utter revulsion at Pence's offensive "slavish hero worship." As he puzzled out the vice president's motivation, Lewis considered two possible explanations for Pence's behavior. The first assumed he was so eager to ascend to the presidency that he was willing to humiliate himself to get ahead. According to the other option Lewis contemplated, Pence was so committed to public service, and thus to soothing the dangerously mercurial—some would say unstable—Trump that he considered self-abnegation a patriotic act. Lewis wrote:

> *Could it be that praising Trump is but a small price to pay for keeping the president on the straight and narrow? Perhaps Pence is making the ultimate sacrifice (his dignity!) in order to keep Trump's agenda from veering into the fever swamps of nationalism. James Carville and Paul Begala once observed that "you never stand so tall as when you stoop to kiss an ass." If that's the case, then Mike Pence is a giant among men.*[6]

Lewis's analysis overlooked a significant signal in the final phrase—"and God bless you"—offered by the vice president when he spoke at the cabinet meeting. Easy to regard as a kind of rhetorical tic, like the "God bless America" that presidents tack on to the end of formal addresses, Pence's call to the deity reminded conservative Christians that their champion was alert to his duty. In fact, as one of Pence's closest aides would explain, the vice president actually believed he could bring Trump to Jesus and, like Jesus, he was willing to do whatever was necessary to help save Trump's soul.

Pence was also calling attention to his own piety, which his supporters valued above all his other qualities. Long disappointed by Republicans who appeared to share their faith but failed to create the society they desired, many Christian Right voters had supported Trump—the most profane candidate in modern times—because of Mike Pence. Like them, the vice president imagined America's conservative Christians to be the modern equivalent of ancient Jews exiled to a wilderness that just happened to look like a comfortable, modern society. This is why Pence said, "No people of faith today face greater hostility or hatred than followers of Christ," he said in 2017.

Pence's hope for the future resided in his faith that, as chosen people, conservative evangelicals would eventually be served by a leader whom God would enable to defeat their enemies and create a Christian nation. Devoted to the dream of a nation guided by Christian Right beliefs, his preternaturally serene presence reminded the devout that Trump was the instrument of God and that they—the Jews of this era—were closer to their goal than ever before. This pursuit would be aided by a host of allies, including Trump's election guru, Stephen Bannon, who would use Facebook and other social media as weapons in a "culture war."

Backed by reclusive billionaires Robert and Rebekah Mercer and their firm, Cambridge Analytica (CA), Bannon would disseminate vast amounts of false information intended to motivate conservative Christian voters and discourage their opponents. The ultimate aim of this information warfare (as described by former CA employee Christopher Wylie) was the election of Trump and Pence, who would then roll back the rights of women and gays while empowering religious conservatives and businesses. In the world at large, Trump and Pence were expected to disengage America from broad agreements on trade, environmental protection, and security.[7]

Key to his election, more than 80 percent of evangelical Christians had voted for Trump. This support perplexed those who considered his lifelong record of sex scandals, bankruptcies, and public displays of cruelty, who wondered how this group could stand with him. The question confounded those who assumed that politically active conservative evangelicals applied conventional morality in a consistent way. In fact, their kind of Christianity placed a higher value on the professions of faith and relied on supernatural assumptions to justify political expediency. Descendants of Luther and Calvin, their emphasis on statements of belief over evidence of personal conduct (with faith, all is forgiven) made it possible to overlook the president's massive and widely publicized record of immorality. At the same time, they yearned for protection, as they lived in what they considered to be the wilderness of national affairs.[8]

Among white conservative Christians of Pence's sort, modern developments such as marriage equality for gay and lesbian citizens, made possible by recent Supreme Court decisions, marked them as latter-day versions of the exiled Israelites of the Bible. Despite their vast numbers and influence and their sense that, like the Jews, they were God's "chosen" people, they saw themselves as victims. Their champions were politicians like Pence, who proclaimed their faith as the basis for their policies. Consistent with Luther's theology, they believed that faith made their actions righteous. This contrasted with Aristotle, whose *Ethics* said good deeds make a good man.

Although these leaders could only do so much against the powerful— as governor, Pence had tried but failed to enact policies to permit antigay discrimination—they were nevertheless revered by the faithful. In the White House, Pence could act on their behalf. As the pastor of Pence's church back home in Indiana once explained, the wily Daniel occupied a place "like the vice presidency" and served both God and the king of Babylon. As the king, Trump could be dangerous and disturbing, but the threat was less frightening with Daniel, or rather, Mike, by his side. Besides, if the worst comes to pass, and the world is engulfed by the apocalypse of Bible prophecy, the chosen will be saved.[9]

For more than a century, American evangelicals of various stripes had forecast the arrival of the apocalypse, often on specific dates, only to find life continuing, and even improving, for most people long after the appointed time. Though others would view these missed deadlines as evidence of errors, the mistaken prophets would be forgiven by believers who consider a profession of faith far more important than any accurate predictions about the end of days. In this way, faith became a substitute for facts and permitted believers to assert their superiority even as they proclaimed their humility. In the same way that President Trump insisted his genes made him better than others, this type of Christian assumed extra insights on an ontological basis: faith, rather than might, makes right.

Such a belief permitted the faithful to claim humility in the shadow of God's grace while also feeling just a little (or a lot) superior to others.[10]

Humble superiority had been Pence's default setting during his twelve years in Congress and four as Indiana's governor, where his blending of religion and politics had alienated fellow Republicans, who noted he could be harsh in his treatment of his opponents and stubborn in his beliefs. When Pence denied climate change or questioned the fact that smoking causes cancer, they saw unseemly and irrational arrogance. His disregard for science and other realms of expertise made him more like President Trump than many Americans understood. It was also consistent with the habits of mind that allowed him to tolerate the scandals that plagued the president and those he brought into his administration.

Dogged by three separate investigations into Russian interference in the 2016 election and possible connections to his campaign, Trump had seen four close associates charged with crimes. White House staff had been fired and replaced at an alarming rate. Amid the churn and uncertainty, the unflappable Pence reassured many that should Trump leave office, someone with a steady temperament would be there. Although it was never stated openly, he was already functioning as a kind of shadow president, taking on so many domestic, foreign, and partisan political assignments that he seemed more engaged in serious matters than the TV-addicted president himself.

With few connections in Washington or to the broader Republican establishment, Trump had relied on Pence to populate his administration. The vice president began this work as he headed the group that managed the transition with the Obama administration. Wherever possible, Pence supported the appointment of like-minded Christians such as Scott Pruitt, who was plucked from his post of attorney general of Oklahoma, to be administrator of the Environmental Protection Agency (EPA).

Pruitt had proved his Christian Right bona fides as a state lawmaker who twice proposed laws that would give fathers property rights over fetuses in the mothers' wombs. These efforts failed in the Oklahoma legislature but succeeded in establishing Pruitt as an antiabortion extremist. In his subsequent position as Oklahoma's attorney general, he repeatedly sued the EPA to challenge its regulation of air and water pollution. Like so many on the Trump team, Pruitt would soon be engulfed by controversy over his spending and relationships with lobbyists. However, he was protected by his Christian Right allies and kept signaling his faith by joining Pence at regular Bible study meetings organized for cabinet members. The sessions were organized by Ralph Drollinger, a seven-foot-two-inch former NBA player turned evangelist who had said women with young children didn't belong in state office and that Catholicism "is one of the primary false religions in the world." Among the other regulars at the prayer meetings were Department of Education Secretary Betsy DeVos, Department of Housing and Urban Development Secretary Ben Carson, Department of Agriculture Secretary Sonny Perdue, and Secretary of Health and Human Services Alex Azar. Azar, DeVos, and Perdue were longtime Pence allies.[11]

The prayer meetings demonstrated to the faithful that their votes had produced real change. Likewise, whenever possible, Pence returned to the theme he had sounded during the campaign—that Trump was God's instrument. The theology behind this notion depended on the Calvinist belief that God elects those who will prosper on earth and that their successes prove they are His favorites. Perfectly circular, this idea credits the powerful with spiritual superiority that cannot be called into question. It also indicates that suffering—poverty, illness, et cetera—is a matter of a destiny determined before one's birth. Of course, determining how God works through a person would depend on when one decides to consider an individual. Viewed at the height of his power, Richard Nixon would have seemed to be blessed. Soon after, God's displeasure would have been there for all to see.

Believers who assume that God chooses winners and losers before they are born typically cite a verse from the Bible's book of Jeremiah: "'For I know the plans I have for you,' declares the Lord, 'Plans to prosper you and not to harm you, plans to give you hope and a future.'" The verse is Pence's favorite bit of scripture, and it is written on a plaque he hung over the fireplace in the vice president's residence in Washington. Depending on the day, he could look at it and take solace in the fact that

God had plans for him to prevail after a momentary setback or find support for his belief that a given triumph fulfilled His plan. Either way, he comes out on top without bearing much responsibility.

Although it wasn't likely that Donald Trump could cite Jeremiah, Calvinism dovetailed with his long-standing belief that he was born to greatness. Conservative Christianity gave him the chance to put a less egoistic gloss on this assumption, and whenever he could, Trump tried to demonstrate piety. At Pence's urging, Trump declared May 3, 2018, as a National Day of Prayer and signed an executive order to ensure that the federal government was partnering with faith-based organizations. This initiative stemmed from the belief promoted by Pence and other conservatives that religious freedom was under attack from the Left. Trump's executive order included a dubious passage that also played up a right-wing theme—that the Founding Fathers had sought to protect America as a Christian nation, that "religious people and institutions were free to practice their faith without fear of discrimination or retaliation by the federal government."

Pence also wanted to leave the impression on his religious base that he was drawing Trump toward a life of faith. Pence, who was not very accessible in general media forums, readily discussed Trump's turn to prayer in an interview on the Christian Broadcasting Network (CBN). "There's prayer going on on a regular basis in this White House," Pence said. "And it's one of the most meaningful things to me, whether it's public meetings or not, I've lost count of the number of times that the president has nudged me, or nudged another member of the cabinet and said, 'Let's start this meeting with prayer.'" Pence sat down for the CBN interview on the same day that Trump acknowledged that he had lied about porn actress Stormy Daniels and that he did know his lawyer Michael Cohen had paid a $130,000 hush payment to her just before the presidential election.[12]

In addition to helping Trump name his team, Pence served as a guide on Capitol Hill. Like Joe Biden before him, who complemented Barack Obama's charisma with a deep understanding of Washington's ways, Pence knew the key figures in the House and Senate and could help Trump navigate toward his goals. The Biden comparison reassured those who feared the worst from Trump, but the example broke down when the two men were examined more closely. Both were lawyers, but while Biden had practiced as a public defender and founded his own firm, Pence had worked in the law only briefly on minor civil cases without distinction. Prior to being elected vice president, Biden had been a senator for thirty-six years, during which he chaired both the Foreign Affairs and Judiciary Committees, becoming highly expert in these two areas of government. A tireless worker, Biden sponsored hundreds of pieces of legislation that became law, including the landmark Violence Against Women Act. Pence was a five-term member of the House who had focused on climbing the ladder of party leadership but never chaired a major committee or authored a single successful piece of legislation. Just as many evangelicals believed that worldly success was a matter of God's favor rather than individual effort, Pence made his choice to become a conservative, pro-business, antiabortion Republican, and he trusted God would make him successful.

As politicians, Biden and Pence established vastly different records, but they were even more distinct as personalities. Biden was an openly emotional man who made his feelings plain at every occasion, and he walked Capitol Hill as if it were his hometown neighborhood. He might have been the most popular senator in the chamber in the time when he served and was beloved by Republicans as well as his fellow Democrats. In the House, Pence was considered likeable enough, but he was not personally popular. His guarded manner combined with his assertive push for a leadership post inside the GOP caucus, despite scant accomplishments, caused some members of his own party to keep him at arm's length. Democrats, even those who were on the Indiana delegation, found him inscrutable. When we spoke, Baron Hill, who served with Pence in Congress for four years, struggled to describe the man. "He was never disagreeable," said Hill in 2018. "He was always nice," he added, echoing comedian George Carlin's bitter riff about people who cover their true personalities with a veneer of niceness. "But I can't say I ever saw past the surface to the real Mike Pence."

The real Mike Pence has been elusive, even to many who support him, throughout three decades of public life. Indeed, the word that is used over and over again when people talk about Pence—"nice"—may be the least distinct descriptor that could be attached to any person, place, or thing on earth. However, according to those who know him well, it does apply. Pence is also well practiced at striking a kindly pose. Study a hundred photos of Mike Pence and you'll see the consistent image of a man who has spent a lifetime learning to avoid offense. It is a style that has permitted him to advance generally unpopular political positions— privatization of Social Security, opposition to gay rights, climate change denial—without alienating too many voters.

A pleasing demeanor made Pence popular in some corners of Indiana politics, where recent history is full of congenial characters, but it's certain that the majority of Americans had little knowledge of Pence, let alone of his political views, prior to the 2016 campaign. Even after Donald Trump selected him as a running mate, Pence was recognized primarily for his demeanor and not his policy priorities. Anyone seeking to know more would have to dig into the public record he had established, and even there, the truth of the man would be difficult to see. Except for a nasty losing campaign for Congress, which he openly regretted, and an ill-fated attempt to legalize discrimination against gay and transgender people, Pence had steered clear of controversy. And though he received thousands of notices in Indiana's press, he had submitted to very few extensive interviews. No major magazine or television show had profiled him in depth. No documentarian had recorded his rise. Instead, for years, Pence controlled and executed the construction of his reputation. This he accomplished as the folksy and well-spoken host of *The Mike Pence Show*, airing daily on statewide talk radio, and as an interviewer on a weekly TV program by the same name. Through these broadcasts, which put him on the public airwaves for thousands of hours each year, he won the trust of people for whom he represented not politics or policies but an indistinct country-kitchen, biscuits-and-gravy kind of comfort.

To sort the pieces of Mike Pence and assemble a clear political picture, one must begin with the understanding that in this age of media proliferation, when vast amounts of information are available about most public figures, his comparatively thin record could only be achieved through a series of deliberate choices. Indeed, Pence was, starting in the 1990s, a careful architect of his own bland image. On his statewide radio show, for which few transcripts or recordings could be found, Pence spoke directly to his audience in such a pleasant way that he called himself "Rush Limbaugh on decaf."

In fact, Pence shared many political views with Limbaugh and other talkers who blustered and bullied their ways across the airwaves, but he was so measured and so respectful of others that even his political opponents seemed to forget that he had smeared Democratic incumbent Phil Sharp in a failed attempt to win his congressional seat and used his campaign's checkbook to pay his own personal bills. *That* Mike Pence seemed all but forgotten, replaced by an agreeable fellow whose hair had turned a premature but distinguished white and who, with each broadcast and chamber of commerce luncheon speech, became a more perfect—perhaps *the* most perfect—Republican candidate for national office, one who could appeal to libertarian economic conservatives as well as right-wing Christian social issue voters without fully alienating those independents and Democrats who might vote for a Republican who doesn't scare them.

Pence's demeanor made him appealing to activists who, beginning in the late 1970s, put together large and well-funded efforts to identify, train, fund, and promote future leaders who would dominate politics and policy on the local, state, and national levels. In the beginning, these programs could be divided into distinct parts. One, symbolized by Rev. Jerry Falwell's Moral Majority, pushed a religious agenda—antiabortion, anti–gay rights, pro–school prayer—and organized through churches and religious broadcasters. Funding for this activity and for favored candidates came from TV viewers, church members, and rich family foundations like the Dick and Betsy DeVos Family Foundation, which was built on the Amway home products company. In explaining their giving, Betsy DeVos noted, in 1997:

> *I have decided to stop taking offense at the suggestion that we are*
> *buying influence. Now I simply concede the point. They are right. We*
> *do expect something in return. We expect to foster a conservative*

governing philosophy consisting of limited government and respect
for traditional American virtues. We expect a return on our in-
vestment.[13]

The second part of the modern right-wing movement advocated
extreme free-market capitalism that would most benefit the megarich
companies, business associations, and individuals who financed them. They
wanted to slash taxes and social programs, eliminate regulations, and
crush labor unions. The leading figures in this part of the right-wing movement were the billionaires Charles and David Koch, who had become
two of the richest people in the world via growing family interests in oil,
chemicals, agriculture, and other industries. Long-term political activists,
the Kochs and their allies pursued political influence on a scale not seen
in America since the start of the twentieth century, when corporate
trusts so dominated politics that some members of the United States Senate
were presumed to represent industries—oil, railroads, steel, and so on—
rather than their constituents.

The modern influence game involves entities with names that are
not immediately associated with a vested interest like an oil company. Instead, candidates and officeholders are supported in various ways by such
organizations as the Heritage Foundation, the Cato Institute, the American Legislative Exchange Council, and the State Policy Network, which
all happen to have been supported by the Kochs. As described by historian
Clayton Coppin, who was hired by Koch Industries to research the family
and its activities, entities were given "obscure and misleading names" so
that their true purpose would be hidden.[14]

Despite concerted effort and substantial spending, neither the economic Right nor the Christian conservatives got what they wanted in the
1980s. Eventually, those with libertarian leanings, who objected to the
freedom-limiting social agenda of the religious activists, made an uneasy
alliance with them in the interest of victory. This accommodation saw both
sides stress areas of agreement and downplay points of difference. Election
wins at the state level allowed for gerrymandering of congressional districts, which, in turn, put more federal offices within reach. However, no

matter how much organizing and support the advocates provided, they still required presentable candidates who could win.

In an era when the political parties wielded less power than they had enjoyed historically, highly motivated individuals who could connect with voters on a personal level and were willing to align themselves with interest groups outside of the party represented the future of politics. When he entered politics, Mike Pence was one of a handful of men and women with the profile—ambitious, conservative Christian, free-market oriented, open to unconventional alliances—that made him an ideal Republican of the modern era. When he eventually made it to Congress in 2000, Pence was remarkable as one House GOP freshman who ticked off all of the Christian Right and economic conservative boxes. More typical was Darrell Issa of California, who came from a traditional Republican businessman background and supported gay rights. However, in the years that followed, Pence's Christian brand of GOP politics would gain against Issa's secular type until, by 2018, Issa would announce his retirement from politics and Pence would hold the second-highest office in the land.[15]

Understanding Mike Pence requires an exploration of his origins, a true sense of how he developed into a political figure, and a grasp of the changing context of his time. He defines himself by his religion, his family life, his politics, and his attachment to his home state of Indiana. When assessing his own personality, he often references an old-fashioned sensibility. On a number of occasions, he has called himself "the frozen man." Although he offered the term as a proud description of a person with unwavering respect for eternal values, it also suggests an icy rigidity he has shown with attempts to impose his values, including some associated with America's bigoted past.[16]

Although Pence presents himself as a deeply moral man, his record indicates both a ruthlessness and a comfort with aggression that belie this pose. It is telling that Pence has claimed Charles Colson as his mentor. Colson was the convicted Watergate conspirator who wrote a so-called enemies list for Richard Nixon and proposed firebombing a Washington think tank in order to obtain documents it held. Pence may have embraced

Colson as a "dear friend and mentor" because he had undergone a religious conversion, but it is just as likely that Pence was drawn to Colson's lingering aggressive tendencies. In 1996, decades after Watergate, Colson wrote that a "showdown between church and state may be inevitable" in order to thwart a secular government that was becoming intolerable for conservative Christians.[17]

Colson wrote of the looming showdown as Mike Pence was growing into the role of conservative Christian politician. Pence was helped in this project by many of the same forces—big donors, activist organizations, and new forms of media—that were changing the overall political landscape. He also benefited from the anger and fear of white conservative Christians who felt their status under threat. These Americans saw demographic trends that were rapidly making them into one minority group like so many others, and they felt alienated in a way that activated them as voters. They hungered for the America of an imagined past—more white, rural, heterosexual, and homogeneous—and which Pence seemed to represent. Put simply, Mike Pence might have been able to rise in another time, but the conditions that prevailed when he decided to make politics his life were especially favorable and became even more congenial as time passed.[18]

Pence's religious beliefs impelled his effort to outlaw abortion and to limit equality for gay Americans. It allowed him to smile while embracing political allies whom others found morally repugnant. According to his faith, everything on earth is predestined by God's will. If God chose to make Trump president, then it was fine for Pence to say and do just about anything to support him. It is the self-justifying theology that also enabled Pence to praise former Arizona sheriff Joe Arpaio's commitment to "the rule of law" as he offered support for Arpaio's bid to become his state's next United States senator. He also said he was "humbled" by Arpaio's presence at the rally where he spoke.

Unmentioned by Pence was the fact that Arpaio's sheriff's department had been notoriously aggressive about detaining Hispanics on the suspicion that they were in the United States illegally, and it was abusive to those who were arrested. Arpaio even operated an outdoor prison where conditions were so bad that he once called it a "concentration camp."

When a federal court ordered him to cease detaining people on the basis of their appearance, Arpaio failed to comply and was convicted of criminal contempt. President Trump had officially pardoned him, and this meant that Pence was happy to stand by the former sheriff, who was the living emblem of hostility toward immigrants, and sing his praises.

The occasion moved *Washington Post* columnist George Will, a conservative icon, to declare Pence "America's most repulsive public figure." After noting how Pence was "oozing unctuousness from every pore," Will warned of the danger in his right-wing Christian populism, adding, "Pence, one of evangelical Christians' favorite pin-ups, genuflects at various altars, as the mobocratic spirit and the vicious portion require." (His reference to the "vicious portion" was borrowed from Abraham Lincoln, who had used it to describe those who threatened the institutions of democracy.)[19]

As noted by Will, Pence represented the epitome of religion joined with politics in service to an extreme partisan faction. The combination was the basis for his self-confidence and righteousness, and it served his ambition. By 2017, he was one of the most effective politicians of the twenty-first century, and a contender to one day be president himself. Mike Pence was all these things, and thus a more complex and consequential figure than either his supporters or detractors knew.

2

MODEL CITIZEN

Look to the rock from which you are hewn and to the quarry
from which you were dug.

—*Isaiah 51:1*

The real Animal House fraternity (not the one in the movie) was at Dartmouth College, where it occupied a sturdy redbrick building with a gray slate gambrel roof and five gable windows. Practically bombproof, the building could withstand everything that the frequently drunk young men of Alpha Delta could do to it. In 1959, the year depicted in the film, frat brother Chris Miller witnessed the apex of the Animal House depravity, much of which found its way into his script for the 1978 film, which inspired imitation at colleges and universities nationwide. Young men and women wrapped themselves in bedsheets for drunken "toga" parties. Food fights became staples of campus life. And across America, the sex anthem "Louie Louie" was bellowed in basements and hallways and from open windows.

Phi Gamma Delta, at Hanover College, was no exception to the Animal House mania. With the same architecture, right down to the five dormers on the third floor, the fraternity house itself was practically a replica of Alpha Delta at Dartmouth. And with a squint, the brothers, among them binge drinkers and drug users, could be imagined as Bluto, Otter, Flounder, and the rest. The exception was Mike Pence, a square-jawed, blue-eyed young man with dark, curly hair and a brand of reticence rare in a college boy. In the movie, he might have been the fellow known as Charming Guy with Guitar, who sat on the stairs and strummed for a gaggle of coeds until the manic Bluto smashed his six-string to smithereens. Pence really did play the acoustic guitar for the young women at his college, but the similarities end there. Guitar Guy wasn't an Animal House brother, while Pence was in fact the president of his fraternity when a much recalled moment of truth arrived.

It was evening, and beer flowed from kegs that had been procured with much planning and subterfuge. The Phi Gams were up to some happy mayhem when a nemesis straight out of central casting appeared at the front door. Although the associate dean's arrival threatened trouble, it also sparked excitement as life came to imitate Animal House art. The brothers scrambled to hide the evidence—mostly booze and plastic cups—in the hope of avoiding shame, discipline, and even expulsion. The straight-and-narrow Pence went to the door. If anyone could persuade the dean that nothing was amiss, it was the chapter president. The guy was contemplating the priesthood and so looked the part of the trustworthy young man that all he had to do was lie a little bit—"Oh, no, that keg party was just a *rumor*"—for the sake of his brothers.

Poised to become a hero in the annals of Phi Gam, Mike Pence looked into the face of authority and immediately ratted everyone out. The sneaking around, the booze, and the scramble to cover it up—Pence spilled it all. Maybe he thought confession, if not contrition, would absolve them. It did not. Punishment was severe, as school officials basically grounded the whole crew for months. The Animal House of southern Indiana became a kind of sober house, and Pence became, in the eyes of some, a narc. Administrators rewarded him with a job offer, which he accepted along with his diploma. (He worked for the admissions office for about a year.) Decades later, the outcome shaded the way his friend from college, Daniel Murphy, described Pence to writer McKay Coppins. "Somewhere in the midst of all that genuine humility and good feeling, this is a guy who's got that ambition," said Murphy. He then added that he wondered if "Mike's religiosity is a way of justifying that ambition to himself."[1]

Many politicians have draped themselves in the flag while carrying a cross, but no modern American office-seeker has deployed faith more fully and successfully than Pence. As Murphy spoke, in 2017, his college friend had risen steadily from Indiana congressman to governor to vice president of the United States. All of this he had accomplished while performing as a middling lawmaker and stumbling so badly as governor that despite his party's big advantages in registration and money, his reelection was in doubt.

Except for the comically ill-prepared Sarah Palin, who ran and lost with John McCain in 2008, Pence had been the least qualified and least known GOP running mate since Spiro Agnew joined Richard Nixon's ticket in 1968. More remarkably, his ballot mate, Donald Trump, was widely regarded as temperamentally unqualified. But though Trump and Pence presented consistently opposing personas—the big-city vulgarian and the small-town squire—they were alike in essential ways. Each had identified national constituencies that were too small to win an election but so rabid that they couldn't be shaken from their commitment. In Pence's case, the core group almost entirely comprised politically conservative evangelical Christians. Trump appealed to antiestablishment voters—he also called them "uneducated"—who had special disdain for elite politicians and the people who voted for them. Both men devoted so much effort to the construction of a façade that these coverings—presented through the mass media—mattered more than the substance of their ideas or their governing skill. Trump held seemingly random and changeable positions on important issues and had never served in government. And while he offered himself as champion of the working class, his economic policies skewed heavily toward the elite. Pence was a long-serving elected official but so inept as a legislator that he couldn't even get his colleagues to support a bill he sponsored to outlaw child pornography.[2]

(Pence's aides had anticipated criticism of his record in Congress and prepared a written response, never released to the public, but obtained by the authors. It cites his advocacy on behalf of his constituents and the praise he had received over the years, from special-interest organizations including the Chamber of Commerce, the Club for Growth, and the American Conservative Union. "Mike has advocated tirelessly for Hoosiers who have been victims of natural disasters, including ice storms, floods and drought, to receive federal assistance to help get them back on their feet," the report noted. It did not describe any successful legislative initiatives.)

In addition to the effort they put into image-building, Trump and Pence, each in his own way, had a remarkable ability to build and maintain a convincing self-image. For Pence, as with Trump, the construction project began in childhood, when he showed a certain natural charm and social skill that would carry him through life. While Trump had pushed and shoved and bullied his way into the public eye by whatever means necessary, including promoting his own sex scandal in the tabloid press, Pence was a well-mannered, conventionally ambitious sort. And where Trump squarely fit the boisterous P. T. Barnum American stereotype, Pence was Sinclair Lewis's George F. Babbitt grown to enormous proportions—the humble man of the Midwest who commits to the American dream, understands how he is supposed to achieve it, and strives to be satisfied with the pursuit.

Considered through the unfocused lens of family legend and lore, Mike Pence seems a rough blend of ethnic stereotypes. Unlike Trump, whose surname was originally Drumpf and who falsely claimed to be Swedish, Pence was certain of his roots. The U.S. chapter of his father's German/Lutheran clan, originally called Bentz, starts with an early eighteenth-century immigrant named Michael, who joined a tide of Germans drawn to the Pennsylvania colony by its liberal acceptance of religious and political refugees. Michael Bentz crossed the Atlantic aboard the British ship *Loyal Judith* in 1732 and settled in the German community of Lancaster, Pennsylvania. The first change in the family name came upon his arrival in Philadelphia, where a local official spelled it "Pents." By the time Michael married another German immigrant, Anna Elizabeth Huber, in May 1738, he was going by "Pence." Nine months later, Anna and Michael had a son, their only child, who was also named Michael.

As frontier farmers, the first few generations of Pences moved to various towns in Pennsylvania, Virginia, Ohio, and Iowa. Hardship was

common. Anna Elizabeth died at age twenty-nine. Another Pence
drowned when his horse bolted off a ferry crossing the Ohio River. The
vice president's grandfather, Edward Joseph Pence, became a wealthy
stockbroker in Chicago. Their grandfather was "a very hard man," according to Mike Pence's brother Gregory, because grandfather Edward
had denied his namesake son, the vice president's father, any help with
college tuition. A loan from an aunt helped, but money problems forced
Edward Jr. to drop out of law school. He served in the army, fought in the
Korean War, and then with his young wife, Mary Jane Cawley, moved to
Columbus, Indiana, where he partnered in a business that sold oil products and operated gas stations and convenience stores.

Although the family carried a German surname, the Irish side dominated its identity. Mike Pence would speak often of his Irish heritage,
and it was his Irish American grandfather who became most important
to him among his extended family. The Pences were Irish American
because of the vivacious Mary, who occupied the center of homelife and
was the main influence on the children. Distinctly Irish in her wit and
sociability, she was popular and admired, and she set the standard for her
children to meet.[3]

Edward Joseph Pence met the slender, auburn-haired Mary Jane Cawley
in a bar in Chicago. A young woman four years younger than her suitor,
her own family's immigrant tale had begun with her father's dream of a
better life, free of the poverty and violence of Ireland. Twenty years old
when he decided to emigrate, Richard Michael Cawley, known as Mike,
was the third of six children. He had been raised in a small stone cottage
planted on a hillside at a country crossroads called Doocastle, about fifteen miles south of what eventually would become the border between
the Irish Republic and Northern Ireland. His father was a tailor.

Although too young to serve in World War I, Cawley had lived
through the violence that began in 1919 with the Irish war for independence. Tubbercurry, the market town closest to Doocastle, was a hotbed
of rebellion. Men from the town and surrounding farms joined so-called
flying columns, which freed prisoners, burned public buildings, and attacked police. After one battle in which a police inspector was killed, Brit-

ish forces, aided by a civilian militia known as the Black and Tans, went on a rampage and burned several buildings, including a church. Although Ireland won independence with the treaty of 1921, fighting continued as factions vied for control. Cawley joined the Free State army force that battled with former comrades and others who had opposed the treaty.[4]

Like many of his fellow soldiers, Cawley was troubled about fighting fellow Irishmen and he was ambivalent about serving in a force he had felt pressured to join. He eventually decided to leave Ireland for the coalfields of Lancashire, England. He lived in Ashton-in-Makerfield and worked in a pit mine where coal was dug by hand, carted behind horses, and loaded on trains for shipment to the industrial hub of Manchester. It was grueling labor in conditions where the dangers included the ever-present threat of a stray spark causing natural gas or coal dust to explode. In neighboring Haydock, a pit mine explosion had killed more than two hundred men and boys in 1878. The risk Cawley undertook in the mines was comparable to the risk he had faced in Ireland. Naturally, like so many young men in that place and time, he was drawn to the idea of America. When he told his mother, her words to him, handed down through generations, were: "There's a future there for you."

With money sent by a brother, James, who was already in New York, Cawley bought a one-way ticket on the RMS *Andania*, a single-stack Cunard steamer that sailed from Liverpool on March 31. Unlike Cunard's speedy *Mauretania*, which could cross the Atlantic in five days, the *Andania* wasn't a swift vessel and didn't arrive at New York Harbor until Wednesday, April 11, 1923.

On the day of Cawley's arrival, the sky was clear, winds were calm, and a warming sun was coaxing the gardens at Ellis Island to life. *The New York Times* reported on its front page the killing by Irish Free State forces of a key leader among a dwindling army of rebels. The local news included an item that suggested sectarian strife could be found in Cawley's new homeland too. PROMISE TO UNMASK KU KLUX IN JERSEY, read a headline about the arrest of Ku Klux Klansmen who had recently set four large crosses ablaze on the New Jersey Palisades overlooking New York.[5]

The Klan represented the extreme edge of a national anti-Catholic/anti-immigrant campaign, which was given legitimacy by mainstream intellectuals who promoted what was called "scientific racism" in such influential books as Madison Grant's *The Passing of the Great Race*. Grant and others ranked nationalities on what was clearly a color scale, with so-called Nordics at the top and Africans at the bottom. His book, which Adolf Hitler came to call "my Bible," would eventually be discredited as a work of pseudoscience, but in the 1920s, it guided new race-based immigration policies, which favored Protestant Europeans and gave groups like the Klan some legitimacy.[6]

The greatest opposition to racial extremism could be found in northern cities like New York where the Klan was answered with anti-masking laws and protests organized by groups including the Catholic Knights of Columbus. Three days after Mike Cawley set foot in New York, a Catholic newspaper editor, Patrick Scanlon, confronted John H. Moore, a preacher who had come to Queens from Dallas to promote his anti-immigrant, anti-Catholic version of Americanism. As Moore tried to rouse the crowd, he was met with silence. Scanlon, who jumped up to denounce him, was cheered. Moore departed under police protection.

With anti-immigrant and anti-Catholic sentiment high, Irish newcomers like Cawley were caught in a cultural and political crossfire. In 1921, Republicans had moved Congress to establish tighter limits on arrivals from newly free Ireland and most other countries. (Mexico was exempted so farmworkers could move freely.) As ships were turned away from American ports, immigration fell by 50 percent. However, lawmakers eager to make America whiter and more Protestant had kept the door open for people coming from Great Britain. When Cawley was admitted at Ellis Island, his last known address, in England, might have helped him pass through.

Leaving his brother James, who stayed in New York, Mike went to Chicago, where he would discover a big, century-old Irish American community on the South Side. Although Irish Americans dominated politics and civil service, the South Siders were resisting newcomers, including black migrants from the South, who wanted to live in the area. Four years prior to Cawley's arrival, thirty-eight people were killed in rioting between the two groups. Afterward, an uneasy peace reigned, but competition for housing and for jobs at the sprawling stockyards remained intense.

In Chicago, Mike Cawley discovered that locals had their own versions of Irish drinking songs and identified themselves according to the Catholic parish they attended. There he would meet his future wife, Mary Elizabeth Maloney, who was four years his junior. A teacher whose own parents had come to America from Doonbeg, County Clare, Mary Elizabeth married Mike in 1931. By 1932, they had two daughters, Ann and Nancy—the vice president's mother. Mike would work as a streetcar and bus driver, earning enough to support his family in a crowded slum neighborhood called Back of the Yards.

The "yards" were the vast and infamous stockyards of Upton Sinclair's 1906 novel *The Jungle*, where cattle, pigs, and sheep were slaughtered at a rate of one million per year and workers labored in what Sinclair called an "inferno of exploitation." (Winston Churchill wrote a glowing review; Jack London called it the *Uncle Tom's Cabin* of "wage slavery.") *The Jungle* accomplished more for meat safety than for workers and the Back of the Yards. However, shortly after Cawley settled there and his daughters were born, activist Saul Alinsky began collaborating with Catholic clergy to organize workers. After a violent struggle—Alinsky's car was shot up—a strong union was installed at the yards and pay and conditions improved. He then helped ethnic groups set aside their differences to form a community council that gradually transformed Back of the Yards into a middle-class community. Though demonized as a communist or a socialist, Alinsky rejected both philosophies, saying, "I've never joined any organization—not even the ones I've organized myself." His work involved prodding the poor toward improving their own lives and then moving on.[7]

As life in Back of the Yards improved, Cawley finally decided to become a citizen, taking the oath in 1941. He became a Franklin Roosevelt/John F. Kennedy Democrat whom relatives in Ireland regarded as a "real Yank," but he retained a touch of a brogue throughout his life and recalled enough Gaelic to teach his grandson Michael Richard to recite the Gaelic version of Humpty Dumpty. Young Mike Pence didn't speak until he was three but soon demonstrated his grandfather's gift for gab.[8]

Mike Pence was the third of six siblings—four boys and two girls—and was born in Columbus in 1959. His mother, Nancy Cawley Pence, was a charming, sociable, and well-liked homemaker. His father, whose law school dreams had been dashed, went to work as an executive in the Kiel Brothers business, first in Indianapolis but then to the small central Indiana town, about forty-five miles south of the capital. The city-bred Nancy hated Columbus at first but adjusted well to this new life. The Pences lived first in a new subdivision built to accommodate the demand created by veterans who were starting families and needed housing. Built at a cost of $12,000, the squatty brick ranch house at 2744 Thirty-first Street had three bedrooms, one and a half baths, and an attached garage set on less than a quarter acre. The tiny backyard ended where a vast cornfield began. To the east, a winding stream called Haw Creek, once home to otters and still fascinating to adventurous children, made its way south toward the Flatrock River. A few blocks south of the subdivision, U.S. Route 31 led to downtown Columbus. This highway, which began at the Canadian border, connected the heart of agricultural America from Mackinaw on Lake Michigan to Mobile on the Gulf of Mexico. (Today, the road can be seen as a strand that links politically conservative "red" America from north to south.)

As with many who lived along Route 31 at the time, though, the Pences were Democrats who would gradually follow their conservative social values into the Republican Party. Homelife was based firmly in the 1950s, not in the 1960s. Greg Pence, one of Mike's older brothers, would recall for Jane Mayer of *The New Yorker* that the Pences whipped their children with a belt if they lied, demanded that they stand when an adult entered the room, and expected them to remain silent at table.

Perhaps because of the strict discipline, by every outward sign, the Pences were an ideal family. Ed Pence was a community leader whose firm sponsored Little League teams and made sure locals were well supplied with heating oil and gasoline even in the midst of the Arab oil embargoes of 1967 and 1973. Ed Pence did have the habit of getting tickets for speeding and errant driving, which earned him occasional mention in the local newspaper. He once also reported to police that one of his credit cards and a coat were stolen at the local Holiday Inn, and another time that the tires of his car had been slashed while parked at home. Nancy Pence was locally famous for organizing community events at the private Harrison Lake Country Club. She served for years as den mother for Cub Scouts Pack 3 and was an officer of the Modern Home Demonstration Club.

Created by the U.S. Department of Agriculture, Modern Home clubs were intended to promote public health and social stability and establish a link between the federal bureaucracy and families across America. The government provided members with program ideas, materials, and even a creed that required members to pledge themselves "to create a home which is morally wholesome, spiritually satisfying, and physically healthful and convenient." The Moderns, as members were called, used USDA materials to coach one another on home economics— Space Savers for Kitchens was one topic of interest. Nancy Pence often hosted the club at her home and offered history lessons on the regular Song of the Month. In 1962, at the height of the Cold War, she gave a presentation on radiation exposure and family health.

Radiation worries aside, the Pence family enjoyed the good life. After Ed Pence became part owner of Kiel Brothers, the family left their modest one-story home for a much bigger house in Parkside, an upper-middle-class Columbus neighborhood. One more move brought them to a seven-bedroom house, which, at five thousand square feet, was three times the size of the median newly built American home and set on one and a half acres. In this same time period, the Pences showed up in the local paper's pre-Christmas features on a regular basis. PENCE CHILDREN SHOPPING WITH OWN MONEY was the banner headline across the top of page 39 of *The Republic* two days before Christmas 1972. Other years, readers learned of the Pences' holiday trips to Chicago to visit relatives and their stay-at-home Christmases when Mike would play the role of Santa Claus and the whole crowd—Ed, Nancy, and six children—would sit down to a home-cooked turkey dinner.

A handsome clan filled with six bright and outgoing kids, the Pences may have been the closest one could get to a Columbus, Indiana, version of the Kennedys. Like matriarch Rose Kennedy, Nancy Pence was a demanding, even tough parent. (One of Mike Pence's peers would describe her as "a nice lady who you also knew would take you outside and kick your ass if you did something she didn't like.") Nancy encouraged her children to make the family proud. They all succeeded, though Mike was the star. In 1966, seven-year-old Mike walked the runway at the downtown Crump Theatre, modeling outfits for the Tempo department store spring fashion show. In 1972, Mike appeared before the local chapter of the Optimist Club, which met at a shopping center cafeteria, to compete in a debate contest. Combining the boosterism of the Gilded Age and the metaphysics of nineteenth-century spiritualists, the Optimists were founded in 1911. The first chartered chapter was in Indiana. The organization's ten-point philosophy was a forerunner of Rev. Norman Vincent Peale's *Power of Positive Thinking*, which would be embraced by the future president Donald Trump. The Optimists' credo called on members "to look at the sunny side of everything and make your optimism come true." Club members were implored to "forget the mistakes of the past and press on to the greater achievements of the future" while offering "every living creature you meet a smile."[9]

At the debate contest one of young Mike's competitors, Monica Gratz, deviated a bit from the Optimists' creed. She spoke about civil rights issues, recommending *Black Like Me*, a popular book at the time by John Howard Griffin, a white journalist who had his skin darkened temporarily to pass as a black man and described his experience in the Deep South. She won the girls' division despite the controversial theme. Pence, hewing to the spirit of the Optimist Club, focused on the world's problems and declared his generation ready to solve them. He won the boys' prize and went home with a silver-colored trophy.[10]

Mike Pence's trophy-winning optimism was consistent not only with the club that sponsored the debate but also with his family's ethos of sunny expectations. Their happiness was reinforced by their deep involvements in the life of St. Columba Roman Catholic Church, where the sacraments offered the promise of spiritual renewal and various lay organizations filled a social calendar. The children attended parochial school through eighth grade, and all the Pences did volunteer work for the parish and its various organizations. The male Pence children were altar boys, and Mike eventually became president of the Catholic Youth Organization (CYO). While in office, his main initiative was a lawn-mowing/weed-cutting project intended to eliminate hiding places for virus-carrying mosquitoes. He devised it after learning that mosquitoes transmitted encephalitis and that infants, like his youngest sister, were especially vulnerable. The tender heart that motivated Mike Pence to defend the babies of Columbus from mosquitoes also moved him to join a group of high schoolers who volunteered to help care for two brothers named Mark and Mike Reardon, who had muscular dystrophy. Mark and Mike Reardon both died before they reached nineteen.[11]

Between the CYO, school, and all the activities St. Columba offered, Mike Pence and his siblings had a sense of belonging and opportunities to excel. In general, the church sheltered local Catholics from religious prejudice in a region where an old-fashioned evangelical Protestantism predominated. "We were discriminated against," said Nancy Pence when she was interviewed by Jane Mayer of The New Yorker. Gregory Pence would recall that bigoted kids had thrown rocks at him simply because they knew he went to St. Columba.

Anti-Catholic sentiment had a long history in southern Indiana. It had surged in the 1920s when one in five male adults in Columbus belonged to the Ku Klux Klan (KKK), which marched against blacks, Jews, and Catholics and advocated for a white, Protestant, American-born country. For a brief period in the middle of the decade, the election of a Klansman governor had given the KKK control of state government. This reign ended when newspapers reported allegations of sexual assault made against the state's top Klan leader. Although scandal eroded the Klan's political power, it continued to terrorize black citizens. In 1930 thousands of white Hoosiers attended the lynching of two black men—Thomas Shipp and Abram Smith—in the farm town of Marion. Arrested on charges of rape and murder, the men were dragged from jail by members of a mob who had used sledgehammers to break through the walls of the building. The hanging, abetted by police, inspired the lyrics to the song "Strange Fruit," made famous by Billie Holiday. No one was charged in the lynching, which was witnessed by a substantial portion of Marion's population and documented by a photographer who worked ten days straight to print enough photos, on postcards, to meet the demand for souvenirs. The Marion spectacle was the last lynching in the state, but KKK activity continued into the 1970s.[12]

The Klan was active in Columbus in 1975, eight years after the Supreme Court struck down so-called anti-miscegenation laws in *Loving v. Virginia*. A cross was planted on an interracial couple's front yard there, with the words RACE MIXING IS A DISEASE scrawled on it. In 1977, Klansmen patrolled the border with Mexico as self-appointed citizen security officers, and forty members of the organization rallied in front of the courthouse in Columbus. Counterprotesters gathered to reject their message that day, and the KKK presence was an affront to the man who occupied the most important address in town, which sat in view of the landmark building. Built to be a dry goods store in 1848, 301 Washington Street is a two-story, redbrick building that became a bank before it was repurposed as an office for J. Irwin Miller, chairman and president of the most important corporation in the region, Cummins Engine Company.

At once a capitalist and a progressive social engineer, Miller was the man most responsible for creating, in Columbus, a widely held belief in the city as an ideal place populated by good people like the Pences and others who presented to the world a well-polished and wholesome image. Everyone in Columbus, including schoolchildren such as Mike Pence, knew about his benevolence and public service. Businesspeople and politicians alike understood that his support could yield great benefits and his opposition was practically the kiss of death any ambition.

Miller dedicated much of his personal fortune to the task of making Columbus a better place. Along the way, he became a power broker who determined much of what could and couldn't happen in the city. He was able to do this because, under his leadership, Cummins became a global, industrial powerhouse that provided the cash he needed to carry out his mission. In true midwestern style, Miller maintained a low-key, even modest public profile and avoided the spotlight. All the while he showed that a strong local leader could use his money to shape not only a physical landscape but also the social and political reality of the people who inhabit it.

Until 1967, Joseph Irwin Miller was essentially two men, and neither was very widely known. The first Miller, call him the Wall Street Miller, prowled the precincts of power in New York, where both his midwestern charm and his education at Yale (he majored in Greek and Latin) and

Oxford were recognized as great assets. He was a Yale trustee and served on the boards at AT&T, Chemical Bank, and Equitable Life Assurance. Miller raised money for Dwight Eisenhower but was friendly with Lyndon Johnson, funded civil rights organizations and, as president of the mainline National Council of Churches, supported Rev. Martin Luther King Jr.'s 1963 March on Washington. (Miller, having abandoned the church where his grandfather had preached against other forms of Christianity, advocated interreligious understanding.)

The other Miller, call him the Main Street Miller, had transformed a modestly successful family business, Cummins Engine Company, into an industrial giant with licensing deals and new plants around the world. By the 1960s, the company was selling engines for trucks, ships, farm equipment, and other purposes in more than ninety countries. At the same time, Miller created and quickly expanded the Cummins Foundation, which began to fund local charities, cultural institutions, and scholarships. The foundation supplied low-cost financing for the local school system, bought equipment for the fire department, and most notably brought in world-renowned architects, including I. M. Pei, Eero Saarinen, Robert A. M. Stern, César Pelli, and others. These architects created a showcase of more than three dozen public buildings and houses of worship. This baby boom–era construction that was followed by the end of World War II brought significant development; Columbus's population more than doubled from about twelve thousand to twenty-six thousand from 1945 and 1970.

Adding public art, like Henry Moore's huge bronze arch, and parks designed by great landscape architects, Miller arranged Columbus in the way that a boy might arrange the layout of a model train set. When locals wanted more recreation options, he gave them a municipal golf course fashioned by the preeminent designer Robert Trent Jones. When housing grew scarce, he purchased 1,200 acres of farmland, pasture, and woods and created a planned community, including the most expensive new construction in the region, built around three man-made lakes.

In every instance, Miller made sure his efforts provided opportunities for all, regardless of race, religion, or politics. In this sense, he counterbalanced one of Indiana's other great engines of social action, the John

Birch Society of Indianapolis, which was founded in 1958 by two immensely wealthy men, Robert Welch and Fred C. Koch. (Koch's sons David and Charles would later build the most formidable private political network in the country.) The Birch Society promoted paranoid conspiracy theories, including one that insisted that communists controlled President Eisenhower, Chief Justice Earl Warren, and almost everyone else in government. This was an embarrassment to Miller and Indiana's other more sober leaders.

As word of Miller's efforts extended beyond Indiana, journalists, academics, government officials, and politicians came to his Athens on the Prairie to study what he had accomplished. This attention eventually led *Esquire*, then one of the most influential magazines in the country, to place a photo of Miller on its cover with the headline THIS MAN OUGHT TO BE THE NEXT PRESIDENT OF THE UNITED STATES. Inside, a long article illustrated with fifteen photos—Miller on a private jet, Miller at the New York Stock Exchange, and so on—exclaimed that the American cognoscenti, including Mayor John Lindsay of New York City, wished Miller would run for office. "He's one of the great people of this world," said Lindsay.

At home in Columbus, Miller's star turn in a national magazine became a point of pride, and fifty years later, locals still cited the endorsement as evidence that their city had been formed and led by a civic genius. In the twenty-first century, people in Columbus extolled Miller's early leadership in race relations and recounted how, beginning in the 1950s, Cummins had opened its doors to African American factory workers and actively recruited black executives. By the 1970s, when this effort was well under way, Columbus and the larger Bartholomew County remained among the least integrated places in America. Blacks in the 1970 census represented 513 out of 27,547 people—less than 2 percent of the population. With Miller's efforts at recruiting blacks at Cummins, the black population of Columbus had tripled forty years later.

Although he was civic-minded and thought that diversity was a public good unto itself, Miller also thought that his efforts were good for business. Cummins benefited from his efforts to make the community more welcoming to outsiders. He readily admitted that his effort to make

Columbus a "forward thinking" community helped Cummins hire business, legal, engineering, and manufacturing professionals recruited from
around the world. People who came to interview for positions inspected
the schools, neighborhoods, and amenities, liked what they discovered,
and happily settled in what they imagined to be an ideal place. Miller also
profited personally from projects like an upscale housing development
called Tipton Lakes, which he built on the outskirts of the city.[13]

Thanks to Miller and the ethos he created, Mike Pence grew up in a city
dedicated to progress: good education, public art, and architectural master-
pieces made possible by J. Irwin Miller. Yet Columbus was a company
town, and the days proceeded as they did in countless small midwestern
cities. Shift times at Cummins set the pattern for local traffic on work-
days, while church services determined the rhythm of life on Sundays.
Civic and fraternal organizations, including the Lions Club, Loyal Order
of Moose, Knights of Columbus, and Kiwanis, thrived, and the local
papers, *The Herald* and *The Republic*, were filled with reports on school
activities and Little League scores. One of the biggest developments in
the city was the construction of a second high school, opened in 1972 to
accommodate expanding enrollments. At that moment, a rivalry was established between what were then named Columbus North and Columbus East. Students at East, who were sent to the new school, thought the
crosstown kids looked down on them. In a state where basketball games
were practically blood feuds, East's first victory over North was such a big
event that more than forty years later, people who had been there still got
excited talking about the game.

Mike Pence entered North High School and tried to succeed as an
athlete. According to his own estimate, Pence was overweight by fifty
pounds but this claim may be a latter-day legend devised to show he had
triumphed over adversity. In fact, a review of the publicly available photos casts doubt on this claim. According to his own estimate, he barely
made the football team. (His standard, self-deprecating quip about this
experience—"I was one grade above the blocking sled"—was something
he would start saying in 1988 and keep saying for decades.) Fortunately
for Pence, North was a big school with lots of extracurricular activities.

He joined the student newspaper as a cartoonist and showed some flair for drawing panels that featured a recurring everyman character named Mortimer who got into the kind of trouble that a good boy like Mike Pence generally avoided. The creation of Mortimer gave Pence a bit of local notoriety. The debate club made him almost famous.

High school debaters like to say their game is football for nerds, which means it is a highly competitive endeavor that requires poise, quick reflexes, and more aggression that a casual observer might imagine. Like that rare high schooler who can throw a football fifty yards, Mike Pence was a natural and already accomplished before he ever enrolled at North. Carefully dressed for each debate—one outfit was a denim leisure suit with a wide collar and an attached belt—he was remarkably composed. In middle school, he did so well in an Optimists' debate that he advanced to a regional competition. When he reached the high school team, he finished near the top in competitions all over the state.

Each debate experience helped Pence grow more confident in his skill; he discovered which methods worked and grew more knowledgeable about the subjects assigned, which generally revolved around civics—the Constitution was a popular topic—and current events. One of Mike's favorite resources was an odd little book called *Growth and Development of the American Constitution*, a self-published volume by a Columbus-born author whose future works would include *Apocalypse: The Revelation—A Historical Rendition*. Intended as a junior college textbook, *Growth and Development of the American Constitution* never entered wide circulation, but Mike Pence read it over and over, and it informed his debate presentations.[14]

Nothing a high schooler might try would be better preparation for a life in politics than the debate club. Pence's success also brought a measure of local fame for him and his family, as each top finish produced at least a snippet in the newspaper, which often reported he was the "son of Mr. and Mrs. Edward Pence." By his senior year at North High School, Mike apparently had shed the excess pounds he claimed to have brought with him from middle school and grown his wavy hair out so that it fell over his ears. In a school where the big men on campus were athletes, he was invisible to classmates like Mike Harris, captain of the football team, who would say, "I didn't really know who he was." But among the earnest nerds, Pence did stand out. He was so self-confident that he ran for class president and actually won. (Pence began to mention to classmates that he might one day become president of the United States.) His gift for public speaking earned him the emcee's spot in the annual talent show, and when he won the state championship in public speaking, the Kiwanis Club asked him to give a talk at its weekly meeting. Finally, at the end of his senior year came a trip to Seattle and a national tournament. The Optimists, Kiwanis, Cummins Engine Company, and others contributed to pay for a teacher to accompany him.

With more than five hundred competitors accompanied by teachers and coming from every state, the scene in Seattle resembled a national spelling bee. When a virus attacked, afflicting many of the competitors with fever and other symptoms, the drama of the event increased. Though so sick his coach, Deborah Shoultz, reported he almost collapsed "after every round," he finished third in one category—impromptu speech—and returned a hometown hero.

Like most young people, Mike Pence wavered in his ambitions, one moment imagining he might get into politics and the next considering broadcasting. Whatever his choice, he knew he would do well to stay in his father's good graces. When his older brother Gregory had come home from college and opted to sleep in rather than get up for Sunday mass, Ed Pence suddenly decided to stop helping to pay his son's tuition. This decision replicated what the elder Pence had experienced himself, when his own strict father refused to support his education. "He was black and white," Gregory Pence told Jane Mayer. "You were never confused where you stood."

When it came time for him to apply to colleges, Mike Pence thought about attending Indiana University, but when he sought advice from a local radio host, he was encouraged to consider smaller schools. He wound up at Hanover, a 1,100-student liberal arts school affiliated with the Presbyterian Church. Founded in 1827 at the time of religious fervor known as the Second Great Awakening, the college was initially a seminary and would maintain its conservative Christian culture. Fraternities and sororities dominated campus life, further reinforcing the traditional feel of the place. Pence joined Phi Gamma, became house president in his sophomore year, and made the fateful keg party decision that signaled where he stood when it came to choosing between his frat brothers and the campus authorities.

Already a very well-behaved and religious young man when he arrived at Hanover, Pence became even more serious about his faith. On his weekly walk to and from Catholic services, he talked with a friend about becoming a priest. Then, in the spring of his freshman year, he went on a weekend trip to Wilmore, Kentucky, outside Lexington, where the tiny Asbury Theological Seminary hosted an annual Christian music festival. Named after the Greek symbol for fish, which stands for Jesus' work as a fisher of men, the Ichthus Festival had begun in 1970 and regularly attracted more than ten thousand attendees. Many were high school students whose parents permitted them to attend what was billed as the Christian Woodstock because, unlike the original festival in upstate New York, Ichthus promised a (mostly) drug-free, sex-free experience.

At Ichthus, Pence heard conservative Christianity's answer to pop rock and folk music. The bill included Daniel Amos, a band that was moving away from a country-inflected style to a rock-and-roll sound, and Phil Keaggy, who began his career in 1960s mainstream music, where he had real success. After a hiatus, during which he lived in a cultlike Christian commune, he returned to performing but focused on evangelical-themed music. The headliner at Ichthus '78 was Larry Norman, regarded as the Bob Dylan of Christian music. Like Keaggy, Norman had played secular music and was so successful that he had opened for the likes of the Doors and Jimi Hendrix. When his group, People!, failed to advance after its only hit single, a cover of the Zombies' song "I Love You," Norman became a salaried songwriter at Capitol Records, experienced a spiritual conversion, and began walking the streets of Hollywood to discuss his faith with whomever he met. In 1978, Norman was at the top of his career as a Christian artist and would soon play on the lawn of the White House at President Carter's request.

For a young Catholic who had, no doubt, heard some awful guitar masses growing up in the 1960s, the Christian music at Ichthus would have been a revelation of sorts. Evangelical acts of the time played loud and sang with emotion. Many of the musicians poured the drama and struggle of their lives into their lyrics. Phil Keaggy, for example, spoke openly of taking plenty of drugs before becoming a born-again Christian. Others were radical in a way that resonated with young people who recognized the hypocrisy around them. One of Norman's most popular songs, "Christmastime," mocked the commercialism of the modern American holiday. The performances at Ichthus went on for two days and included some traditional gospel groups. Mike Pence was moved by what he saw and heard and would credit his experience in Kentucky with beginning his conversion to evangelicalism.

Pence would eventually say that the concert brought about a "deep realization that what had happened on the cross in some infinitesimal way had happened for me." He never offered details about the private and personal suffering this comment suggested. However, the transformation he felt at Ichthus led him toward a more outwardly pious life—more in line with the small-town Indiana Protestants he grew up with and less and less like his Catholic grandfather from Chicago. He voted for Jimmy Carter in 1980 because he admired Carter's religious bona fides and considered Ronald Reagan an actor unqualified for the presidency. Soon after Reagan took office, however, Pence underwent a political conversion similar to his religious one. Soon, Reagan was his hero and role model, and Pence embraced the GOP so fully that, like his religious fervor, it became an obvious and powerful part of his identity. The appeal, as Pence would explain it, was more a matter of perspective and style than specific policies. "His broad-shouldered leadership inspired my life," said Pence.

In Indiana, being a Republican would make Pence's path to political success much easier; the GOP had won the governor's office in four straight elections and, save for 1964, dominated the vote for president going all the way back to 1940. Republicans also controlled both houses of the state assembly by big majorities. Inside the party, evangelical Protestant Christians of the sort Pence met at Ichthus were the largest religious group. Their influence was growing with the recent development of political groups like Moral Majority, which turned church congregations into hotbeds of activism. Pence claimed it all as he embraced his new faith, but he hedged his bets by retaining some Catholic identity.

He would call himself a "born-again, evangelical Catholic," combining two generally exclusive faiths into one that suited him. This was an unusual but not unique choice, as Protestant conservatives were luring Catholics into new so-called megachurches where members could attend lively services and access gyms, schools, adult education classes, and sports leagues. As a self-proclaimed evangelical Catholic, Pence sought to have it all, including a religion that did not require the moral action inherent to Catholicism, while retaining a connection to his roots. By all accounts, his deeply religious Catholic mother was not pleased, but among the believers in his new faith, Pence could count on finding instant and broad acceptance.[15]

Embarked on a religious journey that would lead him away from the Catholic Church, Pence set aside the idea of the priesthood and focused on the political ambition he harbored while still in high school—he wanted to be president of the United States. The choice was a matter of matching talents to vocation. In 1994 Pence would tell the *Indiana Business Journal* he believed his best assets were "my gifts: to articulate, to advocate."[16] The logical direction for a former high school debater was law school, but he encountered his first roadblock after graduation—he failed the admissions test for the Indiana University Robert H. McKinney School of Law. Hanover College, where his tattling had aided administrators, came through with a job in the admissions office, which gave him two years to study and then pass the exam on his second try at the Indianapolis school. Once admitted, though, he hated his law school classes. "It was a bad experience," he later said. On a personal level, though, the move to Indianapolis changed his life. He attended St. Thomas Aquinas Catholic Church, where one day he spotted Karen Sue Batten Whitaker, a pretty young woman who sometimes played the guitar at mass. He fell in love.[17]

Two years older than Pence, Karen was a second-grade teacher and had been previously married. Ambitious and competitive, she too had competed in speech contests in her high school days, but she had also been an excellent student while he had bumped along with a B average. Whitaker had met her first husband, John Steven Whitaker, at Butler University. They were married at Big Bend National Park in Texas and then returned to Indiana, where he studied medicine. After they were divorced, Dr. Whitaker became a drug company executive responsible, in part, for the development of the erectile dysfunction drug Cialis. He later said the marriage ended because he and Karen grew apart. "We were kids," he told *The Washington Post* in 2016. "We probably didn't know what we were doing."

After she had dated Mike Pence for almost a year, Karen expected they would one day marry. She bought a small gold cross, had it engraved with the word *"Yes,"* and placed it in her purse. Determined to propose in a memorable way, he bought a ring and hid it inside a loaf of bread, which he brought on a walk to feed the ducks who floated in a local canal. When the moment arrived, he fished for the ring and asked for her hand. She gave him the cross. The loaf of bread, shellacked to preserve it, became a memento. Their June 1985 wedding was at St. Christopher's, a Catholic church two blocks from Indianapolis Motor Speedway. Karen had seven attendants. Mike was accompanied by a best man and six groomsmen. The reception party was held at a modest venue called the Midway Motor Lodge, where a Plexiglas dome covered the swimming pool and the restaurant overlooked a small lake.

Newly married, Pence returned to law school and a clerk position at a local firm. The law would be not a career but a step on the road to fulfilling his political ambitions. Karen returned to teaching second graders at Acton Elementary School in southeast Indianapolis. Mike graduated from law school in 1986 and was ready to make his move in politics. Karen was ready to help.

3

MUDSLINGER

For everyone who exalts himself will be humbled.

—*Luke 14:11*

One day, Mike Pence would be considered the most famous person ever to have visited Fountain City, Indiana. On a cloudless one hundred–degree day in July 1988, he was just an apparition in the shimmering heat on two-lane Route 27. Ahead waited a tiny community—shops on the main highway, neat side streets—of roughly seven hundred.

A little too old for his short-shorts and a little too big for his fat-tire mountain bike, Pence struggled against the drafts created by passing 18-wheelers. When he reached a slight incline, which passed for a hill in the flat terrain, he stood to use the weight of his body against the pedals. A sticker pasted onto the front of his plaid short-sleeve shirt read, "Mike Pence Congress."

An attorney who hated the law and a native son with the grandest political ambition, it had been inevitable that Pence would run for office. He started by visiting Republican grandees to seek their blessings. One, an irascible former Nixon man named Keith Bulen, received him in a basement office Pence described as a "bat cave" illuminated only by a single desk lamp. With a gift for drama that hid his own insecurities, Bulen liked to test others. He asked why Pence thought he could succeed at politics. Pence replied, "Well, I've won several awards for public speaking."

"What the hell does public speaking have to do with winning an election?" shot back Bulen.[1]

Although Bulen was on to something, Pence didn't hesitate to bypass the training grounds of city and state politics, where men and women traditionally paid their dues, made connections, established reputations, and honed their craft. Just as Bulen had once been an upstart challenging the party elders, Pence presumed he was ready to shoot for the top. At age twenty-nine, Pence showed he had the stamina to conduct an aggressive campaign, including the bike tour, which brought him face-to-face with voters across the Second Congressional District. He was often accompanied by Karen, who rode a matching bike and wore a white PENCE FOR CONGRESS T-shirt. Every bit as bright and assertive as her husband, Karen was a political advisor as well as a spouse. Together they looked like a nice young couple sweatily committed to a dream, which is exactly what they were.

In politics, as in showbiz, backstage planning makes a performance seem spontaneous. So it was with the Mike-on-a-bike show. An advance man or woman drove ahead of the bikers to arrange meetings and press interviews at photo-friendly sites—a grain silo, a general store, a diner. Behind them, a staffer followed in a van emblazoned with the campaign sign: PENCE FOR CONGRESS. Trouper that he was, Pence stayed in character. Why spoil it for the audience and voters? "I think people responded well to someone who comes riding along down the street straddling a bicycle," he told a reporter for his hometown newspaper, *The Republic*. "It's nothing more than one person relating to another and I don't think you can get any more effective in campaigning than that."[2]

The tour did offer unplanned encounters. On open stretches of road, the campaigning couple would pause to chat with a man mowing his lawn or a woman collecting letters from her mailbox. Here, Mike could blend Midwest charm with the poise of a skillful public speaker, creating just the right impression. Even die-hard Democrats liked him. "He stopped at the house and asked for a glass of water," recalled Tracy Souza, whose father, then-congressman Lee Hamilton, was a giant in the state's

Democratic Party. "He came across as a really nice guy." Pence came across well with donors too. Individual contributions poured in from wealthy Indiana supporters along with other well-heeled midwesterners, such as Mary Kohler of the Kohler plumbing fortune. She and her husband were deeply engaged in politics and giving money to candidates and causes, though Mary Kohler had her own distinct brand of private funding. She used her private jet, for example, to transport rare bird eggs around the country to help restore species that had been wiped out in regions where development and industries destroyed their habitat.[3]

Mike's father, Ed, had been a tough sell when Mike sought his support. Mike and his family told the story that Ed Pence had been against his son's decision to run. Mike held his ground when his father peppered him with questions. Finally satisfied, Ed was all in. By the spring of 1988, with the primary approaching, Ed was touring the district with a trunkful of campaign yard signs as he introduced his son to everyone he knew.

On April 12, Ed decided to take a break and play golf at Harrison Lakes Country Club. Somewhere out on the course, he suffered a heart attack. The fire department ambulance brought him to the emergency room at Bartholomew County Hospital, which was less than ten miles away. Although he got immediate attention, the damage to Pence's heart muscle was too great. He was pronounced dead soon after arriving. He was fifty-eight years old. Mike suspended his campaign for a few days so that he could be with his family and Karen. Her own father, a former United Airlines executive who had moved to Las Vegas, had died only a month earlier.

Coming weeks before primary voting, the break didn't affect Pence's momentum. Thanks in part to his father's enthusiastic support, Pence enjoyed a five-to-one funding advantage over his primary election rival, an accountant named Raymond Schwab. Executives at Cummins and other corporations rallied donations for Pence. In political campaigning, money attracts money, and Republican Party bosses recognized Mike's ability to make the system work. Ten of the eleven county chairmen in the district announced their support. Pence defeated Schwab by more than two to one. Flush with victory, Pence declared himself a natural-born winner.

"What you are seeing is the genesis of a consensus candidacy, a candidacy that the vast majority of Republicans can say, 'This is the guy who can beat Phil Sharp and we're going to get behind him.'"[4]

A Democrat who kept getting reelected, Philip Sharp, a professor at Ball State University, first went to Congress in 1974 as part of the huge post-Watergate class. (Voters punished President Nixon's GOP by electing dozens of new Democrats to Congress.) Sharp's party affiliation and his doctorate in foreign policy made him a bit of an anomaly in a state where Republicans dominated. But with impeccable manners and a long fuse, Sharp had the neighborly demeanor Indiana voters seemed to favor. He counted farmers in his immediate family and understood the concerns of his constituents and the way they looked at the world.[5]

Sensitive to Tip O'Neill's old saw, "All politics is local," Sharp hired more aides to work in Indiana than in Washington and assigned some of them to travel the district in a van offering on-the-spot constituent services. People got so accustomed to turning to him for help that all sorts of strange requests came in. (In one instance when a worker fell into a big water tank, Sharp's office got the first emergency call.) Constituent services helped the Democrat win over just enough Republicans and independents to come out on top in seven straight elections.

In addition to his modest style, Sharp cultivated a middle-of-the-road voting record that gave opponents little to attack. During his time in Congress, both parties counted substantial numbers of moderates who frequently crossed party lines to support legislation. Northern Republicans voted for social programs. Southern Democrats eagerly funded the military and cut taxes. In this environment, Sharp was remarkably successful at devising proposals that would be adopted by Congress. After analyzing the records of the state's House members, *The Indianapolis News* judged him the most effective of them all, noting that ten of the thirteen bills he proposed passed. The runner-up had managed only five legislative successes. At the bottom of the rankings, Representative Andy Jacobs went three for sixty-four.

Sharp's total package—personality, performance, perspective—made him such a formidable incumbent that established politicians feared running against him. In seven elections, he had squared off against a farmer, a shoe salesman turned state bureaucrat, and a Ball State University public affairs officer. Conservative third-party candidates such as Libertarian Cecil Bohannon sometimes complicated things for the GOP and split the vote, making victory even more difficult. The net result was that in a district where 56 percent of the voters were registered Republicans, Sharp had achieved victory every time, with margins that ranged from seven to twenty-five percentage points.

The GOP's advantage in registration meant that national party leaders generally considered Sharp one of the more vulnerable Democrats in the House, and he was always among the thirty or forty members targeted for special attention. However, none of the candidates put forward against him since 1974 had proved to have much charisma or skill. Young, handsome, and gifted on the stump, Pence had more promise, but anyone willing to take the chance knew that, in all likelihood, the result would be a losing campaign that would only yield valuable experience and, perhaps, some useful contacts.[6]

In 1988, a young Republican couldn't hope for a better point of contact than President Reagan, and thus many made their way to the Capitol seeking a handshake and photo opportunity. All presidents do this kind of duty, giving candidates both a reward and a trophy in the form of a story to tell about how "I was just with the president." During a lifetime of celebrity, Reagan had so perfected his meet-and-greet technique that he seemed to enjoy every encounter; perhaps he did, or perhaps it was his Hollywood training. The party's slate of congressional contenders was invited to attend a reception in the Blue Room. With its French Empire furnishings, acquired in the refurbishing done after the mansion was burned by the British in the War of 1812, the room overlooks the South Lawn and is often used for receiving lines.

As he waited in his dark suit and red tie, Pence prepared, as he would recall, "to say something of meaning to the great man." For a president who no doubt heard thousands of attempts at meaning in reception lines, the brief exchanges that occurred as hand met hand and cameras clicked were not memorable. Pence, however, recounted the moment for the *Congressional Record*, upon Reagan's death, in 2004:

I had the privilege in 1988 as a candidate for Congress to sit with the president in the Blue Room of the White House and speak to him personally, and on that occasion, that great privilege of my life, I was able to look the president in the eye as he asked me how my campaign was going. I said, "Mr. President, it is going fine, but I just want to thank you for everything you have done for our country and to encourage my generation of Americans to believe in this country again."

In other tellings, Pence would add that Reagan demonstrated "real humility," which he admired. "He seemed surprised," Pence said of Reagan. "His cheeks appeared to redden with embarrassment, and he said, "'Well, Mike, that's a very nice thing for you to say.'"

In the Blue Room, Reagan and Pence sat side by side in matching gilded chairs, which had been placed in front of a fireplace. A French bronze doré clock, acquired by James Madison, kept time on the carved white mantel behind them. When the White House photographer moved in to capture the moment, neither Reagan and Pence struck very different poses. The smiling Reagan set himself in perfect profile with his chin slightly raised and his eyes focused over Pence's shoulder. He looked like he had his face toward the sun and it had lit him up. Pence, his curly, dark hair cut short, grasped one arm of his chair and looked down at the hands of the seventy-seven-year-old president. In this image, they could have been grandfather and grandson.

After all the photos were taken, Reagan spoke to the assembly of young Republicans, saying, "Many of you have thanked me for what I did for America, but I want you to know I don't think I did anything. The American people decided it was time to right the ship, and I was just the captain they put on the bridge when they did it."

Back home in Indiana, candidate Pence resumed his bike tour, though as the novelty faded, it gained him less and less attention. With no record of his own to defend, Pence played offense on the campaign. He criticized Sharp for taking money from political action committees (PACs), which presumably gave donations in hopes of advancing their interests. Pence vowed not to take any money from PACs, but his wealthy supporters gave him more than $425,000, a sizeable sum at the time and about the same amount that Sharp took in. In a sign of his rookie status, Pence provoked his own campaign finance snafu by repeatedly missing the filing deadline to report on his fund-raising. When he finally did submit his papers to state and federal officials, they were riddled with errors. His campaign aides blamed Pence's mother and a friend, who had handled these responsibilities. They said the problems were not a matter of intent but rather the result of inexperience and poor arithmetic skills.

Pence and Sharp differed on basic issues. Pence opposed abortion and wanted it outlawed. Sharp was pro-choice. The voters were so closely divided that neither candidate got much advantage out of any issue, even such a contentious one. For every fervent antiabortion voter who might choose Pence solely on this issue, a comparable number could have voted for Phil Sharp because he was among the first to talk about defending the earth from pollution-caused climate change. In this era, when people were more likely to identify themselves as political moderates than in later years, elections were not likely to be determined by any single issue. Voters tended to pick among individual candidates rather than mark straight party tickets. Pence understood this, saying, "I never had a whole lot of faith in people who said, 'Vote for me because I'm a Republican or Democrat.' I think it's a lot more important to tell who you are and what you stand for. The reason I became a Republican is because it was their ideas I agreed with."

Besides his opposition to abortion, Pence advanced a standard Republican platform, which called for increased defense spending, tax cuts, and curbs on federal regulations. Faced with an incumbent who was a whiz at bringing projects home to Indiana, he pledged that getting funds to widen a local highway—he called it "four-laning" the road—would be his number one priority. Of course, there was no reason why Sharp couldn't deliver the same highway funds, and given his seniority in the party that controlled the Congress, he might have been expected to have an easier time of it.

As the election drew closer, Pence could not find traction against Sharp. Few voters seemed moved by road projects or his stance on campaign finance. At the same time, his pleasant personality was so similar to Sharp's that they could have been brothers. When newspaper articles began to note that many voters didn't seem to know much at all about him, Pence tried to win over Republicans by appealing to party identity. That didn't work well either. When he complained that Sharp's votes in Congress too often aligned with his Democratic colleagues, he was met with the fact that Sharp actually voted with House Republicans almost 30 percent of the time. On the opposite side of the ledger, Pence had to admit that he had admired certain Democrats, especially President Kennedy, who "meant something to me because he was a leader and not simply a politician. He stood for a lot of things I believe in. If you look at the record, you'll see he cut taxes, was strong in defense, and stood up to the Russians."

Pence also used the Republican argument that he was more likely than a Democrat to hold strong against America's adversaries, and he suggested that some of his resolve in life developed in response to hard times in childhood. "I had a lot of experiences in life that were very difficult," he said. "I was very chubby and unpopular when I was a kid. And I had a hard time keeping up with the rest of the guys my age." Although he overcame his difficulties, Pence said, "I've never forgot what it's like to be in that position, to be looked down upon because I was fat, or a fourth-string center, or in shop class." In a state where factory work remained an essential part of the economy, the shop class note probably sounded sour to some voters, but Pence's intention—to claim that despite all appearances he had experienced some suffering in life—was clear. "Having gone through that," he continued, "has taught me that every person in this world has value, no matter what their position or status. I'll never forget that."

Pence's life story, as he recalled it, would have sounded odd to anyone who knew him well. This was the same person who modeled spring clothes as a child, won debates, led the CYO, was elected president of his high school class, and became president of his fraternity at an expensive private college. His family had been sufficiently well off to live in ever-larger homes and to belong to the private country club in Columbus.

The challenge Pence faced—to connect with voters personally *and* politically—would have been daunting in a race for city council. In a sprawling rural congressional district with small cities like Muncie and rural expanses of rolling farmland, he could, at best, present a series of clichés about himself. "Conservative, energetic, and earnest young man" was what he chose to offer. Sometimes he tried to mix in a bit of humor, but the tactic came with its own risks. After answering questions at Franklin College, a small liberal arts school, he spotted a student wearing an armband bearing Sharp's name. "Ah, Hitler Youth, I see," said the candidate.[7]

Pence wasn't alone in the struggle to make a good impression. Sharp was the incumbent but could not let his guard down. As a former college professor, his biographical sketch suggested the image of "experience, intelligence, and open-mindedness." Of course, a sizeable number of voters would consider these to be negative traits indicating he was a wishy-washy, out-of-touch political insider. No one who hoped to be known would be satisfied with a chalk-outline identity, but as expediency forced them to choose these traits, the process revealed something meaningful. Their selected traits reflected an idealized self—the one they strived to achieve— and also brought attention to what they left out. Politics is a game of ego and ambition, but both men avoided being identified by either of those. Error and incompetence are also normal in politics, but admitting them is anathema.

All the posturing made Sharp and Pence easy targets for the jibes delivered at a traditional election year roast sponsored by local journalists. The event was held at a convention center in downtown Muncie, where about 175 people sat at big round tables dining on banquet food and ready to laugh. Sharp and Pence were required to sit there facing the audience, smiling and chuckling as roasters stood and mocked them from a lectern.

Sharp is "so broad-minded he can't even take his own side in an argument."
Pence is so conservative "he doesn't try anything first."
Sharp's first election victory came against an opponent who campaigned like a "dead squirrel."
Pence "rides through this district on a tricycle. Sharp walks because he can't ride" a bike.

"Phil reminds me of a cat watching a canary fall into a goldfish bowl. He knows if he waits long enough, he can have two meals at once."[8]

Pence and Sharp also faced off in two televised debates. A panel of journalists went through the issues. Sharp responded testily to a question about campaign contributions, saying the suggestion that he was somehow bought by special interests was "sleazy." Pence, true to his nice-guy image, wouldn't go so far as to contradict Sharp's claim that he was his own person, but he did say that "special interest groups exist to influence Congress." The two debates found the men often meeting in the political middle. Noting that two-worker families struggled to arrange childcare, Pence wanted the government to help. This was hardly a Republican position. Sharp was critical of labor unions even though they were a central Democratic constituency. Pence tied himself to the most popular politicians in the state, Senators Richard Lugar and Dan Quayle, and to President Reagan. The message was that these were all splendid leaders and Republicans. Since he was a Republican too, he deserved to be elected.

Perhaps it was the vague quality of his argument, or maybe it was his youthful demeanor, but Pence did nothing in his campaign to score points in a way that would help him actually defeat Sharp. Then, with time running out, he began an advertising blitz that delivered two negative messages about Sharp. In one TV ad, a hand filled out a $1 million check on an account held by "Influence Peddlers" and signed with the words D. C. LOBBYISTS. The ad closed with the message, "Mike Pence—nobody's congressman but yours."

The second spot was Pence's own version of the infamous "Willie Horton" ad, which then-Republican candidate for president Vice President George Herbert Walker Bush was using to suggest that his Democratic opponent, Governor Michael Dukakis of Massachusetts, was soft on crime. William Horton, who never went by Willie, was a black man who committed murder while on furlough from a Massachusetts prison. The advertisement, which featured an image of a scowling, disheveled Horton, was widely deemed to be racist. Bush's campaign manager, Lee Atwater, was proud of the spot and bragged about its effect. The ad's creator, Larry

McCarthy, would say, "The guy looked like an animal" and was "every suburban mother's greatest fear."

Mike Pence's Horton-style ad was shot in a schoolyard. The video focused on a scary version of a still life: a razor blade, a rolled-up dollar bill, lines of white powder. Red letters bled over the picture, declaring, "There's something Phil Sharp isn't telling you about his record on drugs." The spot ended with the words "It's weak" written in white powder. The print version of the ad featured a lovely photo of Mike Pence in a jacket and tie, arms folded across his chest, a determined and confident look on his face opposite images of the same props—razor, powder, rolled-up bill. The piece claimed that Sharp was responsible for "1,200 convicted drug pushers . . . being set free." Instead of protecting "our children, Phil Sharp has supported the rights of drug pushers."

Pence's ad presented no explanation for Phil Sharp's alleged disregard for children in the war on drugs. Maybe Sharp was well intentioned but wrong on policy. Maybe he was just evil. The reason didn't matter. All that mattered was that Sharp was trying to hide a weak record. Who had a strong record? Well, Pence couldn't claim any record at all, because he had never served in any office. However, he had called for the execution of convicted drug "kingpins," whomever *they* were, and this proposal was something he repeated often. (Decades later, President Donald Trump would advocate the same policy—execution—for dealers.)

As with all art forms, campaign ads communicate as much with what's left out as with what's included. In these two instances, Pence left out the fact that Sharp had received $1 million in PAC money *over fourteen years* and that his vote on violent offenders had not been against the idea of treating them firmly but in favor of having a committee work on a tough-minded proposal. Sharp was irritated by the blizzard of negative TV spots, which Pence bought at a cost of about $100,000, but they were not enough to tilt the election.

On Election Night, Pence was tantalized by early returns from the most heavily Republican corners of the district, which showed him with a lead of more than thirteen thousand votes. However, as larger cities such as Muncie began to complete their tallies, the balance shifted. At 10:30 P.M., Sharp was so far ahead that Pence called his opponent's campaign headquarters to congratulate him. Sharp, who had been home playing Monopoly with his wife and two children, wasn't there. When they finally spoke, both were gracious, but Sharp remained annoyed, telling reporters that many voters he had spoken to had "expressed disgust at all the negativism" coming from his challenger. Pence had a different take. "We didn't run a negative campaign," he said. "We've run one that was bluntly honest."

The result, a six-point win for Sharp, came even as the top of the GOP ticket—George Bush and Indiana's native son Dan Quayle—won the state by twenty points. While Pence was surely frustrated, he resisted those who expressed "condolences" on Election Night. "Nobody's dead," he said, a reminder that he had endured his father's death earlier in the year. Compared with that experience, an election loss was easy. Besides, Pence could take comfort in the fact that he had come closer to beating Sharp than any previous challenger. He also established himself as an attractive candidate who could manage a campaign and stand up to the rigors of the contest. He understood the political capital he had amassed, and so, even on a night when he lost, he declared a victory of sorts. "Nine months ago, I was an unknown lawyer, and nine months later, we were able to convince 100,000 people. I think we just ran out of time."

Mike Pence's 1988 Election Night "ran out of time" line echoed the words of countless coaches and athletes who respond to defeat by saying they were beaten by the timer on the scoreboard. This perspective helps competitors sustain the confidence they need to play the next game. In this instance, Pence immediately began talking about his next run. In the summer of 1989, he went to Washington and met with Lee Atwater himself, who had become chairman of the Republican National Committee on the strength of his success as the architect of George H. W. Bush's 1988 presidential campaign. A notoriously ruthless operative, Atwater was the type of swaggering political hit man who said of Democratic nominee Michael Dukakis that he would "strip the bark off the little bastard and make Willie Horton his running mate." Atwater also understood that the success of the GOP's so-called Southern Strategy depended on the party's ability to appeal to the racist underpinnings of white voters.[9]

Still riding high from the 1988 campaign and eighteen months away from his death from brain cancer at the age of forty, Atwater advised Pence to prepare for a 1990 rematch with Sharp. (In the final months of his life, Atwater began a rapid journey toward repentance, which would culminate in an apology to Michael Dukakis and a public confession that "while I didn't invent negative politics, I am one of its most ardent practitioners.") By the fall of 1989, Pence was organizing fund-raisers and acknowledging that he was likely to declare his candidacy. This time around, Pence's donor list showed that he appealed to the two main factions in conservative politics: right-wing Christians and pro-business activists. Corporate executives, especially those in the government-regulated health care and oil industries, gave generously. Among the religiously motivated were billionaire Richard DeVos, Christian Right campaigner Richard Viguerie, and evangelist Jacqueline Yockey, whose radio station beamed Christian messages to listeners in Israel and neighboring states. Far more strident than the moderates they hoped to supplant, at every level of the GOP, activists in these two camps were becoming more intently engaged in campaigns.

On a national level, major Republican donors, including the DeVos, Koch, and Scaife families, backed Christian Right organizations such as the Family Research Council (FRC) and the Council for National Policy (CNP), which, despite their bland names, advocated radical religiously inspired policies. The CNP, to take just one, was created in 1981 to support "a united conservative movement to assure, by 2020, policy leadership and governance that restores religious and economic freedom, a strong national defense, and Judeo-Christian values under the Constitution." Its founder, Rev. Tim LaHaye, accepted that Bible prophecy of the apocalypse was at hand and that a conspiracy of a mythical group called the Illuminati controlled much of world affairs. (His famous "Left Behind" series of books imagined a future when evangelical Christians have been brought to heaven and the people left behind suffer and battle with the Antichrist.) Though it kept its membership private, documents leaked to the press showed the CNF was supported by a who's who of conservative America.[10]

The national elements of the religious Right were matched on the state level across the country. In Indiana, the Pence campaign received financial and moral backing from leaders such as Rev. Gene Hood of Independent Nazarene Church, who was part of a growing movement of wealthy, politically conservative Christians. The energy for these activists was different from the traditional evangelizing, gospel-preaching devotion to saving as many souls as possible. Hood, like national leaders such as Jerry Falwell and Pat Robertson, was an alarmist who used fear to mobilize. This was accomplished by dividing the world into Us and Them and then interpreting changes that brought rights to others, especially gay Americans, as losses for their side. Thus, laws barring discrimination became attacks on conservative Christians' rights to discrimination on religious grounds. Hood benefited from the privileges of a pastor, living in a church-owned home and enjoying special tax breaks afforded to clergy. He was also a wealthy businessman who owned companies involved in insurance, real estate, radio, and electronics. The insurance company alone took in $25 million in revenue annually.[11]

In 1986, an assistant pastor at Hood's church, Rev. Donald Lynch, became one of the first hard-Right neophytes to use provocative social issues to storm the GOP and win an important primary. (He had run against Sharp one cycle before Pence in the general election.) Lynch's main campaign issue was HIV/AIDS, and he advocated "isolation and quarantine" of people who contracted the virus. He also proposed that cities that failed to forcibly close "bathhouses and pleasure dens" be denied all federal funds. In the May 1986 primary, he knocked off a conventional Republican named Jay Wickliff. Facing Sharp in the general elections, Lynch's campaign tried to present a more mainstream image, even demanding he not be referred to as "Pastor" or "Reverend." It didn't work. Sharp swamped Lynch 62 to 38.[12]

Lynch's defeat, combined with losses by others who ran as part of the Indiana religious Right, signaled the limited political appeal of an overtly conservative Christian message. Preaching and protest—rather than running for office—became the focus for activists. No one in Indiana was better known for this kind of action than Lynch's boss at Independent Nazarene. Rev. Hood was arrested at a clinic where abortions were performed and led a crowd of two hundred that stormed the famous Indiana

Roof Ballroom to disrupt the 1988 Miss Gay America pageant. Some demonstrators with him wore surgical masks to signal their fear of HIV/AIDS. Others held Bibles aloft. But the flamboyant Hood issued an extremist warning of violence on behalf of those who could not abide the thought of a national drag queen pageant occurring in their community. He said, "If they try this another time, I'm telling you, there's going to be bloodshed. We mean business. There are some red-blooded men in Indianapolis, and we won't stand for this."[13]

The pageant protest reflected the local conservative Christian community's response to changing social mores and a belief that the HIV/AIDS epidemic, which was first noted in the gay community, indicated God's punishment for liberal views on sex in general and homosexuality in particular. Indiana became a focal point for public conflict on HIV/AIDS when Ryan White, a hemophiliac infected via transfusion, was barred from school in Kokomo, Indiana, by officials who didn't accept the science that showed his presence did not present a health risk to others. The boy's parents successfully sued the school system, and Ryan White's condition changed the perspective on HIV/AIDS, no longer a "gay disease." Though White's case gained international attention, it did not settle the culture war waged by activists like Hood who, besides speaking out on social issues, gave contributions to Pence and other like-minded politicians.[14]

Mike Pence began to develop ties with admired national figures on the hard-core libertarian Right, including the billionaire DeVos and Koch families. In addition to unfettered free enterprise, the DeVoses promoted right-wing Christianity. The Kochs were not much interested in religion but pushed libertarian tax and regulation slashing with the zeal of crusaders. As they turned Koch Industries, their father's oil refining business, into one of the largest privately held companies in the world, they used their billions to build political organizations and support candidates that would shrink government and promote capitalism in its place. Ironically, Fred Koch built his business by making deals in the 1920s and 1930s in the competition-free Soviet Union. His sons David and Charles Koch opposed all regulation, especially all laws that aimed to protect the environment. Not coincidentally, Koch Industries was one of the most prolific polluters in the country and did business so ruthlessly—even cheating sellers in the way crude oil was weighed—that they proved the need for government oversight and regulation.[15]

In the 1980s, the Kochs' national political focus extended to state-level organizations, promoting the same doctrine and seeking out candidates who performed according to their agenda. The network they created would eventually function like a shadow political party, nurturing and promoting candidates who challenged regular Republicans and pushed the GOP ever rightward. In Indiana, Mike Pence was an obvious choice.

Pence also attracted the financial and political aid of Charles S. Quilhot, who had cofounded a new organization, the Indiana Policy Review Foundation. The IPR, as it was known, was part of a new wave of state-level political organizations created to promote policies such as the privatization of schools and other government activities, rolling back environmental and business regulation, and lowering taxes. The IPR also provided jobs for people who moved in and out of political campaigns and government. They replicated, on the state level, older national organizations like the conservative Hudson Institute in Washington, which, for example, welcomed Indiana businessman/politician Mark Lubbers as he moved between the public and private sectors. Lubbers, in turn, donated campaign money to Mike Pence, among others.

IPR's origin story, told to *The Indianapolis Star*, described a dozen conservative businessmen gathered like the apostles at a Mexican restaurant in Indianapolis, Acapulco Joe's, to conceive of a way to get more out of a state political system that was already friendly to their interests. Soon, they had engaged one of the nation's most prominent young conservative agitators, Dinesh D'Souza, as their chief consultant. Not yet thirty years old, D'Souza had gained notoriety as a student at Dartmouth, where he edited a newspaper that outed gay students, mocked African Americans, and parodied mainstream politics. (Unaffiliated with Dartmouth, the paper was supported financially by conservative alumni.) After college, D'Souza had embarked on a high-flying career that had already included a stint at the Heritage Foundation. In 2014, his reputation would be tarnished by a plea of guilty in a case involving violation of campaign laws, even though four years later, in May 2018, Trump singled him out and issued a pardon. But at the time when D'Souza advised the founders of IPR, he was among the most admired conservative activists of his generation. He steered the Acapulco Joe schemers to a conference in California, where the Heritage Foundation taught attendees from around the country how to plant and nourish state-level organizations so a right-wing agenda could be pushed at every level of society. Major foundations in Indiana shied away from IPR, but smaller ones did support the group. One such foundation was a trust organized by an Indiana-based manufacturing firm called Dekko. A Dekko official, Linda Speakman, described IPR's mission as aligned with its own. "One of our beliefs," she said, "is that we feel, in a sense, government is our enemy."[16]

As with many state think tanks around the country that emerged in the late 1980s, IPR was affiliated with the State Policy Network (SPN), which was backed with donations from a variety of right-wing foundations, including groups created by Charles and David Koch. Ironically, U.S. law considered such "educational" or "public welfare" nonprofits as tax-exempt. Such free-market, anti-government funders would say they were merely playing by the established rules and would be foolish to do otherwise. At this time, the Kochs and like-minded people with huge sums to invest in politics were creating new initiatives to deliver change that the Republican Party had failed to provide. In general, they wanted to shrink government at all levels, while encouraging profit-driven entities to dominate every other sector of society. A key figure in the SPN was the same Fort Wayne businessman, Byron S. Lamm, who helped create IPR.

Free marketeers were generally wary and had no interest in the religious goals of the Christian Right. Libertarians were especially resistant to the religious movement's efforts to police sex and reproduction and had no interest in funding protests and marches against abortion or gay rights. They chose instead to fund think tanks and writers who could produce position papers and contribute to journals. Pence immediately began to cultivate both sides. He certainly wanted to outlaw abortion and aligned with groups that wanted to limit gay rights. Yet he was also the son of a successful businessman and the product of Columbus, a company town that gave him connections to industry. Pence's background appealed to entrepreneurs and capitalists. He won campaign support from Cummins, which was based in Columbus, and from other major Indiana firms, including American Lawn Mower and the giant drug-maker Eli Lilly and Company, whose executives flocked to give him campaign cash.

Drug and health care executives would, over time, become essential to Pence's fund-raising efforts. Heavily regulated by the government and also extremely profitable, these industries were often maligned for price gouging but also protected from the kind of government action that would rein in prices. The ultimate example of this dynamic would come in 2003 when a Republican Congress and president created a new drug benefit program for seniors on Medicare and simultaneously barred the government from negotiating on prices. This move destroyed buyers' power in the typical marketplace relationship and meant that no discounts could be had for the massive volume of purchases made by Medicare. The price set by the sellers was the price paid, and profits soared at the companies where execs were such loyal political donors. In his political life, assorted drug companies, health care firms, and people working in these fields would give Pence more than $400,000 in campaign contributions. Tony Moravec, owner of Blairex Laboratories and Applied Laboratories, based in Columbus, Indiana, would eventually give Pence more than $430,000. (Among the companies' biggest-selling products were an ointment called Boudroux's Butt Paste and Encare, a spermicidal suppository.)[17]

In 1990 and later, Pence also received donations from politically connected corporate lawyers, including Tom Huston of the powerful firm Barnes & Thornburg, which had become briefly famous during the Watergate scandal for drawing up a plan to use criminal means—burglary, illegal surveillance, tampering with mail—against President Nixon's political foes. With money coming in greater volume than it had in 1988, Pence engaged in some questionable financial arrangements, which led to one of his biggest mistakes in the 1990 election rematch with Phil Sharp.[18]

Pence took the unusual step of creating two campaign organizations to accept donations. One—the Mike Pence for Congress Committee—was an ordinary nonprofit. The other—People for Mike Pence Inc.—was set up as a business that was able to take out loans and make payments, including personal payments for his own use. Reporters found that this

entity had made payments on Pence's personal credit card bills and mort-
gage, for the loan on his wife's car, and paid for groceries, parking tickets, and golf outings. Sharp pounced on the issue, demanding local
prosecutors investigate possible campaign law violations.

The candidate's formation of a for-profit committee, which was legal
but controversial, caught Pence's campaign manager, Sherman Johnson,
by surprise. Years later, he would recall, "That was something Mike did
completely on his own. I think only two people in the campaign knew
about it." When the issue arose, Pence responded with a testy "I need to
make a living." His aides then stepped in, saying that the candidate's
openness about the campaign company signaled it was an aboveboard
enterprise. And, in fact, there was nothing illegal about it. However, the
controversy deprived Pence of the advantage he believed he held when it
came to campaign finance and gave Sharp something to talk about for
months.

In this rematch of their 1988 contest, Pence looked noticeably older.
His brown hair had started to turn gray, and he now wore glasses. He put
his bicycle away but maintained his commitment to direct contact with
voters. He used a counting device to keep track of the number of hands
he shook. His goal of one hundred per day was modest considering he
would need the support of about seventy-five thousand people to win.
Voters who questioned Pence on his priorities heard the same list he offered in 1988, only the candidate was a bit more strident. This time, he
wasn't just opposed to abortion; he advocated an amendment to the Constitution, except in cases of rape and incest or when a pregnancy endan-
gers a woman's life. He opposed the Clean Air Act, which regulated
emissions from vehicles and industry, and favored a permanent ban on
deficit spending, even though many economists support it when used, for
example, to stimulate the economy during recession.

Among Pence's other positions were many GOP standards, including reductions in the federal estate tax and a rollback on the capital gains
tax. During a debate, Sharp reached for the name of a famous plutocrat
to criticize his economic ideas. "Donald Trump will be delighted to hear
your commitment," said Sharp, "because 80 percent of the capital gains
tax [reduction] will go to people who make $100,000 a year."[19]

Although their policy differences were real, once more, the candidates did not attract the kind of attention that might come with more dramatic issues. Determined to avoid a second defeat, Pence began to play rough. In early March 1990, he argued that Sharp was akin to an oligarch "choosing to be part of a system that gives control of our government to just a few inside special interests and takes power away from the people." At the end of the month, he said his opponent was selling out his constituents. "While we in central Indiana need honest, decent representation, Sharp has gone off and left us to get the money these groups dole out."

Sharp had been prepared for a tough fight and was more assertive than he had been in 1988. From the start, he tried to tie Pence to unpopular out-of-state Republicans and to the consultant Ed Rollins, who came in from Washington to help Pence. He crowed about Pence's fund-raising prowess and said that Pence had raised more money from donors than any Republican challenger in the country. (With the aid of informal groups like Auto Dealers for Pence, he had pulled ahead of Sharp in contributions.) Rollins was known as a political streetfighter in the style of Lee Atwater, but he did not appear to lay heavy hands on the Pence-Sharp race. "It wasn't a campaign directed by consultants without the candidate's input," said Sherman Johnson. "It was dirty; it was a campaign that had consultant input. And . . . the final decision was made by Mike." Undoubtedly, Mike's closest advisor, Sherman said, was Karen. "They do make a terrific team," he said.

The dirt began flying when Pence accused Sharp of planning to sell a family farm in Illinois that could be a future nuclear waste depository. (Pence raised the issue in broadcast ads and with mailers featuring green cows.) The property at issue wasn't far from the Illinois border with Indiana, and thus Pence implied that Sharp was risking the health and safety of those who lived nearby. The truth was that Sharp didn't own the farm and was not involved with it. The land was subject to a possible forced sale under eminent domain, as federal authorities were eyeing the area for a waste repository. The development never came to pass.

When the farm story failed to excite voters, Pence's team went lower, developing a TV ad that was remembered decades later. It became almost an opening self-defining explanation when someone asked Indiana politicians or journalists about Mike Pence. "Well, do you know about the sheik?"

The "sheik" was a robe-wearing figure in sunglasses posed before a desert backdrop. When he spoke, he excitedly credited the incumbent congressman with rising sales of Arab oil to the United States, which were making him rich. "Thank you, Phil Sharp," he said. Arab American groups condemned the ad as an ethnic slur. Sharp ran his own TV spot, saying, "Mike Pence's negative TV ads about Phil Sharp are not true." In response, Pence's campaign manager said the sheik ad was supposed to be regarded as a joke. "It's delivered with a degree of comedy," said Sherman Johnson as he refused to stop running it. This decision only increased the animosity between the two camps. When aides to the candidates found themselves at the same campaign stop, they got into a shouting match that escalated to pushing and shoving.

In retrospect, the 1990 version of Pence might be regarded as a boxer who knew he was losing and desperately threw some low blows. Two days before the election, the district was flooded with automated phone calls, which delivered a recorded message saying that a group called the Martinsville Environmental League was so outraged by the Phil Sharp farm-sale issue that it had switched its endorsement and was backing Pence. Just as there was no effort by Sharp to aid the development of a waste site, the Martinsville Environmental League did not exist. Sherman Johnson told reporters that, as far as he knew, his campaign had nothing to do with the calls, which came from a telemarketing outfit in Utah called Matrixx Stats. (Actually, the calls were recommended by a national GOP consultant and arranged by associates of Republican U.S. senator Dan Coats, whose campaign paid for them. The two aides who arranged them were fired.) Johnson also said that published polls showing Sharp with an insurmountable lead were wrong.

On Election Day, the Pence team sent a life-size model of a mother elephant with her baby careening around the district on a trailer pulled by a pickup truck. The idea was to soften the candidate's image after months of mudslinging. It didn't work. Sharp trounced Pence, winning with 60 percent of the vote. For the first time, he actually won Pence's home area, Bartholomew County, where a five thousand–vote swing indicated that voters were turned off by the Mike Pence they got to know the second time around. In the moments after his defeat was announced, Pence seemed defensive, saying, "I don't think our campaign ever had a choice but to go straight at Phil Sharp."

Eight months later, Pence reversed himself, publishing a document unique to Indiana politics. Titled "Confessions of a Negative Campaigner," it noted that "the mantra of a modern political campaign is 'drive up the negatives,'" where an opponent is concerned. Pence said this was wrong because "a campaign ought to demonstrate the basic human decency of the candidate. That means your First Amendment rights end at the tip of your opponent's nose—even in the matter of political rhetoric."

The other points Pence made in this public confession included acknowledging that "a campaign ought to be about the advancement of issues whose success or failure is more significant than that of the candidate." This kind of campaign would create a lasting "foundation of arguments" whether a candidate wins or loses. The main personal failing Pence noted was his embrace of a winning-is-everything notion. "Negative campaigning is born of that trap."

Although many considered the brief essay to be an apology, it was not. Instead, it was a "confession" of the sort that religiously oriented people would understand as a "declaration" rather than a mea culpa. Like a confession of faith, Pence's statement announced he favored positive political messaging and not attack dog–style campaigning. And though he said that, in general, "negative campaigning is wrong," he didn't describe his own specific transgressions. More remarkably, he argued, like a boy who says "The other guy hit me first," that Democrats were worse offenders than Republicans. This was, said Pence, because GOP voters expect their side to be "above that sort of thing." The implication was that if Pence had won, he would not have ever written the confession.

The better option suggested in Pence's declaration would come from those who campaign simply to advance certain ideas, with personal victory remaining a lesser goal. He wrote, "But one day soon the new candidates will step forward, faces as fresh as the morning and hearts as brave as the dawn. This breed will turn away from running 'to win' and toward running 'to stand.' And its representatives will see the inside of as many offices as their party will nominate them to fill."[20]

In his prediction, Pence laid out for himself the identity he might craft and bring back to the political arena. In the meantime, Phil Sharp considered the document to be the self-serving kind of thing offered by people who offend and seek forgiveness before actual repentance because they just can't bear to admit their sins. This was consistent with the man Sharp described, years later, as "Indiana nice." By this, he meant to indicate a person "who won't take the last cookie on the plate but will stab you in the back." Pence was, in Sharp's estimate, profoundly and personally ambitious.

The Christianity Sharp observed in Pence wasn't the humble, turn-the-other-cheek sort. Instead, said Sharp, "Pence believes that God is on his side." The most troubling aspect of this belief, he added, was that Pence "can tolerate any amount of darkness to get his way."

4

LIMBAUGH LIGHT

Cry aloud; do not hold back; lift up your voice like a trumpet.

—Isaiah 58:1

In 1991, Mike Pence, two-time election loser, was looking for something new to do with his time. Other defeated congressional candidates would return to their prior work in business or a profession, but Pence had no particular interest in practicing law, which was what he had trained to do. He lacked the standing to land a teaching gig (another common choice for defeated politicians), and nothing in his experience suggested he was qualified to work in government. Pence was left looking for some other way for him to stay true to the career mantra of his generation— "Do what you love"—and to make a livelihood out of work that he could enjoy.

What Mike Pence enjoyed was arguing. This didn't mean he liked to fight, although he had shown he would make verbal attacks when necessary. What he preferred was to charm and persuade, and he was good at it. Like a kid who learns in Little League that he can hit a baseball better than most grown men, Pence had found his preternatural public speaking talent in the high school debate club. And, unlike athletes, who rarely get much better after they become adults, Pence possessed skills that could be developed for decades to come. It was his good fortune to find himself adrift and looking for somewhere to attach himself at a time when a great effort was being made to create comfortable homes for well-spoken young conservatives.

By 1991, foundations and wealthy individuals had nearly completed the construction of an alternative infrastructure for the development of people and arguments to advance an agenda of low taxes, deregulation, curtailed government, and Christian Right morality. Conceived to oppose colleges and universities, which were considered irredeemably biased against conservative thought, these institutions ranged from nationally oriented centers such as the Heritage Foundation to dozens of state and local groups scattered around the country. Year after year, donors kept these think tanks operating with millions of dollars. Corporate backers represented the tobacco, drug, and technology industries, among others. Family foundations included the names DeVos, Coors, Olin, Scaife, and Koch.

The conservative organizations funded writers and researchers—many were given academic-sounding titles such as "distinguished fellow"—who generally devoted themselves to completing manuscripts that supported preset policy goals. Among the notions spawned in these places, the granddaddy of them all was "supply side" economics, which found little support among economists but justified such policy prescriptions as tax cuts for the rich, which also happened to benefit the wealthy and big business. (Put simply, this theory suggests that rather than dampen prices, abundance stimulates demand, so tax cuts would rev up the economy. This is the opposite of what happens in the real world, where once buyers have what they want, they close their wallets.) The salesmanship practiced by the institutes that distributed papers backing supply-side economics and other partisan ideas reduced policy to a matter of marketing, with victory going to the argument packaged with the right slogan and adequate budget.[1]

At the national and local levels, the think tanks were filled with young people who were groomed for lifelong service to conservative causes and somewhat older men and women who used them as temporary homes when they were between campaigns or jobs in government. Mike Pence fit into both categories and within weeks of losing the 1990 election got a position as president of the Indiana Policy Review Foundation. Funded by many of the same benefactors who supported the national organizations, IPR claimed to commission studies but more typically funded political broadsides. As a Republican budget expert told *The Indianapolis Star,* "They've thrown out some ideas, but so far, everything's fairly loose." When Pence took over, the review operated with a budget of $200,000 per year. Its main activities were publishing a journal and submitting articles to newspapers. In general, the group favored businesses and Republicans and opposed Democrats, unions, and government agencies.

The position at IPR required that Pence oversee the operation of the foundation and serve as its principal cheerleader. Friendly and soft-spoken, Pence excelled as a promoter. Within two years, he increased funding to $500,000. During the same time, the little institute gained wider notice in the press and greater influence in the state capitol. Much of this progress was due to Pence's mild but also determined advocacy, which sometimes required a bit of debate club trickery. When a critic noted that the IPR pledged to "exalt the truths of the Declaration of Independence, especially those concerning the interrelated freedoms of religion, enterprise, and speech" though none of these truths are referenced in the declaration, Pence was steadfast in defense. "We talk about the freedoms *of* the Declaration, not *in* the Declaration," he said. Such sophistry was nonsense.

Under Pence, the IPR became more provocative, adding social commentary to its otherwise dry menu of proposals on taxation and municipal services. In one paper, Douglas Kmiec, a law professor at Notre Dame, used the news that basketball star Magic Johnson had been diagnosed with HIV to argue that "the only genuine morality" in sex occurred in marriage. He went on to criticize President Bush for praising Johnson's public statements on his condition. Under Pence, the IPR alleged "systemic corruption" at state universities based on a study of instructor salaries that erroneously included administrators and physicians at university hospitals. The author of the study complained that the IPR had released a draft that wasn't ready for publication and gave it a title he felt was inaccurate. He told a local paper that because of this experience, he hoped to have "little or nothing to do" with the think tank in the future.

Seemingly modeled after the snide and provocative *American Spectator,* the *Indiana Policy Review*'s opinion pieces often reeked of derision and prejudice. Its writers seemed especially vexed by gay Americans' demands for equal rights. In one piece, which included what was undoubtedly the most extensive, prurient, and graphic descriptions of sex acts ever printed in a "policy" magazine, retired colonel Ronald Ray insisted that "homosexuality is a grave threat to our national health and our national security" because it made people vulnerable to blackmail.[2]

Another essay published by Pence decried the idea that "gaydom be elevated from a pathological condition or mere sexual preference to the status of one of several natural human divergences such as hair or skin color." (In fact, medical authorities *had abandoned the idea that homosexuality was a pathology* in 1973.) The magazine was also irked by efforts by the disabled to reach equal status, criticizing President Bush for supporting the Americans with Disabilities Act. The latter piece was credited to a "senior fellow" who had recently been a staffer at the Indiana Chamber of Commerce. The same author, who was called an economist but didn't have a doctorate, was a frequent critic of public schools and argued forcefully for proposals that shifted tax dollars to private schools under the rubric of "choice" in education.[3]

In his own writing, Pence initially avoided controversies by taking people-pleasing positions. In one article, he defended native son Vice President Dan Quayle against those who would push him off the GOP ticket. In another, he advocated term limits for elected state officials and members of Congress. Term limits would reduce the power of entrenched incumbents like his nemesis Phil Sharp. (Pence did not consider the argument that long-serving members of Congress often use their seniority to benefit the folks back home.) When he eventually sharpened his focus, Pence aimed at an easy target—a local talk radio host named Stan Solomon. In a piece published in *The Indianapolis Star*, Pence criticized Solomon for making personal attacks and concluded he was a crank.

New to the Indiana airwaves, Solomon was a conspiracy-minded provocateur whose politics fit well with Pence's but whose style couldn't have been more different. Solomon said he believed the Central Intelligence Agency armed civil rights protesters and that the men who carried out the bombing of a federal building in Oklahoma City were part of a federal plot. He called Rev. Jesse Jackson a "pimp," declared Anita Hill a "slut," and said a local critic got his ideas "out of an enema bag." He also theorized that the Holocaust occurred in part because "influential Jewish people started promoting as fact that homosexuality is just as acceptable as heterosexuality." To keep himself safe, Solomon always carried a pistol.[4]

Solomon had a six-day-a-week outlet on a prominent Indianapolis station, WIBC. His job proved the moneymaking power of provocative radio personalities who energized both those who agreed with their views and those who were repelled. The trend toward this kind of on-air talk had been established by the nationally syndicated Rush Limbaugh, whose acidic schtick was more sophisticated but no less pointed than Solomon's. Among the imitators who arose across the country, Solomon was one of the most extreme and made an easy target for the outrage of those who wanted to position themselves as more moderate.

As he criticized Solomon, Mike Pence was starting his own broadcasting career at WXIR, a tiny station owned by the American Bible Radio Group and which was devoted to the broadcast of sermons and Christian music. In a short time, he moved to a bigger station that gave him a weekly show. Pence performed in a style that he admitted "rips off Rush Limbaugh." Limbaugh's record of stoking outrage and intensifying the political divide made him an odd role model for a man who had just published his "Confessions of a Negative Campaigner," and Pence promoted right-wing views with an Indiana focus. Add the periodic publication of his own *Mike Pence Report* on politics—about 250 people paid the $19.95 per year to subscribe—and it was obvious that he was building a personal brand that competed with the Indiana Policy Review Foundation. By the end of 1993, Pence decided to leave the little think tank. The break was apparently hastened by a disagreement over founder Charles Quilhot's increasing criticism of Senator Richard Lugar. A moderate in a GOP that was leaning ever more Right, Lugar wasn't conservative enough for Quilhot, who called for the senator to resign. (This was the opening salvo in what would be a long assault on Lugar from his Right flank.) Pence objected to the attack, and by January 1994, he was finished as the boss at IPR, which he said was becoming too conservative for him. He was, apparently, a Lugar Republican.[5]

When *The Mike Pence Show* went daily in April 1994, the host said he didn't expect to run for public office again. The "restraints on my ability to be candid are very frustrating," said Pence as he wondered aloud whether he ever had the temperament for campaigning. In a newspaper interview, he seemed embarrassed by his performance as a candidate. "I don't think there was any style of negative campaigning I didn't use," he confessed. The only campaign mistake he blamed on others was his use of the for-profit committee that paid his bills. He smelled something fishy in the fact that the law permitted these practices even though they were toxic in the minds of voters. "It's one of those rabbit traps that the political classes laid for challengers," he complained, and it taught him that politics was a game he would rather not play. Broadcasting was a career choice, he said, not a step toward another run. He said he wasn't a "good and effective politician" and he felt that all his ambition for office had disappeared. "If I was trying to rehabilitate myself, this would be an interesting way to do it," he allowed. "I'm just not."

On the radio, Pence spent 180 minutes daily (minus commercials) sharing his views, interviewing guests, and taking calls from listeners. Folksy in a way Limbaugh could never be, Pence opened his show with the words, "Greetings across the waves of amber grain," and he talked about everything from basketball to the weather, but his most frequent topics revolved around a bleak vision of American society.

"Our nation is in decline," he said as he complained about abortion, teen pregnancy, and divorce. Where others saw economic factors—stalled wages, rising prices—requiring parents to work more and putting families under stress, Pence imagined that political liberals were to blame. In his mind, feminism wasn't a struggle for equality but rather an attack on the way things should be. Social programs weren't intended to address human needs but rather deliberate efforts to undermine families. "The epicenter of our cultural decline is the decline of the family," said Pence. "Welfare regulation, illegitimacy, outcome-based education, too much government; all are directly related to the decline of the family." (An approach that assessed students on their mastery of course materials, outcome-based education was backed by business leaders and many Republicans but then became a bogeyman for Christian conservatives who believed it undermined religion.)[6]

Radio Mike stood reliably on the Right and often sought to get ahead of whatever trends moved the GOP. When fellow Christian Right activist Newt Gingrich mounted a drive to become Speaker of the House of Representatives in 1994, Pence supported him on the radio. When Pat Buchanan ran well in the 1996 Iowa caucuses, Pence ignored William F. Buckley's denunciation of Buchanan as an extremist (because he had questioned the historical record of the Holocaust) to say he was "four square in the mainstream." On the broadcast where he defended Buchanan, Pence also interviewed Chris Dickson of a local organization called Family First, whom he said "proudly falls into the category" of the Christian Right and thanked him for leaving his "horns and pitchfork" at home. Dickson's main concern was America's "moral decay," which he said could be repaired by "conservative evangelicals." Toward this end, he quizzed candidates on their positions, distributed literature, and ran two failed campaigns for local office. He didn't like the press and sought to counteract its influence by purchasing airtime on a radio station where he broadcast his views and read from the Bible.[7]

Skepticism about the news media was a frequent topic for Mike Pence, who said that journalists "vilified" people who applied their religious convictions to politics. Of course, he was not above vilifying others for values that conflicted with his. He declared Dr. Jack Kevorkian "a monster" for assisting a dying woman's suicide. And a news item about a female officer breaking a military rule against adultery led him to a discussion of the Ten Commandments, "the normalization" of adultery, and whether women should be permitted to serve. "I for one," said Pence, "believe the seventh commandment contained in the Ten Commandments is still a big deal." He couldn't help but mock the woman involved in the affair as both a "grizzled feminist" and a "doe-eyed hapless victim." He asked, "What could possibly be a bigger deal?" than her affair with a civilian man.

With pop and country music bumpers announcing the start and end of segments, Pence beckoned people to call 1-800-603-MIKE and leafed through the newspapers. As he gained confidence as a broadcaster, Pence tried out some impressions—he did a good Bill Clinton—and put some distance between himself and the likes of Solomon and Limbaugh, who, he said, took things too personally. His show was "infotainment," he added. "I'm conservative, but not in a bad way." Pence talked of Solomon as someone who lived in the "paranoid little tributaries" of politics.

Opposite as they were in style, Pence and Solomon were sometimes bonded on issues such as gays serving the military, and they were both outspoken in their hope that conservative Christianity would guide government officials. The main difference was that while Solomon ranted and railed, Pence expressed himself in an indoor voice. After the 1996 Republican National Convention, Pence lamented the low TV ratings and blamed them on appearances and speeches by "an endless line of pro-choice women, AIDS activists, and proponents of affirmative action." The party needed to remember, he wrote, that "traditional Pro-Family conservatives make up the bedrock of modern Republican electoral success."[8]

Solomon and Pence were also both temporarily employed by the same Rev. Gene Hood who had stormed the Miss Gay America pageant, been arrested at a women's health clinic, and donated to Pence's failed campaign for Congress. Hood, of the Independent Nazarene Church, controlled a string of Christian radio stations, including two in Indiana. One of his stations carried Pence in 1995 but dropped him when Pence refused to stop booking a guest named Harrison Ullman, who promoted more liberal-leaning views. "I want my show to be fair, civil, and open to all sides of an issue," Pence had said. Solomon was on the same station as Pence and would remain with Rev. Hood for years despite both his political vitriol and personal attacks. Nothing Solomon said seemed to trouble Hood. Speaking of one local businessman, Solomon said, without offering any evidence, "He can't keep his hands off very young girls." When contacted by the press, Rev. Hood said he thought Solomon should "lay off that tacky stuff" but kept Solomon on the air for three hours nightly.[9]

At the more powerful WIBC, Pence was more Indiana than the state fair, promoting local institutions, from the Indianapolis 500 car race to Indiana University basketball coach Bob Knight. Though hotheaded, profane, and physically abusive, Knight was a living legend in Indiana thanks to three national championships. When players began leaving the team because they couldn't adapt to Knight, Pence was among those who took the coach's side. Within three years, after further complaints and video and audio evidence became public, Knight was fired for behavior deemed "uncivil, defiant, and unacceptable."

Although Knight proved to be in the wrong and undeserving of support, Pence was on firm ground lining up behind him. For one thing, plenty of Hoosiers thought Knight's success and his position of authority meant he could do what he wanted with his players. Besides, Pence was himself becoming such a comfortable presence with his audience that he didn't have to worry much about any single comment. He was so well liked that when a station in Kokomo celebrated its fiftieth anniversary, Pence was brought in to do his show from the parking lot.

By the time he was broadcasting from a Kokomo parking lot, Pence was syndicated statewide on the Indiana Network, which was the property of Wabash Valley Broadcasting.

The tone of Pence's broadcasts helped attract advertisers who made the show profitable. Pence's income depended in part on the revenue, and he needed the salary to support a growing family. The Pences had always wanted children. However, in the first six years of their marriage, they had been disappointed by their inability to conceive. They had even tried gamete intrafallopian transfer, which is used by some Catholics to get around theological objections to procedures that involve fertilizing eggs outside the body.

GIFT, as the treatment is called, was not accepted by all Catholic authorities. Some objected to it on the grounds that it defied conception via the "marital act," even though the semen was collected in a condom during sex. Despite their extraordinary efforts, the Pences didn't conceive, and Karen would say she experienced a crisis of faith. Finally, after ending GIFT, she became pregnant at age thirty-four. A son, Michael Jr., was born in 1991. He was followed by two daughters named Audrey and Charlotte. Karen was no longer teaching, leaving her husband as the sole wage earner for the family. His prospects improved when his employer made him an offer to get into television.

Wabash Valley Broadcasting was owned by one of the wealthiest families in the country, the Hulman-George clan, which was also involved in real estate, finance, energy, and food processing. Its Indianapolis TV station, WNDY, was not affiliated with a major network. It aired mainly reruns of wholesome family shows. The station was a perfect fit for Pence, whose talk show was a mild-mannered version of national political round-table programs like *Meet the Press*. It was taped once weekly and aired at odd hours, when it competed against the likes of *Flipper, The Lawrence Welk Show, Teletubbies,* and *Barney and Friends.*

On TV, Pence used humor to turn his cornstalk image into an asset. Introduced as "the man who would have been the next James Bond, if his mom had let him," Pence worked hard to cultivate a connection with people who might share his perspective, which included a bit of anxiety if not resentment when it came to the world beyond Indiana. His first show, inspired by the debut of a racy new film called *Showgirls,* was set up as a battle between midwestern decency and the straw man of a de-praved entertainment industry.

Titled "Hollywood vs. Indiana," as if the film business had organized itself to hurt the people in Pence's audience, the entire half hour amounted to an alarm occasioned by a movie that was so bad that hardly anyone went to see it and it ruined the career of its star, Elizabeth Berkley. The little controversy around *Showgirls* was stimulated by the fact that the perky, blond-haired Berkley was previously known for her part in the squeaky-clean TV show *Saved by the Bell,* which presented a saccharine version of high school life. In *Showgirls,* Berkley's character, a stripper, was often nude or having sex of one sort or another. The contrast with her previous TV role was both intentional and disturbing for parents who had been happy for their kids to be fans of *Saved by the Bell.*

The panelists on Pence's first TV show generally agreed with the host's assault on Hollywood. Some called for regulations to control film and TV. They didn't seem to be aware that some of what was proposed had been tested before and found by courts to be unconstitutional. The high point of the program may have been Pence's imitation of national talk show host David Letterman's "Top Ten" list. In this version, Pence offered the Top Five Differences Between Indiana and Hollywood.

Among them were "In Indiana, people with paranoid delusions get therapy; in Hollywood, they write scripts for Oliver Stone" and "In Hollywood, people think Dan Quayle can't spell *potato;* in Indiana, people think Elizabeth Taylor can't spell *commitment*."

Setting aside the fact that Vice President Quayle actually misspelled *potato* on national TV and the elderly Taylor had been reduced to doing voice-overs for *The Simpsons,* Pence's Top Five was a pale imitation. The self-deprecating part of his presentation was warm and even charming. The Us vs. Them flavor of the Hollywood bashing seemed purposely crude. Besides, Pence was an avid consumer of Hollywood's products. He loved *The Wizard of Oz,* despite the feminist power of its main characters and the occult themes deployed by writer L. Frank Baum, who was a member of the pre–new age Theosophical Society. If he could find something beautiful in *Oz,* it was disingenuous to encourage a culture war between Hollywood and the Heartland. Supply and demand drove the production of films and television programs, and people in Indiana supplied some of the demand.

As on the radio, on TV Pence rarely wandered beyond Indiana, but when he did, he was likely to fix his attention on Bill Clinton, who, as president, was a favorite target of right-wing broadcasters. Unlike Limbaugh and others, Pence tried to confine his critique to policy, but then came the Monica Lewinsky sex scandal and impeachment proceedings. Pence expressed revulsion whenever Clinton was mentioned, and when Clinton was acquitted, he became convinced that the problem was too much democracy. According to Pence, things went awry with the Seventeenth Amendment to the Constitution, which, in 1913, required that United States senators be elected and not appointed. The amendment had been adopted in response to vote-buying and bribery scandals. The unfortunate result, in Pence's view, was that senators were too concerned about public opinion and thus wouldn't vote to strip a popular president of his office. He thought more presidents had been more vulnerable to impeachment under the previous system (history showed this was not true) and that this was beneficial.[10]

In the Indianapolis TV market, Pence's half-hour shows couldn't compete with the nightly news programs. However, week after week, the program gave him the chance to practice and polish his public persona. Ann DeLaney, a prominent Indiana Democrat, was a regular guest who would recall Pence as a man who "was using his personality to make a living, and so it was in his interest, it seems to me, to get along more with people." Decades later, she would compare the 2018 version of Pence with the one she knew in the 1990s and find she liked the old one better. "He didn't have the same kind of saccharine sincerity that he evidences now in his public speaking," she said. "So, he was fine to deal with in that context. You know, you could disagree with him then, and certainly we did. I did. But there wasn't any animus involved."

Four times each year, Pence the TV host presented one-hour specials, which brought him into elite circles in business and politics. In 1995, the first of these shows was recorded at the home of Stephen Hilbert, who headed Conseco Financial, which at the time invested in projects across the country, including a building bought with Donald Trump. At the time Hoosiers knew Trump as a New York–based real estate promoter. High flying and highly leveraged, Conseco's stock was nearing the top of a stunning run that would take it from one dollar in 1989 to fifty-eight dollars in 1998. Named one of America's "shrewdest dealmakers" by *Fortune* magazine, Hilbert's main personal asset was, according to one colleague, "an uncanny ability to get people to believe," which made him an Indiana version of Donald Trump.

In four years, Hilbert would be fired, as, under his leadership, the firm headed for a crash in the form of the third-biggest bankruptcy in American history, which would wipe out billions in investor equity and render the stock virtually worthless. But in the moment, Hilbert, who earned $117 million in 1994, was one of the most influential executives in America. He was also famously erratic in his personal life. When Pence met him, Hilbert was just beginning his sixth marriage and in the midst of a physical transformation that included a fifty-pound weight loss and surgery to allow him to stop wearing glasses. He was forty-nine. His wife was twenty-four and still practiced an instrument—the saxophone— she'd played in her high school's marching band. The Hilberts lived in the most expensive home in the state, which was decorated with a mural of Alexander the Great and portraits of nudes painted by French masters. Built at a cost of $35 million, the compound included a separate barn that housed an indoor basketball court and a three-thousand-square-foot guardhouse. Hilbert was personally involved in the local horse racing and casino industries, which depended on state licensing, and was partner in a race car team. He frequently hosted the state's political elite at his home and regularly donated to their campaigns. He favored the GOP but sometimes gave to Democrats, including Governor Evan Bayh, who appointed Hilbert to the Indiana State University board of trustees and defended him when he was criticized for not attending the board's meetings.[11]

When Pence taped his show at Hilbert's home, the program was arranged as a group discussion with the Conseco chief and seven other executives from big locally based firms, including Mitchell Daniels of Eli Lilly. Daniels had previously been Senator Richard Lugar's chief of staff. One of the execs caused a little stir when he agreed that "family" was the most important thing in life but added that he considered business associates to be part of his family. Hilbert may have offered the most candid reply to one of Pence's questions when he confessed that he was motivated by "fear of failure." At moments the show verged on parody. Longtime local television reporter Jim Shella described it as "movers and shakers sit around a dinner table and hold a conversation. I think it was really bad TV."

Where DeLaney sensed in Pence a pleasant get-along guy, others detected in him an overeager desire to please. Local political reporter John Krull said Pence had a "puppyish desire to ingratiate himself and oversell everything he does." Among the powerful, Pence posed as a "good professional son," added Krull. "He will approach those political figures and say, 'Please lead me, guide me.' He's got the gift of giving them credit, whatever he might accomplish, even if he ended up not taking their advice."

Taken together, Pence's broadcasting career—radio, weekly television, occasional specials—made him famous across the state, put him in contact with top political figures, and allowed him to approach men and women who were wealthy potential campaign donors with access to vast networks of like-minded and similarly wealthy people. In every encounter, Pence could offer access to his airwaves in trade for whatever these powerful people gave him. Along the way, he could test out various positions on issues and receive what were essentially instant poll results in the form of listener responses and ratings.

The mostly positive responses helped Pence make adjustments. Bruce Stinebrickner, from his post as a political science professor at DePauw University in Terre Haute, watched Pence's development and saw a remarkable example of self-invention. "It strikes me if you were drawing up a composite portrait of what a president might look like, Pence was pretty close to it—extremely conservative but also opportunistic." With decades of experience watching the political process, Stinebrickner had admiration for "principled conservatives." This was not the main trait he detected in Pence. "I think he's more political than the average politician. And those are not words of praise."

The politics practiced by Pence reflected his professed "evangelical Catholic" faith, which allowed him to keep one foot planted in the state's largest faith group and another in its second largest and most well organized. He and Karen demonstrated their Protestant/evangelical preference by attending Grace Evangelical Church. A large Indianapolis congregation located on the south side of the city in a suburban neighborhood, Grace was a small denomination—the Evangelical Free Church of America—that stressed that the Bible is literal truth handed down by God and completely free of error. Church leaders taught that Satan is a real being with a personality who is the enemy of God. They anticipated Jesus's return to Earth to reign over one thousand years of peace. In the meantime, the denomination sought to help individuals and communities conform to a conservative Christian way of life.

Grace's pastor, Bryan Hult, was a clean-cut young man whose short hair and firm posture indicated his past as an army officer and helicopter pilot and his present as a chaplain in the National Guard. Hult was not just a minister but also a counselor certified by the National Association of Nouthetic Counselors. The term *nouthetic* related to a Greek word for *confrontation*. The counseling is not psychological but religious, which explains why the association's founder, Rev. Jay Adams, regarded mental illness as one of many "euphemisms that exist in the area of psychiatry and psychology, which have confused the public so greatly."

In their rejection of mainstream mental health concepts, Adams and his students were similar to Scientologists, who saw spiritual problems where others saw neurosis or psychosis. Treatment involved getting one's life aligned with God's will, as Adams's ministry determined it. Students of his "institute" were not required to write papers, take exams, or conduct research. God was presumed to monitor their mastery of the material. Certificates were granted on request to those who paid.[12]

People who joined Grace could immerse themselves in a community devoted to supporting their commitment to a conservative Christian way of life. In the time when Mike and Karen Pence joined, Grace was growing at a rate that would make it one of the first so-called "megachurches" in the state, a phenomenon that began in the South and spread across the country. The trend toward large congregations turned churches into communities where members worshipped, prayed, did business, and even voted together. (The prototypical megachurch was Rev. Jerry Falwell's Thomas Road Baptist Church in Lynchburg, Virginia, which hosted his *Old Time Gospel Hour* TV show.) The rise of these big congregations was accompanied by new concern for politics marked by opposition to abortion and an embrace of Republican policies and candidates. Homeschooling was popular among some believers who wanted to remove their children from the influence of public school teachers and students. Others agitated for new laws to permit public funding for private, church-based schools so their kids could learn among the like-minded with the state paying their tuition.

Although the ministers at Grace were not as openly political as the nation's most overtly partisan pastors, members harbored little doubt that their faith favored conservative Republicans. Their beliefs also commanded them to arrange their marriages so that wives would yield to their husbands and children would show consistent obedience. (The relevant scripture reads, "Wives, submit to your own husbands, as to the Lord. For the husband is the head of the wife even as Christ is the head of the church, his body, and is himself its Savior.") They were also expected to go into the world to make it more in step with the Bible as they read it. For Mike and Karen Pence, as well as their fellow congregants, the strict ethos preached at Grace supplied boundaries that could make life seem more ordered and support their preexisting beliefs.

For Karen Pence, one key preexisting belief regarded homosexuality as a sinful state, and she was opposed to efforts to gain acceptance for gays and lesbians. In the summer of 1991, she was offended by a newspaper article that gave six young people who were gay an opportunity to describe their experiences as teens. They generally focused on the difficulties they had endured, and the article was titled, BEING GAY COMPOUNDS TEENS' PROBLEMS. A sidebar reported on a hotline that provides "help amid terror" (hardly an endorsement of homosexuality) for young people with questions.

Although the Children's Express page in *The Indianapolis Star* was punctuated by cautions, Karen Pence noted one nineteen-year-old's anecdote about a crush he had on a male teacher when he was eight: "I knew I was different from then on." In a letter to the editor, Mrs. Pence wrote, "No wonder our youth are confused. I only pray that most parents were able to intercept your article before their children were encouraged to call the Gay/Lesbian Youth Hotline which encourages them to 'accept their homosexuality' instead of encouraging them that they are not." Pence wrote that, as a teacher, she had encouraged her elementary school pupils to read Children's Express, but in the future she would not.[13]

Having left her teaching career, Karen Pence wouldn't have to deal with schoolchildren who were concerned about their sexual identity or worry about anything they might read. However, she didn't entirely withdraw from public issues. In 1998, she helped put together a fund-raiser for a local jeweler named Gary Hofmeister who had decided to run for Congress against Democratic incumbent Julia Carson. Hofmeister was a divorced man who nevertheless decried the social change of the 1960s, when divorce lost its stigma. This record mattered little to his supporters in local evangelical groups, who were firmly behind his campaign. Their faith required only that one profess to be a believer today. Their politics demanded that they share the positions he advocated, including the creation of vouchers to allow parents to direct tax money to private and religious schools and opposition to abortion rights. Despite help from a national organization called the Christian Coalition and local groups such as Good Shepherd Community Ministries, Hofmeister lost by 18 percent.[14]

Anyone looking at the Hofmeister/Carson election would have been

hard-pressed to see any sign that Mike Pence was wavering on his decision to stay out of politics. Karen's work indirectly reminded politicos
that her husband might return to the game. She helped organize a circus
fund-raiser in July and then, later in the campaign, helped put together a
rally and luncheon where former vice president Dan Quayle and his
wife, Marilyn, were the honored guests. These activities brought her
close to the state GOP elite, where she could judge the mood of the
party, measure the caliber of its ambitious men and women, and, perhaps,
imagine where her husband might rank in comparison.

5

GUNS, GOD, AND MONEY

For the Lord your God is the one who goes with you to fight
for you against your enemies to give you victory.

—*Deuteronomy 20:4*

Walking into a shooting club in Columbus, Indiana, one day in the spring
of 2000, Mike Pence did his best to look like a regular guy. He took off
his jacket, but he could do nothing about his crisp, white button-down
shirt. He donned protective glasses, stuck his hands in his pockets, and
slouched a bit to show he was comfortable in the macho confines of the
Hoosier Hills Rifle and Pistol Club. The sound of gunshots echoed off
the cinder-block walls.

Pence visited the range to make a pitch for votes. Home to a national champion, Elisha Hoover, whose weapon of choice was a military-
style AR-15 rifle, the club was an ideal hunting ground for the vote-seeking
Pence, who was ardent in his support for the National Rifle Association's
rigid opposition to every proposal to regulate guns. Once known only as a
sporting organization, in 1977 the NRA adopted a single-issue political
mission that involved continually sounding an alarm about efforts to
limit gun purchases and funding candidates who embraced their agenda
of antiregulation. With gun manufacturers pouring millions of dollars into

this effort, enthusiasts bought more weapons. By 2000, the number of guns in private hands was about to exceed the U.S. population even as the percentage of households where a gun was present steadily declined. The NRA had become one of the most powerful single-issue groups in the country.[1]

Politicized and frequently mobilized by the NRA, gun owners formed a reliable voting bloc, and clubs like Hoosier Hills became perfect points of contact for campaigning politicians who had received the national organization's approval. As they arrived at shooting ranges and clubhouses, the vote-seekers entered a subculture where guns were symbolic of all sorts of conservative values, including a lock-'em-up approach to crime and a devotion to right-wing Christianity (hence such organizations as Christian Deer Hunters and Christian Hunters and Anglers). Pence needed the men at Hoosier Hills because, despite declaring he was through with the dirty rotten world of election campaigns—"I've had all of the political ambition knocked out of me," he said—he wasn't. Indeed, in the summer of 1999, Mike Pence had sent paperwork to the Federal Election Commission to start the process of running for Congress again.[2]

What had changed besides Pence's mind? First, thanks to his TV and radio gigs, he was locally famous—a statewide celebrity, actually. Second, the congressional seat he wanted was going to be unoccupied. His nemesis Phil Sharp had retired in 1994, to be replaced by Republican David McIntosh, who intended to run for governor in 2000. In the summer of 1999, McIntosh had discussed his decision over breakfast with a group of powerful Republican activists, including Van Smith, who ran a manufacturing and real estate empire from a headquarters in Muncie. As chairman of the U.S. Chamber of Commerce, Smith was also a national political figure with access to a network of conservative donors. After breakfast, he called Pence to say he should get back into politics. As Smith would later recall, Pence "said he wouldn't do it without Karen's blessing." It came quickly.[3]

When Pence and Karen surveyed the political landscape, they could see that no one else in Indiana's Second District was as well known or well connected to the political power and money elite as Mike. In fact, since his losing effort in 1990, Mike Pence had fashioned himself into an ideal candidate for the seat. Three weeks after McIntosh said he was leaving the House of Representatives, news reports indicated Pence was considering a run for his seat.

The opportunism was obvious, but there was more at work. Former campaign manager Sherman Johnson would recall sensing that Pence still thought the Christian conservative agenda was best for the country. He remained adamant about outlawing abortion, determined to cut taxes, and worried about the strength of the U.S. military, even if the end of the Cold War had left the nation with no major adversary. These beliefs were still powerful, even if he was also motivated by ego.

"If Mike were driven by *pure* ambition and the lust for public adulation, he would have run again much sooner for something," Johnson said. Instead, Pence had been rocked by his early experience, which included not only the back-to-back defeats but the realization that he had betrayed his own personal ideals with negative tactics. "A reasonable person would certainly step back and take stock of things, as did Mike," added Johnson. "Then, as time moves forward, one decides what one wants to still accomplish and how best to achieve those goals."

Along with Pence, the Republican field for the open seat included four lawyers, two local politicians, and a retired teacher who hosted a radio gospel program. With party affiliation favoring the GOP, the Republican nominee would be the favorite to win the general election. Pence pursued it with a caution missing when he was younger and with the aid of more powerful friends. Among them was Bill Smith, former aide to Indiana Republican Congressman Dan Burton and founder of the Christian Right organization called the Indiana Family Institute.

Smith and Pence had become close friends in the 1990s. They were amused by the fact that they each were married to women named Karen and had family pets, dogs, named Buddy. Like so many like-minded activists, Smith was involved in a range of activities that included a radio program, a newsletter, and speaking tours. During one of these tours, prior to joining Pence as his 2000 campaign manager, Smith accompanied author Frank Peretti to gatherings across the state. Peretti was the Stephen King of the conservative Christian world. His most popular books included a series of horror stories for young readers. They imagined a community overtaken by demons whom young believers, aided by angels, must kill.

Smith's political background and Christian Right beliefs made him an ideal person to advise a candidate who wanted to blend politics and religion to win votes. When Smith accepted the job of campaign manager he signaled to all other Republicans that Pence was the front-runner. The first competition among the potential candidates involved the scramble for campaign money. In the early going, the man or woman who amasses the biggest war chest looks like the one with the most power, and this creates a kind of momentum.

Candidates generally insist that their political positions and votes are not for sale and that people who fund their campaigns are simply backing the one who already supports their priorities. No one in politics believes this is true, which is why, in 1988 and 1990, Pence made a big deal out of Phil Sharp's habit of accepting donations from political action committees. Everyone knows that committees and individuals give to gain access and influence. Pence's first campaigns were funded mainly by businesspeople—many from local industries like Cummins Engine—who had their own interests, but they were harder to discern than the goals of a PAC named for a labor group, a commercial association, or policy priority. Nevertheless, the donors would make their wishes clear, and it would be understood that future support depended on performance.

After nearly a decade of making connections as Radio Mike, Pence knew the big players who could give and also connect him to others who would make donations. However, no one can function as both the chief fund-raiser and the candidate for a campaign. Pence relied on an Indiana-based manufacturing executive, Kelly Stanley, to guide fund-raising. Kelly was also vice chairman of the United States Chamber of Commerce. He raised $100,000 in a single month at the end of 1999.

At about this time, Pence interviewed with a key national political action committee called the Club for Growth that had been created with the aid of the Koch brothers' political machine and advised about 1,500 wealthy donors, a number of whom were Wall Street investors. Most of these people had never met Mike Pence or any of the other candidates they were backing, but they agreed with the club's priorities—tax cuts and deregulating business—and were guided by its endorsements. They sent checks to the organization, which in turn sent them to campaigns in twice-monthly Federal Express shipments. For example, in 2000, first-time candidate for Congress Jeff Flake said that every two weeks as much as $15,000 just arrived at his doorstep in Arizona in the form of checks from people he didn't know. This terrified moderate incumbent Republicans who understood that the club used primary elections to oust GOPers who were insufficiently right-wing. As founder Stephen Moore would say in 2003, "We say we're going to run someone against them, and they start wetting their pants."[4]

Candidates who wanted Club for Growth's money appeared at gatherings where they were inspected like political livestock. They were quizzed about their positions, and their appearance and speaking style were examined with an eye toward their abilities as campaigners. One of the participants in 1999, who had been on Pence's radio show in Indiana, would recall that Pence "wowed the audience." At the time, the organization was smarting from Republican president George H. W. Bush's tax hike, which was made despite his "read my lips" promise to never raise federal revenues. Founder Moore, who considered politicians "cowards" at heart, wanted to scare those who were Republicans into becoming extremists when it came to cutting taxes and regulation to favor business and investors. He was so uninterested in social issues that he banned the word *abortion* from club meetings and so determined that when he went after one senator, he said he wanted a "scalp on the wall."

In the 2000 election, the men and women of Moore's club wanted to help elect members of Congress who would resist the gravitational pull of the middle ground of politics where, historically, the spirit of compromise led to policy. From their perspective, the game in Washington was a win-or-lose affair, and they were willing to pay for victory. However, this required candidates who were more than committed to the cause. They needed to be persuasive, presentable, and personable. In other words, they needed to be like Mike Pence. After he appeared for inspection, Pence was selected to be one of ten newcomers favored by the club. Two of the members were Ric Keller of Florida and Scott Garrett of New Jersey, who, like Pence, were clean-cut men with law degrees, brilliant smiles, and a gift for public speaking. Like him, they were also fervently opposed to both abortion rights and the legalization of same-sex marriages.

With the club's acceptance, Pence and the others became eligible to receive shipments of checks. Pence would eventually receive a bit more than $3,100 from a Club for Growth account and an additional $62,400 in checks that the club collected from its members and forwarded to him. PACs representing tobacco companies, financial firms, auto dealers, and others filled his coffers with what would eventually be more than $1 million. Pence's list of contributors would include stalwarts of the Christian Right like Amway heir Richard DeVos and J. Patrick Rooney of the insurance company Golden Rule Financial, who compared his conflicts with regulators to Jesus Christ's preaching. "Jesus was put to death not for his miracle," noted Rooney, "but for his criticism of those in power." Rooney advocated replacing government health care programs like Medicare and Medicaid with private insurance.

In his part of Indiana, Pence got money from Cummins executives, including his own brother Edward. High-level people at Conseco donated. Among them was another brother, Thomas J. Pence, who had been hired by the high-flying Stephen Hilbert's firm. Many contributions came from the wealthy Rose family of Indianapolis, including two checks from Thomas Rose, publisher of *The Jerusalem Post* in Israel. Rose shared Pence's adamant positions against abortion and gay rights. He said that English should be made "the official language of the United States" and imagined there was a "secular assault on God" taking place in American society.

While Rose and others stood for certain religious values, the libertarian movement was represented in the Pence campaign by the likes of T. Alan Russell of the Indianapolis-based Liberty Fund. The fund used its $300 million endowment to back candidates, treat judges to vacations and seminars, and publish books like the works of Ludwig von Mises. A twentieth-century economic theorist who found a limited number of followers in his profession, von Mises was made into a hero by anti-government businesspeople and politicians who held that the unfettered pursuit of wealth produced the best result for society.[5]

Ludwig von Mises would have regarded the Pence campaign's fund-raising as an effective form of political capitalism. The candidate had identified his market, supplied the promise of his ideology, and netted much more than the national average for congressional races. In Indiana, where everything from advertising to office space came at a discount compared with the coasts, the money meant he could blanket the airwaves with ads. In the Republican primary, his advantages helped him sail to victory when voters cast their ballots in early May. The Democratic Party nominated Bob Rock, a former Marine and a successful lawyer, as their candidate. Rock was a political newcomer whose reputation, one voter noted, was marked by his inherent "kindness." Hard-pressed to match Pence in any of the campaign arts, from stump speeches to fund-raising, his entire campaign would be run with a little less than $380,000.[6]

As Pence turned to the general election, his campaign team built a website where they presented "The Pence Agenda: A Guide to Restoring the American Dream." The agenda was fourteen pages of bullet-pointed directions for congressional actions. Of the eleven points collected under the headline "Restoring Moral Integrity," ten referenced abortion. One point was a call for a constitutional amendment to make the procedure illegal nationwide. The eleventh item called for a ban on physician-assisted suicide. Pence made mention of no other moral issues, but elsewhere in this document he called for policies to favor two-parent families and to ban marriage for anyone but heterosexual couples. He also asked that federal funds go to groups devoted to changing the sexual behavior of gay people.

If the Pence moral agenda seemed to have been written by Catholic bishops, and it did, other parts of the document could have been cribbed from PowerPoint presentations made at meetings of the Club for Growth. Pence called for tax cuts and more treaties like the North American Free Trade Agreement, which promoted open global markets. (Among his ideas was a Free Trade Agreement of the Americas that would span the Western Hemisphere.) He promised to support all the items pushed by the Club for Growth and others who wanted government functions shifted to profit-making businesses, and he sounded an alarm about federal debt, which at the time stood at $5.6 trillion—a little less than 60 percent of the gross domestic product.

All of Pence's business and economic positions were standard GOP issue. The arguments for them were many years old and once memorized could be offered in succinct portions. Where he strayed was in the emphasis he put on social issues. Noting the "cultural primacy" of the "two-parent family," he opposed civil rights protections for gay Americans and promised to fight funding for any AIDS programs that "celebrate and encourage" same-sex relationships. This language reflected a rhetorical twist often used in the conservative Christian world, where many considered AIDS God's punishment for sin and regarded homosexuality as both a disorder and a public health problem. With this in mind, Pence called for the government to fund programs that would assist "those seeking to change their sexual behavior." Overwhelming evidence indicated that at best these programs failed and at worst they traumatized participants. The only foreign policy point Pence stressed was support for Israel, and here he went to great lengths to explain his commitment, which included expanding aid to Israel even if it required cuts in aid to others.

Pence rarely explained his agenda, or any item in it, in detail. At larger events, including rallies and debates, he stressed instead the feel-good message of TV ads, which announced, "He believes that America is one nation, under God, rich with a purpose yet to be fulfilled. Renewing the American dream." When needed, this big-picture inspiration was supplemented with carefully targeted messages meant to excite small groups of special-interest voters. One mailer, sent to just ten thousand gun enthusiasts, featured an image of the Bill of Rights with several bullet holes. "Some politicians in Washington, D.C. would like to choose what liberties we have," noted the text in the mailer. "Mike Pence believes they are all worth protecting."[7]

Voters who combined religion and politics once again became key to Pence's campaign, as he stressed his opposition to abortion rights. At many churches and church-affiliated colleges, Pence stirred excitement among those who shared his fears about the country's moral direction, especially in the areas of sex and reproduction. At Indiana Wesleyan University, students eagerly volunteered for the campaign and followed Pence closely. Then a junior preparing to be a youth minister, Chris Warren, noted that "the idea was that we were going to get 'one of ours' into

Congress and he would advocate for what we believed." Warren would become an enthusiastic Pence supporter and volunteer. Upon graduation in 2001, he would become a youth minister for a Church of the Brethren congregation in Madison County, Indiana. Related to the Mennonites and Amish, the Brethren were similarly devoted to plain living, which they expressed in the way they dressed and their focus on their spiritual lives. Warren grew up in this denomination, and since it stressed an even more constrained way of life than he found at the university, he was not surprised by the way students there were monitored and policed.

At Indiana Wesleyan, students were expected to avoid alcohol, drugs, dancing, and sex of all kinds. The Wesleyan lifestyle was enforced by official university policies and peer pressure that was formalized to include a kind of buddy system that required confession and counseling that reinforced abstinence in times of temptation. Students regularly consulted each other on the power of their urges and shared strategies for dealing with them. The sense of crisis that attended an unmarried student's pregnancy was heightened by the community's belief, which Pence voiced in political terms, that except in rare cases, all abortion was murder.

This position, which countenanced a few abortions, actually put Pence at odds with the formal teaching of the Catholic Church, which had joined forces with the right wing to address the abortion issue. Unlike their allies, including Pence, Catholic leaders considered every fertilized egg and developing fetus to be equally divine and thus opposed abortion even in cases of rape and incest. The Catholic hierarchy was logically consistent, but its view was so far out of the American political mainstream that it was untenable for most politicians. So it was that Mike Pence would endorse the idea of certain fetuses being aborted because they were conceived through crime. Would his version of Christ agree? Probably not.

Although Indiana was assumed to lean toward conservative Christianity, public opinion on abortion mirrored the nation with a little more than half favoring a woman's right to choose freely, at least during the first three months of pregnancy. When surveyed, fewer than half of the state voters said the issue motivated them when they went to the polls; however, the number was greater among GOP primary voters, who were more likely to share Pence's view. This sentiment also explained why all the other Republicans hoping to win the nomination for the Second District seat held the exact same position. Antiabortion voters were motivated voters, and no one wanted to risk alienating them.

Generally willing to go further than his rivals, Pence told a gathering of teens at a youth center in his hometown of Columbus that he was opposed to laws that would make attacks on gay people hate crimes worthy of extra punishment. (Comparable laws already established extra penalties in crimes motivated by racial or religious animus.) He also said that he would fight efforts to give same-sex couples who sought to marry legal status and access to all the benefits that state and federal laws afforded heterosexual married couples. Heterosexual marriage "should be elevated, held higher than, esteemed more under the law than any other relationship," he explained.

In standing against both marriage equality and hate crime protections for gay Americans, Pence flashed signals to voters who cared most about social changes that offended their sense of order, especially when it came to issues around sex and gender. Sexual morality and the roles of men and women have long been motivating concerns for religious conservatives who saw an unfolding disaster in feminism, birth control, abortion, widespread divorce, single-parent households, and sexual equality. As preaching crusades gave way to televangelism, the alarm about social change grew louder, and believers' political engagement grew more intense. For some, a so-called biblical worldview justified rejecting science, history, and democratic norms in the pursuit of a Christian America that reflected God's rule. Others thought they were preparing for an actual conflict with an Antichrist who might already be walking the earth. They considered the Muslim world to be aligned with this evil force and considered modern Israel's creation, with Jerusalem as its capital, as a precondition for the battle of Armageddon, the return of Jesus, and the conversion of Jews.

Whether they were hoping to make America a Christian nation or preparing for the so-called end of days, politically inspired Christian Right activists felt God's call to action. This feeling made them willing to make common cause—even with those who seemed to worship money rather than the deity—if such alliances brought them closer to fulfilling God's plan. Few politicians voiced the belief that the apocalypse of prophecy was imminent. Instead, they indicated their Christian Right bona fides by expressing affection for an American past favored by the Christian Right, including children standing at their desks and reciting the Lord's Prayer as they did in most places prior to a 1963 Supreme Court ruling that determined the practice violated the separation of church and state. Decades later, Pence used a pair of creative arguments to breathe life into this issue.

At the Columbus youth center, Pence first talked about the state religions that existed in the colonies *before* the United States came into being. (Pence didn't mention the fact that the founders explicitly opposed state religions in their new nation.) Then he added some blood-and-guts patriotism to the argument, saying, "The idea that the blood spilled on the battlefields from Gettysburg to Iwo Jima was spilled to prevent [school prayer] from happening is ridiculous." Since these battles were fought *before* the Supreme Court determined that school prayer was unconstitutional, they weren't connected in any way. But Pence's point pleased seventeen-year-old Tim Hollowell, who told the local paper he too was a "real strong Christian." He considered Pence's views "cool," adding, "I could tell he was very firm on his values and wasn't going to compromise them."[8]

Religious compromise was anathema for conservative Christians who were certain they had the one true faith. In Republican congressional circles as well, *compromise* was becoming a dirty word. This generation of Republicans had followed Newt Gingrich of Georgia to a new level of partisanship and a controlling majority in the House of Representatives for the first time in forty years. They did so not through compromise but by lockstep opposition to all of Democratic president Bill Clinton's initiatives, adherence to a deeply conservative national agenda, and a crescendo of inflammatory language against anyone, including Republicans, who disagreed with them.

Gingrich would flame out after an ethics scandal forced him to abandon his post as Speaker of the House in 1998 and leave Congress in 1999. Nevertheless, the direction he established for the GOP was set, and it became ever more conservative and ever less willing to reach bipartisan

consensus with the Democrats. Within the party, moderates would be replaced by conservatives, and conservatives would be usurped by archcon-
servatives who reveled in shocking opponents with claims flirting with
flat-earth-style extremism. This rhetoric included strained efforts to deny
the vast and persuasive evidence that human activity caused dangerous
changes in the earth's climate. In a convenient marriage of religion and
libertarian business interests, Christian conservatives argued that God
had given humanity dominion over the earth and predetermined its destiny. This meant that efforts to combat climate change were not just foolish but unchristian. Of course, antipollution rules could also be costly to
industrialists who owned oil and chemical refineries. Little wonder that
funds from these firms and their owners, including the famous billionaire Koch brothers, supported right-wing organizations and candidates
who denied the reality of a warming planet and all the havoc this phenomenon would wreak on the lives of its inhabitants.

Pence was a climate change denier who saw behind the concerns
raised by scientists a secret effort to increase government control over
people's lives for some unstated diabolical purpose. In his campaign, he
refuted the vast amounts of science done on the topic with the claim that
the earth was growing cooler and not warmer, as the widely accepted data
indicated. He refused to acknowledge that human activity created much
of the increase in greenhouse gases in the atmosphere. Instead, he blamed
"underwater geological displacements" as well as volcanoes and hurricanes.
In Indiana, one of his chief allies in this argument was a retired chemist
named Jay Wile, who also contested evolution and published books for
homeschooled children. Wile promoted himself as a former atheist who
became an evangelical Christian. After Wile backed Pence's 2000 campaign, J. C. Randolph, an Indiana University expert in the field, described
the candidate's position as an example of antiscience paranoia. When
contacted by Muncie's *Star Press,* a playful Randolph said, "I'm sure the
black helicopter folks view this as a United Nations attempt to take over
with a new world order."[9]

Many on the Christian Right cited their faith in God as the basis
for denying climate science, arguing that the deity gave man dominion
over the earth and should be trusted to deal with the consequences. As

with so many issues, the extreme believers sometimes brought the Antichrist of Bible prophecy into the equation. Historically, the Antichrist has been regarded as a demon, a person, or an institution. Luther considered the Roman Catholic Church an Antichrist. One patriarch of Moscow said Peter the Great was the Antichrist. In this case, some evangelists said the Antichrist existed in those who would supposedly exploit public concern over the issue of climate change to impose their will on the people of the earth.

Pence didn't talk openly about the Antichrist, but he could be extreme in his opposition to science. In the 2000 campaign, Mike Pence's antiscientism went a step further, with the upside-down-and-backward declaration that "despite the hysteria from the political class and media, smoking doesn't kill." For proof, Pence pointed to the fact that the vast majority of smokers do not contract lung cancer, and two-thirds die of something other than smoking-related disease. In fact, the connection between smoking and deadly disease was incontestable. In 1965, the government placed health warnings on all cigarette packages, and in 1982, the Reagan administration's surgeon general said that secondhand smoke likely caused cancer in nonsmokers.[10] The Centers for Disease Control estimates that 80 to 90 percent of lung cancer cases are related to smoking.

The occasion for Pence's statement was Washington's consideration of an agreement to settle litigation against tobacco companies that had hidden from consumers and regulators evidence that the nicotine in their products is addictive. (This explained why it is so difficult for people to stop smoking once they start.) The legal action was undertaken by officials in forty states who were trying to recover the cost of health care provided to people who had been injured by tobacco. Pence saw in these efforts a government attempting "to protect us from our own stubborn wills" and he begged voters to ask which was the greater threat, "secondhand smoke or backhanded big government disguised in do-gooder health care rhetoric."

That statement gave Pence's opponent an easy topic for the general election. Reporters examined campaign finance reports and found that Pence had received $13,000 from cigarette-makers Brown & Williamson, Philip Morris, R. J. Reynolds, and US Tobacco. Overlooked was another reason to support big tobacco: through Kiel Brothers, the Pence clan still co-owned hundreds of convenience stores, including many named Tobacco Road, where cigarettes, cigars, snuff, and chewing tobacco were big revenue producers. The company was under pressure from state officials for TV advertisements that relied on kittens and sly language obviously crafted to get around a law that had banned advertising of tobacco on TV since 1971.

"We can't talk about some of the things we sell at Tobacco Road," intoned an announcer at the start of one TV spot.

On the screen flashed videos of a monster, a lounge singer, and playful kittens.

"Tobacco Road," the announcer continued. "Gas and cheap prices on, well, you know."

Officials in Indiana, where tobacco-related illnesses soaked up millions in tax dollars devoted to health care and drove up insurance premiums, complained about the ads to federal authorities who were charged with enforcing the law. A news story about the ad in the Pence hometown newspaper, *The Republic,* said Gregory Pence, the president of Kiel Brothers, was not available for comment. It did not report that he was the brother of Mike Pence, the local Republican candidate for Congress.[11]

Democrat Bob Rock tried to capitalize on the tobacco issue but was unable to drive a wedge between Pence and his supporters. At a debate in Columbus, Pence said his remarks were taken out of context, because his main argument was about the role of "government protecting me from myself." But Pence then repeated the essential falsehood: he claimed there is no "scientific causal link" between lung cancer and smoking. The U.S. National Institutes of Health had determined that even secondhand exposure to smoke could cause cancer. Pence had no basis for what he said.[12]

The smoking/cancer issue didn't stick, nor did any of the other criticisms Rock offered. A Marine Corps veteran, Rock chided Pence for failing to serve in the military. That didn't catch on. Meanwhile, a successful Democrat in Indiana couldn't sound like a liberal. Knowing he couldn't win if he seemed very liberal, Rock made sure voters knew that he agreed with Pence's stance against abortion, opposed gun regulations, and supported tax cuts and using the Clinton administration's budget surplus to cut the federal deficit. With few real differences between them, the two candidates decided to make an issue out of the national leaders of the Republican and Democratic parties. Pence complained that Rock would be led around Washington by the likes of his party's congressional leader, Representative Dick Gephardt of Missouri. Rock argued that Pence would follow departing representative David McIntosh's lead, and he thought McIntosh had done poorly.

Between Rock and Pence, the election seemed to be a contest over who could be more friendly and affable. The only spice in the race came from the entry of Bill Frazier, populist independent, who made his opposition to NAFTA, which he said hurt workers, almost his only issue. A farmer and businessman, Frazier spent $300,000 of his own money on anti-NAFTA TV advertisements. Remarkably, this was almost as much as Bob Rock raised and spent as a candidate with the backing of one of the two major parties. This was, perhaps, a sign of what all the experts assumed about the election, which was that Rock's inexperience and mild manner would put him at a disadvantage against any regular Republican and at extreme disadvantage against a well-spoken and telegenic man like Pence.

With all that he had going for him, Pence was recognized as a potential star in the Republican universe, a fact that was affirmed when he was given a chance to stand on the big stage at the 2000 presidential nominating convention in Philadelphia, where George Bush and his running mate, Dick Cheney, would be acclaimed. The occasion moved him to wear a red-white-and-blue-striped tie with a sober blue suit.

Given just a minute to speak on the first day of the four-day gathering, Pence suffered the bad luck of being introduced as someone else—namely, John Kline, a candidate for Congress from Minnesota. As the Minnesota delegation cheered and waved red signs with Kline's name written in big white letters, Pence strode to the podium, gripped it with both hands, and flashed a smile.

"With apologies to John Kline," he said, "I'm Mike Pence, and I'm running for Congress from the great state of Indiana."

Loud, resonant, and steady, Pence's voice sounded with the announcer's quality that he had perfected during his years on the air. The words "Mike" and "Pence" rang with special force and clarity. Combined with his looks, the delivery evoked a trusted local TV news anchor or perhaps the emerging breed of televangelists who were handsome enough to be soap opera stars and dressed so well they would fit in on Wall Street. Pence's message was little more than generalities, which meant that it didn't get in the way of the messenger. He said:

> *Our nation is in need of renewal as never before. We must renew the American dream, and I believe we can.*
>
> *We can renew the American dream by lifting the burden of taxes on families, small businesses, and family farms so they can once again dream and build a better life for their children and their grandchildren.*
>
> *We can renew the American dream by rebuilding the military after years of reckless cutbacks, rekindling the fires of men, matériel, and morale that warm the warriors who stand on liberty's ramparts protecting our families.*
>
> *Why am I running for Congress?*
> *To renew the dream of a strong and good America.*
> *I'm from Indiana, and I'm Mike Pence.*

The brief speech moved just a few people to applaud but one could imagine that the recording would be valuable to the Pence campaign. Others with minor roles at the convention attracted much more attention than Pence. Former pro football quarterback Steve Young and pro wrestler Dwayne "The Rock" Johnson won over the sports fans. Hollywood actress Bo Derek captured those who were looking for glamour. She got lots of applause and prime-time TV coverage when she appeared to introduce Abel Maldonado, an assemblyman from California. (In 2000, the GOP was making an effort to appeal to Hispanic voters, and Maldonado delivered his entire address in Spanish.)

Although Pence couldn't match the star power displayed by the celebrities, his poise reassured donors like the Club for Growth group that he was an able competitor. Pence's talent was also recognized by mainstream GOP leaders like Speaker of the House Dennis Hastert, which meant he drew frequent visits from top party officials, including majority leader Dick Armey and Republican whip Tom DeLay. Armey, a member of Congress from Texas, was especially enthusiastic about visiting Indiana to attend rallies and boost Pence.

A pugnacious campaigner and rigid conservative, Armey was famously bigoted about gay people. In 1995, he gained national attention by calling Massachusetts Representative Barney Frank "Barney Fag." He was such a hawk where Israel was concerned that he wanted all Palestinians driven out of the territories that were seized to create the Israeli state. His economic priorities included privatization of Social Security. These kinds of ideas earned him a spot among what political columnist Dave Rossie termed "the party's Talibans," who were mostly kept out of sight at the convention by Republican leaders who wanted to appeal to a more moderate national electorate.

After the big gathering in Philadelphia, Armey took to the road to boost candidates in districts where his views were less of a liability. When Armey visited Indiana just after the national convention, he raised a quick $10,000 at a gathering of donors and spoke at a rally where a band played "Yellow Rose of Texas" and the decorations leaned heavily toward red, white, and blue balloons. His remarks amounted to generic praise for Pence and criticism of Democrats. When the candidate spoke, he all but adopted Armey as a mentor. "Other than David McIntosh, there is not a member of Congress I admire more and want to emulate more than Dick Armey," said Pence.

Pence wouldn't get much chance to learn from the Texas congressman, as Armey would announce his retirement in 2002 and enter the world of consulting and organizing for big-money donors. And soon, DeLay and Hastert would each be disgraced by scandal. Hastert would confess to violating banking laws to cover up payments made to buy the silence of boys he had sexually abused when he was their school wrestling coach. DeLay would leave politics amid allegations of financial wrongdoing that were eventually rejected in the courts. However, in the moment, these men were political celebrities who could entice donors to write checks, which DeLay did, and draw crowds to rallies, which Hastert did. In September, Hastert campaigned with Pence at events where he touted GOP efforts to improve Medicare coverage for the poor and the elderly. Hastert also defended Republican support for trade agreements like NAFTA and expanded trade with China. In the future, these positions would be abandoned by many in the party, including Pence, but at the time, he and Hastert agreed on all of them.

By Election Day, Pence was so well positioned that the only matter to be resolved would be the size of his victory. In fact he was so confident that he spent the day with with gubernatorial candidate David McIntosh, doing what he could to help him against an incumbent governor, Frank O'Bannon, whose folksy touch made him an ideal Democrat for Indiana. (McIntosh would be defeated.) A victorious Pence ended the day with campaign aides, volunteers, and supporters who filled a ballroom at the Ramada Inn in Columbus. Spotting a TV camera crew setting up, he shouted to anyone who listened, "Will everybody move behind Mike so it looks like there is a crowd of adoring people behind him? The five dollars will be handed out later." When he was declared the winner by a margin of 12 percent, he took a look at the stage, which was so crowded some standees almost fell off, and quipped that he was happy to be surrounded by family. "Of course, this is actually just my immediate family."

When he went to Washington in late 2000 for some orientation sessions, Pence told reporters that the House of Representatives was a place "I never thought I would be except as a tourist." He said that he was no longer "enamored of the trappings of power" as he had been in 1988 and 1990. He had Karen worried about how Washington would affect their family life, and, as he explained, they saw in the examples set by others that it is possible "to keep families strong and marriages strong."

Faced with the prospect of actually filling a job he had first sought fourteen years earlier, Pence persuaded his campaign guru, Bill Smith, to serve as chief of staff. Smith would stay in the job for twelve years. He joked that after he won the office, "I didn't know what to worry about."

Pence's profession of humility reflected the attitude that won him praise during the campaign. (One newspaper described him as a "model citizen" in the race.) It was a smart pose for an incoming freshman, and others adopted it. However, every congressional class includes some freshmen who eventually become powerful through incumbency, committee assignments, leadership posts, and their work with their peers. In Pence's class, the Republicans included fellow Club for Growth favorites Jeff Flake and Todd Aikin and those who followed more ordinary paths, such as Darrell Issa of California and Mark Kirk of Illinois. Together on the day their class photo was taken on the steps of the Capitol, their paths would diverge almost immediately and lead in directions that not one of them could imagine.[13]

6

THE FROZEN MAN

Do nothing out of selfish ambition or vain conceit. Rather, in
humility value others above ourselves.

—*Philippians 2:3*

Bright eyes sparkling, his unlined face framed by neatly clipped white
hair, Mike Pence bubbled over with charm and enthusiasm as he led the
summer interns from his office on a tour of the United States Capitol.
Although he could be icy when it came to ideology and his moral focus,
Pence's personality set point was toasty warm. Interns, who gave lots of
Capitol tours themselves, were expected to be warm and enthusiastic too.

When the tour reached the West Front of the Capitol, where a special pole is used to run American flags up and down so they can be given
away as souvenirs, Pence reminded his charges that this was also where
presidents and vice presidents took the oath of office. Anyone standing
on the white marble expanse of the Capitol, where daylight bounces
off the stone and the great expanse of the Mall stretches toward the
Washington Monument, would feel the history and majesty.

Although every inauguration in the interns' memories had occurred
at the West Front, it wasn't always so. Prior to Ronald Reagan, the ceremonies had been held on the east side of the building, which faces the

Supreme Court and the Library of Congress. It was there, in 1841, that William Henry Harrison gave the longest inaugural address ever and caught the cold that developed into pneumonia, which killed him. Though born in Virginia, Harrison had become famous as commander of a force that defeated Tecumseh in Tippecanoe County, Indiana. His running mate was John Tyler, hence the famous slogan and campaign song "Tippecanoe and Tyler Too."

Indiana's only native-born president, Harrison's grandson Benjamin also took the oath on the east side of the Capitol, in 1889. Though historians judge him to have been, at best, a middling president, Benjamin Harrison did live to finish his first term and to be defeated when he sought reelection. He is nevertheless beloved in his home state, where his likeness stands near the Indianapolis War Memorial, his home is a national landmark, and a state park bears his name. Indiana's schoolchildren, including those who became interns at Pence's office, are taught his biography.

It's possible that Pence had both Harrisons in mind when he explained to the interns that were he to be elected president, he would prefer to be sworn in at the Capitol's East Front. One intern would recall that he said it was all about the light. In January, the noontime sunlight on the west-facing side of the building was just too bright, explained Pence. The glare forced presidents to squint and made every line and wrinkle in every face look more pronounced. On the east side, the indirect rays made everyone look better. And no squinting.

In retrospect, the intern would say that Pence might have been attempting some humor. Why else would he risk sounding like a bridesmaid musing about just how *her* wedding would go? Also, this episode happened in 2010, and at that time, the congressman from Indiana was just one of 435 members of the House of Representatives. Add a hundred United States senators, fifty governors, and countless other famous leaders and debate club champions, and he was just another person who dreamed of becoming president. What reasonable chance did he have of actually seeing his fantasy come true?

Actually, Pence's chances were better than the casual observer could imagine. Two years before he daydreamed aloud about his future inauguration, *Esquire* magazine had included him among its "ten best" members of Congress. The generally liberal magazine liked Mike because he was a conservative who didn't come across as hard-edged and because he was against the practice of "earmarking," which members of Congress had long used to send federal money home for specific purposes. Before it was canceled, the most infamous earmark in history would have sent almost $400 million to Alaska to build a bridge—dubbed the Bridge to Nowhere—to an island with about fifty inhabitants.

Esquire also liked Pence because he had once struck a humane tone on the matter of undocumented immigrants, mostly Latin Americans, who had put down roots in the United States. Pence addressed the issue in June 2006 at the Heritage Foundation, one of the primary conservative advocacy groups in the country. Contemplating the immigrants hiding from authorities, Pence declared that "mass deportation is a nonstarter" because "it is not logistically possible to round up twelve million illegal aliens." He proposed offering incentives for "really good people" who left voluntarily for as little as one week to return legally after applying at centers established in their home countries. Granted temporary work permits, the immigrants would eventually become eligible for more permanent status.

Similar to a proposal made by President George W. Bush, the plan outlined by Pence would have ended a debate over immigration that had begun almost as soon as Ronald Reagan signed the Immigration Reform and Control Act of 1986, which granted legal status to millions of people. Reagan had acted out of humanitarian concern and in response to businesspeople who relied on the immigrants for labor in agriculture, construction, and other industries. In the ensuing years, America had grown even more dependent on the labor provided by undocumented workers, so when Pence spoke up, he expressed a position that was favored by the farmers and business managers who were among his most ardent backers at home.

However, Pence's immigration stance provoked the anger of those Republicans who were hardliners on the issue. Former Nixon speechwriter and onetime presidential candidate Pat Buchanan lacerated Pence in a column published by the conservative weekly *Human Events*.

A well-practiced fulminator who had reached his sarcastic prime, Buchanan likened Pence to the character Tessio in *The Godfather*, who betrayed the Corleone family. While using words such as *fraudulent* and *capitulation*, Buchanan wrote, "What makes the Pence plan insidious is that Mike Pence has an unimpeachable pedigree." He concluded that Pence was swayed by "the White House, the ethnic lobbies, the Big Media, mainstream churches, the U.S. Chamber of Commerce and the 'conservative' front groups and foundations they finance, and corporate contributors to congressmen who fear law enforcement." (Five years earlier, Buchanan had announced, in a book called *The Death of the West*, that immigration and the decline of white birth rates constituted a threat to the survival of American and European societies. "The pill and condom have become the hammer and sickle of the cultural revolution," he wrote, adding, "Western women are terminating their pregnancies at a rate that represents autogenocide for peoples of European ancestry.")[1]

The remarkable thing about Buchanan's list was that it represented a huge swath of American society, from the Chamber of Commerce to churches to corporations to organizations representing Hispanics. If Pence was courting these groups with his immigration position, it may have been a wise choice, as they represented a great many votes and potential campaign donations. At the same time, Indiana was not substantially affected by undocumented immigrants. The best estimates suggested that between fifty-five thousand and eighty-five thousand undocumented people, including children and the unemployed, lived in Indiana. The small number meant that their effect on jobs, ages, and government services was quite minor, and the issue did not matter much to rank-and-file voters in Indiana. For them, especially those who were part of Pence's Republican base, it was far more important that he preserve his bona fides on issues like abortion and to associate himself with figures whom they respected and admired.[2]

Abortion was the topic that welded many evangelical Christians to the Republican Party, and over the years, their importance as a voting bloc had in turn pushed the GOP to adopt opposition to abortion rights as a central tenet. (This despite the fact that significant numbers of Republicans identify as pro-choice.) Among Pence's early speeches on the House floor was a statement called "The Case for Life," which was a meandering tour of world history from an antiabortion point of view. It included approving references to John Quincy Adams and Cicero, who "actually placed it beyond doubt that the offense of abortion was a capital offense punishable even by death." In addition to the history, the speech was a complete amalgam of talking points from the antichoice movement, including a callout to the Holocaust with his side of the debate on the role of Oskar Schindler, who saved Jews from the Nazis. He also sounded an alarm about "post-abortion stress syndrome," which he claimed was seen by "psychologists across America" but was not recognized as an actual pathology by either medical or mental health experts.[3]

Like his claim about the supposed post-abortion syndrome, much of what Pence argued in his abortion speech, and elsewhere, was drawn from the subculture of Christian Right authorities and could not withstand factual analysis. However, on the floor of the House of Representatives, he was free to say what he liked, and it became part of the Congressional Record. This process resembled his experience on talk radio, where, for hours every day, he was permitted to say pretty much anything, and except on rare occasions, it went unchallenged.

Radio was Pence's medium and as soon as he had arrived in Washington, he made sure he would maintain some presence on the airwaves back home. With $3,000 from the budget he got to outfit his office, he bought a desk, headphones, a special microphone, and other equipment to establish a broadcast-quality radio studio in a hallway next to the washroom. Within weeks, he was appearing every Monday on the show hosted by his replacement on the Indiana Network, a lawyer named Greg Garrison. On Wednesdays, he called in to stations in Anderson and Columbus, and on occasion, he subbed for weekend hosts at outlets around the state. He also used this little setup to fill in for nationally syndicated radio host Oliver North.

North was a combat veteran and thus even more respected among culture warriors who admired his machismo and bravado. He had been a central figure in the Reagan-era Iran-Contra Scandal, for which he was fired by the president. He was convicted of three felonies, but the convictions were overturned when a judge found his trial could have been tainted by prior testimony he gave to Congress, for which he had received a promise of immunity from prosecution. A pariah to those who saw him as a rogue officer who broke the law, North was regarded as a defiant hero by many on the hyperpartisan Right. As Pence became his occasional substitute, he made himself known to a national audience of listeners who enjoyed North's pugnacious style. Although Pence would never match the temperament that moved North to, for example, call the Clinton admin-istration "white trash," some of the tough-guy aura attached to him merely because he hosted the show. For a politician with a milquetoast image, it was a valuable bit of spice.

The association with North affirmed for fierce conservatives, espe-cially those back home, that Pence was someone whom they could trust. (Pence's long friendship with Watergate felon turned evangelist Chuck Colson served a similar purpose.) At the same time, people who were put off by Oliver North weren't likely to ever listen to the program and dis-cover their congressman playing substitute host.

In the mainstream press and in his public appearances, Pence built an identity as the straightest arrow in Congress, a man so concerned about propriety that he told the newspaper *The Hill* that without his wife by his side, he wouldn't attend an event where alcohol was served or sit down to a meal with a woman. He said these practices were about avoiding even suspicions of impropriety, adding that he kept in mind the "little old ladies [who] come and say, 'Honey, whatever you need to do, keep your family together.'" This comment, and Pence's effort to isolate himself, re-called the ancient Christian regard for women as occasions of sin. This notion, and the matching idea that men are ever poised on the edge of perdition, energizes the sexism that has forever constrained the lives of women and advanced the power of men. In Pence's case, he was signal-ing to his religiously oriented supporters that he lived in this world but was not of it, and if he could return society to a past when men and women remained in their separate spheres, he would.[4]

The puritanism Pence practiced in his personal life was matched by the watchdog role he chose when it came to his peers. He frequently com-plained about the GOP's supposed drift away from what he deemed to be its core principles of small government, low taxes, and Christian Right social values. Inside the party caucus, House members waged a continual contest over which items their leaders would push. In this internal fight, Pence chose to stand with a small but loud group that claimed to represent the principled core of the party and attacked those who cooperated with moderates and liberals. He also promoted the interest of major political donors who opposed limits on the money they could pour into candidates' campaigns.

Campaign spending had begun a steady rise in the mid-1980s, far outpacing inflation, and would soon exceed the rate of growth in health care costs, which was considered a national crisis. By 2000, winning House candidates spent about $1 million to get their jobs, which was almost three times the figure for 1990. Common sense would hold that the candidates who raise and spend the most money are more likely to win *and* that donors give in order to gain some benefit, whether it is a representative who votes for their interests or will listen when they call.

Political scientists had found that having more money is only a slight advantage in campaigns. (They also confirmed that donors do get attention from politicians.) However, even those who conducted empirical research noted that the psychological effects of fund-raising were greater. "The *belief* that money is the key to electoral success is almost as damaging as a scenario in which money really does matter," wrote Steven Levitt in 1994. "As long as conventional wisdom views money as critical, the pattern of behavior that has led to widespread criticism will prevail."[5]

The practices that concerned Levitt included all the phone calls, meetings, and travel that House members devoted to raising money, which was amassed in part to intimidate foes. Although senators and representatives generally complained about the duty, it was an accepted part of the job. Like many of his colleagues, Pence made raising campaign funds a regular occupation, even in odd-numbered years when no actual election would be conducted. After winning in 2000, he would raise more than $1 million every year to defeat opponents who ran with ever smaller budgets. In 2010, he would accumulate more than $2.7 million to defeat a rival who reported collecting only 115 dollars. Besides his own campaigns, Pence raised money for his own political action committee (PAC), which then gave money to other Republicans. Borrowing from a Bible verse, this so-called "leadership PAC" was called Principles Exalt a Nation. Essentially a funnel, it took money from the usual Pence donors, including the Kochs, Club for Growth, Cummins, and Erik Prince, and delivered it to politicians, including Christian Right champions such as Michele Bachmann of Minnesota.[6]

Leadership PACs facilitated the flow of money among politicians who could turn indebted colleagues into allies by funding their election efforts. They also helped donors get around the limits on giving imposed by campaign finance laws. Intended to give the public some sense of how politicians raised money and to limit the appearance of impropriety, these regulations irritated Pence, who was a gifted fund-raiser. In 2002, Pence put his name on a Supreme Court lawsuit filed in response to campaign finance limits proposed by Senator John McCain, an Arizona Republican, and Russ Feingold, a Democrat from Wisconsin. The lead complainant was then Senate minority leader Mitch McConnell, who would become famous for teaching that the three keys to politics are "money, money, money." The argument, which he and Pence would make, was that money was the equivalent of speech and that the free speech clause of the First Amendment to the Constitution barred limits on its use to advance candidates. On the first Monday in September 2003, Pence sat in the court to observe the arguments in a case that his side lost. However, he had signaled where he stood.[7]

As Pence picked his spots on issues and occasionally seized the chance to get ahead of like-minded conservatives, he distinguished himself from others who entered the House in January 2001. Just three years after he arrived in Washington, he got the prized opening-remarks slot at the annual Conservative Political Action Conference. (Among the other speakers at CPAC were white supremacist Richard Spencer and Wayne LaPierre of the National Rifle Association.) Pence, whose talk was preserved on the CPAC website, began his remarks with imagery he borrowed (uncredited) from Ronald Reagan:

> Picture a ship at sea. A proud captain steps onto the sunlit deck as it
> plies the open seas of a simpler time. Its sails full and straining in

the wind, its crew is tried and true, its hull, mast, and keel are strong,
but beneath the waves, almost imperceptibly, the rudder has veered off
course and, in time, the captain and crew will face unexpected peril.
The conservative movement today is like that ship with its proud cap-
tain, strong, accomplished, but veering off course into the dangerous
and uncharted waters of big-government Republicanism.

According to Pence, expediency had found members of the party embracing programs to solve problems they should stay away from and using tax dollars to fund them. Pence preferred the ethos of the GOP circa
1995, which was led by fire-breathing Speaker of the House Newt Gingrich, who pushed hard for cuts in federal programs to benefit the poor.

"When I was finally elected in 2000, it was like I had been frozen
before the revolution and thawed after it was over. When I first ran,
Republicans dreamed of eliminating the Department of Education and
returning control of our schools to parents, communities, and states. Ten
years later, I was thawed out, took my oath of office, and they handed me
a copy of H.R.1. One as in our Republican Congress' number-one priority. It was the No Child Left Behind Act."

Intended to benefit kids in poorly performing public schools, the act
was proposed by GOP president George Bush and supported by Republican leaders in Congress. It required that states create standards that
would have to be met if schools were to get federal funding. The account-
ability imposed by the act and its focus on basic education were considered conservative policies, and in the first few years, it was credited with
raising test scores. However, Pence objected to the spending attached to
the bill and voted against it. His side lost.

In the subsequent Congress, after he easily won reelection over
Melina Fox, a farmer who had not run for office before, Pence was confronted by a second H.R.1. This one gave senior citizens receiving Medicare a big new benefit for prescription medicines. "To the frozen man,"
recalled Pence, "it was obvious: another Congress, another H.R.1, another
example of the ship of our movement veering off course." Pence described
Republicans who opposed this Bush plan as "twenty-five rebels [who]
made a stand for limited government. When all the votes were counted, we

were one rebel short, and the ship of conservative government veered further off course."

Mixing his military metaphors, Pence briefly evoked the Alamo as he recalled his fellow H.R.1 opponents and then went back to sea—and described a possible mutiny—for the big finish to his talk. He said:

> *When a ship is approaching a rocky coast, the life of the ship and its crew depends on the navigator with his sextant to counsel the captain and crew to steer clear of the shoals and, if need be, to forcefully oppose the captain when the fate of the ship hangs in the balance. This is our cause. To stand with our captain as he leads us well. And to right the ship where she is adrift.*[8]

A politician who identified himself as a conservative before he was a Republican, Pence put his ideology above his party, his GOP colleagues, and the president. In this way, he stood against the tradition of politics and compromise that marked the entire history of a body charged with serving a vast and diverse nation. Pence affirmed this view by joining the Republican Study Committee (RSC), which was one of many groups with bland names but extreme goals founded in the 1970s by Christian Right activist Paul Weyrich. (Others included the Heritage Foundation and the Moral Majority, the American Legislative Exchange Council, and the Krieble Institute, which focused on politics in Russia and Ukraine.) Weyrich was among the first to woo wealthy benefactors to the work of building conservative institutions. Mike Pence considered him a mentor and a close friend.

Weyrich believed that God gave Christians dominion over the earth and that this meant they had been chosen to govern according to their beliefs. He also understood this was a minority view and it might not go over well with an electorate composed of people of many faiths, no faith, and broadly held concern for the separation of church and state. For this reason, he famously complained that "many of our Christians have what I call the 'goo-goo syndrome.' Good government. They want everybody to vote. I don't want everybody to vote. Elections are not won by a majority of people. They never have been from the beginning of our country, and they are not now. As a matter of fact, our leverage in the elections quite candidly goes up as the voting populace goes down."[9]

In 2002, one of Weyrich's organizations, the Free Congress Foundation (later called the American Opportunity Foundation), urged members to become propagandists who understand "the truth of an idea is not the primary reason for its acceptance." America was afflicted by "sickness and decay," wrote Weyrich protégé Eric Heubeck, as he called conservative elites to a constant effort to tear down basic structures of society. "We will not try to reform the existing institutions," he wrote. "We only intend to weaken them, and eventually destroy them. . . . We will use guerrilla tactics to undermine the legitimacy of the dominant regime."

The tactics Heubeck suggested might include, he wrote, having "every member of the movement put a bumper sticker on his car that says something to the effect of 'Public Education is Rotten; Homeschool Your Kids.' This will change nobody's mind immediately; no one will choose to stop sending his children to public schools immediately after seeing such a bumper sticker; but it will raise awareness and consciousness that there is a problem. Most of all, it will contribute to a vague sense of uneasiness and dissatisfaction with existing society. We need this if we hope to start picking people off and bringing them over to our side. We need to break down before we can build up. We must first clear away the flotsam of a decayed culture."

Besides sowing dissatisfaction, Heubeck's advocacy jujitsu called for Christian conservatives to assume the posture of a persecuted victim "only interested in being left alone." With this pose, "we will surely gain the sympathy of the public. The dominant culture will see its life-force being sapped, and it will grow terrified. It will do whatever it takes to destroy its assailant. This will lead to the perception that the dominant leftist culture is empty, hollow, desperate, and has lost its mandate to rule, because its only basis for authority is coercion, much like the communist East Bloc. Sympathy from the American people will increase as our opponents try to persecute us, which means our strength will increase at an accelerating rate due to more defections—and the enemy will collapse as a result."

The persecution drama Heubeck described was a poor fit for a foundation that had received tens of millions of dollars from wealthy donors, but it was consistent with other narratives promoted by conservative activists. The Christian Right, which operated in a nation where God is mentioned in the Pledge of Allegiance and is printed on its currency, nevertheless claimed victim status. This way of thinking saw a "war on Christmas" in the phrase "Happy Holidays" and a threat to heterosexuals in extending the legal right to marry to gay and lesbian couples. In this way, every time society granted more people fuller participation in any realm, Heubeck and others could claim that their side was losing something. By building up a sense of threat and loss, Heubeck could create a dramatic, energizing narrative of a people in the wilderness fighting a terrible foe. "Popular culture now acts as a giant narcotic, offering an escape from the difficulty and hard work of realizing our higher selves," he announced. "Our movement's intention is to break that addiction for as many individuals as possible."[10]

Like Heubeck, Mike Pence had a flair for the dramatic. However, he possessed a limited repertoire and tended to repeat himself. After joining Paul Weyrich's Republican Study Committee, which sought to push GOP House members ever rightward, Pence repeated his seafaring story in another speech on the dangerous state of public affairs. He began, "Picture, if you will, a ship at sea. Shoulders back, a proud captain steps onto the sunlit deck of a tall ship plying the open seas of a simpler time. Its sails are full and straining in the wind. Its crew is tried and true; its hull, mast, and keel are strong. But beneath the waves . . ."

One again calling himself the "frozen man," Pence again described his two rebellious votes against GOP leaders as heroic choices. He ended, however, with an optimistic observation about what he saw as President Bush's course correction. "After weeks of confusion from Massachusetts to California," Pence said, "this president has brought moral clarity to the debate over same-sex marriage by calling on Congress to pass a constitutional amendment to protect marriage. The president rightly called marriage 'the most enduring human institution,' and so it is. Marriage was ordained by God, confirmed by law, is the glue of the American family, and is the safest harbor for children."

The danger children faced, and which required "safe harbor," in

Pence's view, was same-sex marriage. In Massachusetts, the State Supreme Court had recently determined that gay citizens should be permitted to marry, noting that "barring an individual from the protections, benefits, and obligations of civil marriage solely because that person would marry a person of the same sex violates the Massachusetts Constitution." In California, a new civil partnership law had given gay couples all the legal rights and benefits of marriage. President Bush's response, which Pence supported, came at a press conference where he said, "I believe marriage is between a man and a woman, and I think we ought to codify that one way or another."

Bush sounded as if he favored the social conservatives in the matter, but he moderated his statement with the observation that he thought it was "important for society to welcome each individual." Society *had* been moving in this direction, granting ever-greater acceptance to gay Americans. In 2003, the United States Supreme Court had struck down state laws that criminalized homosexual behavior, and public opinion polls were beginning to show a gradual, steady rise in public acceptance of homosexuality. However, this trend was being driven by a faster shift in opinion among younger people, who were not as likely to vote as older citizens. Also, the Supreme Court ruling and changes in certain states had alarmed Christian Right activists who once again saw that liberal courts were working against them. GOP strategists, believing these voters could be mobilized by appeals to their fear, just as gun owners were rallied by NRA warnings about the specter of regulations, moved to make opposition to marriage equality a centerpiece of 2004 political campaigns.[11]

Bush's chief policy advisor, Karl Rove, concluded that conservative Christians, who naturally favored his candidate, would be more likely to come to the polls if they had a chance to fight the acceptance of gay citizens by voting to amend state constitutions to ban same-sex unions. (Writer Andrew Sullivan reported that Rove "told gay Republicans . . . the only thing that mattered to him was there were more votes in gay-bashing than in standing up to the bigots in his base.") In prior election cycles, Rove-run campaigns, assuming they could energize bigoted voters, had used rumormongering to suggest opponents were homosexual.

This tactic was especially wicked as used by Rove, since his parents had divorced when his father announced he was gay.[12]

In 2004, the Rove-led GOP would push for anti–gay marriage amendments to state constitutions. This state-by-state approach promised anti-equality Republicans a better chance to pick up votes in key spots, even though the national tide was moving against them. This problem was borne out by a January 2004 poll commissioned by the Christian Right–oriented American Family Association, which showed that 60 percent of respondents favored legalizing gay marriage, 8 percent approved of civil unions for gay people, and only 32 percent wanted to ban legal status for gay couples.[13]

In social and political terms, Indiana seemed a likely place for an anti–gay marriage amendment. However, statutes already barred same-sex unions, and no judges, clergy, or couples had attempted to defy the law. With nothing to rile Christian Right activists, no groundswell developed to drive an amendment campaign. However, Congressman Pence, spying an opportunity, moved quickly to identify himself with the issue. At the start of 2004, he announced he was a coauthor of an anti–marriage equality amendment to the U.S. Constitution and began promoting it across his district.

On a Thursday night in February 2004, Pence faced a crowd of people at a local civic center in Columbus and tried to get them interested in the gay marriage issue. It was a struggle, as they were far more interested in the war in Iraq. Already costing far more than the Bush administration had projected, the war was part of America's response to the terror attacks on September 11, 2001. However, Iraq had no link to the attacks, and administration claims that its dictator, Saddam Hussein, possessed weapons of mass destruction had proven to be false. "Weapons of mass disappearance" was how a veteran who stood to address Pence described them. Pence replied that Saddam was himself a dangerous weapon. This argument didn't impress the crowd, but Pence had little to worry about with voters. Having defeated his previous opponent by thirty points, he didn't yet have an opponent for November. Still, he had made a continuous effort to raise money and, in the off year, had collected $570,000. When a challenger finally arose, she was able to collect only $50,000 for her entire campaign and was swamped by thirty-seven points.[14]

In 2004, in each of the eleven states where they were proposed, voters approved anti–gay marriage initiatives. However, each one of them would eventually be overturned by the courts. In the meantime, the federal constitutional amendment Pence proposed never became more than something to talk about. President Bush all but declared the proposal to be a political stunt when, two months after the election, he announced he wouldn't push for it because he had come to deem it unnecessary. Mike Pence did not follow Bush. Secure in his district, which he kept winning by higher margins, Pence kept talking about gay marriage and other social issues even in places like his hometown of Columbus, where Cummins Engine had promoted a more liberal social agenda and voters did not prioritize these concerns.

Pence's great power at the ballot box was enhanced by the squeaky-clean image he maintained in the press. Where others were damaged by personal problems, family difficulties, or financial issues, he went untouched by these kinds of challenges. The closest he came to this kind of trouble might have been on the occasion of the bankruptcy that announced the abrupt death of the Pence family business, Kiel Brothers. With more than two hundred convenience stores/gas stations and a wholesale petroleum business, the company had lost the confidence of the bankers who provided the credit to keep it going. In part, the trouble was a matter of the difficulty of competing in a business with little room for error. However, under Pence's brother Greg, who ran it after their father died, Kiel Brothers had not kept pace with rivals who had newer stores in better locations. Despite doing more than $340 million per year in business, the firm went into decline.

As one of the lawyers who worked with Kiel Brothers would eventually recall, only a steady effort to rejuvenate the chain would have extended its life, and in the end, the bankers wouldn't back such an effort. But even considering the causes, the firm's condition was remarkably bad. Kiel Brothers owed vendors, workers, and others more than $100 million, with $9 million due to the State of Indiana, mainly for environmental cleanups at its facilities. When the assets were finally liquidated, most of the creditors received about fifty cents on the dollar. One of the losers was Mike Pence, who previously had income from his ownership stake but lost the value of his stock, which had been estimated between $100,000 and $250,000.[15]

While some political opponents tried to make an issue out of Kiel Brothers, it never caused much trouble for Pence in elections. Indeed, every time he ran, he won by a greater margin, and this popularity with voters freed him to do things that might have been difficult for another conservative. An example arose in the weeks after the 2004 election, when a woman from Sierra Leone was stopped for speeding in her car in Muncie and was arrested when police discovered a fifteen-year-old deportation order issued when she had been divorced and her husband reported her to authorities. Pence's intervention with the Department of Homeland Security worked: the deportation order was dropped. The congressman said he was moved to tears by the outcome. She "belongs with her family," he said.[16]

As he helped a woman whose dilemma had become a cause célèbre in Indiana, Pence showed himself to be a compassionate conservative at home even as he struck a more doctrinaire pose in Washington. In 2005, he was elected chairman of Weyrich's Republican Study Committee, which had grown to more than one hundred members and sometimes challenged party leaders for control of the GOP agenda in the House. More committed to ideological purity than rank-and-file Republicans, the RSC functioned much like other interest groups that pushed the party rightward. While electioneering organizations like the Club for Growth used money and primary challenges to this purpose, the RSC organized its members to vote as a bloc, thereby threatening efforts that House leaders might make to pass legislation.

On social issues, the group took cues from leading Christian Right organizations like Focus on the Family, which was run by psychologist James Dobson. The son of a traveling evangelist, Dobson first gained fame in the 1970s as a proponent of corporal punishment for children. With broadcasts, publications, conferences, and other activities, Focus on the Family promoted prayer in public schools, abstinence-only sex education, and the notion that God's acts and not evolution accounted for life on Earth. Dobson was stridently opposed to marriage equality and even operated a ministry that sought to change the sexual orientation of gay men and women. (After it was sold to other operators, this ministry was shut down and its managers apologized for harming participants in its programs.)

Under Pence, the study committee pushed for spending cuts to offset billions in relief after Hurricane Katrina (the proposal was defeated) and mounted a failing effort to allow some Social Security funds to be invested in private accounts. Both ideas were political poison with general election voters, and GOP leaders were never going to let them be approved. The push-pull between the study committee and GOP leaders often strained their relationships. At one point, after his old friends Dennis Hastert and Tom DeLay read him the riot act, a chastened Pence hustled to an engagement at the Longworth House Office Building, where he abandoned the text of a speech he was about to give on the "massive spending splurges" indulged by his colleagues. Instead, he told a crowd of young conservatives, "I believe in the leadership of this Congress. I believe in the men and women who lead the House of Representatives and the Senate. I see them as men and women of integrity and principle, who work every day to bring the ideals of our Founders into the well of the people's house."[17] This abject pandering was noted in the press as something that should have embarrassed Pence but it foreshadowed much more craven capitulation to come.

Embarrassing as it may have been to read about it in the newspaper, Pence's tail-between-the-legs retreat showed he knew how to be a team player when it was required. Pence wanted to become more powerful within the GOP establishment, and to that end, he had tried to get along with Hastert and DeLay when he could and did what he could to help his party raise money. Whenever possible, he showed his support for his colleagues, even if it meant answering tough questions back in Indiana. For example, when he voted to increase the salaries paid to members of Congress, which was not a popular cause among fiscal conservatives, he explained it by saying, "I fear Mrs. Pence more than I fear voters." This was, no doubt, true.[18]

In 2006, as his party lost control of the House, which they had captured in 1994, Pence saw his chance to reach for a big prize: the post of minority leader. "We didn't just lose our majority," said Pence as he announced his bid, "we lost our way. In recent years, our majority voted to expand the federal government's role in education, entitlements, and pursued spending policies that created record deficits and national debt."

Unmentioned, but obviously the target of Pence's critique, were outgoing Speaker Dennis Hastert and majority leader Representative John Boehner of Ohio. (Boehner had assumed the office when predecessor Tom DeLay had been indicted and resigned.) Ten years Pence's senior in the House, Boehner was one of the best-liked members of Congress. An old-school politician, he was willing to practice give-and-take within his party, which meant that he had helped many members, including lots of those who belonged to the RSC. However, as the two men pursued the job, Pence only seemed to win over people who couldn't cast votes. Archconservative pundits like Phil Kerpen of *Human Events* favored him because he had supported their agenda by voting against Medicare drug benefits and seeking to change Social Security. Politicians who were sensitive to what voters preferred tended to oppose these ideas, which might explain why they failed and why Boehner clobbered Pence in the leadership race by 168 to 27.[19]

Some congressional Republicans suspected that Pence's bid for the minority leader post was not truly sincere and that he might have acted with Boehner's secret encouragement. Better to have a contest, went this line, than a coronation. Two years later, when Pence wanted the job of House conference chairman, Boehner supported him. The office was concerned with making sure the process of lawmaking worked smoothly, and Pence would do it well. Pence would also do well by colleagues who wanted to make sure that donations from wealthy Christian conservatives continued to flow. This work required the ability to speak the religiously imbued dialect of Christian Right politics and a willingness to stroke egos when necessary.

In December 2007, Pence showed his flair for ego-stroking when he organized House members to hold a reception for wealthy heir and businessman Erik Prince, the founder of Blackwater USA, a private military company that had contracted with the U.S. military to provide security services. Four months before Pence's show of support, on September 16, 2007, Blackwater guards had opened fire while accompanying a U.S. convoy at Nisour Square in Baghdad, killing seventeen civilians and wounding twenty others. (Four Blackwater guards were eventually charged, convicted, and sentenced to prison for their roles in the massacre. One of these men successfully petitioned to have his conviction voided and was to be retried.)

In addition to being Pence's friend, Prince had given more than $230,000 to GOP causes between 1992 and the time of the get-together. (His family, likely the wealthiest in the state of Michigan—his sister was billionaire education funder Betsy DeVos—had given more.) Prince's private military force had a $1 billion contract to provide services in Iraq. It billed the U.S. taxpayers roughly $450,000 per year per man deployed in the country, which was about six times the amount paid to an American soldier. This was privatization—the concept of transferring government functions to businesses—in action.[20]

For Blackwater's Prince, politics, business, and religion flowed together in a life that found him in frequent contact with the same people; Mike Pence shared values with Prince and like-minded friends, including James Dobson, whose Focus on the Family also received Prince's money, and broadcaster/evangelist D. James Kennedy. The mutual support in these relationships formed an informal circuit that was common to the Christian Right political subculture and reinforced by money and displays of mutual admiration. Donors like Prince gave comparatively small sums to see their views promoted and, in his case, received $1 billion worth of government work. Politicians and advocates advanced thanks to the contributions from their benefactors.

Receptions like the one Pence arranged with Republicans in Congress were part of the exchange that kept the Christian Right movement going. So too was the award Pence received—Distinguished Christian Statesman—from D. James Kennedy's Center for Christian Statesmanship. The center offered a three-week course to attendees, who were called "fellows" but who paid ($16,000 as of 2018), to study subjects such as Bible-based economics and strategies to oppose equal rights for lesbian, gay, and transgender citizens. Previous award winners included Judge Roy Moore of Alabama, who was removed as chief justice of the Alabama Supreme Court after he refused a federal court order to remove a Ten Commandments monument from state grounds. (Moore later lost a run for U.S. Senate after testimony from women who said he had inappropriate sexual or social contact with them as teenagers when he was a prosecutor in the 1970s.)[21]

Roy Moore and Mike Pence were not likely candidates for the types of honors bestowed on public servants by great institutions. Distinguished Christian Statesman was not comparable to, say, an honorary doctorate at an Ivy League university. However, for the cost of a plaque, a photo opportunity could be created, which might be useful to both the giver and receiver. In this case, supporters gathered at a dinner where, afterward, Pence and his wife, Karen, stood for a picture that was then distributed nationwide by an outfit called PR Newswire, which functions as a self-promoter's version of the Associated Press.

The statesman award was one of many signs of Pence's high status within the Christian Right movement. More significant was his involvement with a secretive group known as both the Family and the Fellowship, which spread a kind of elitist fundamentalism by cultivating powerful believers and gathering them together. Led by a charismatic figure named Douglas Coe, the Family housed members of Congress at a house on Capitol Hill, offered leadership training and other services at its headquarters in Virginia, and maintained a network of thousands of members and friends who helped one another with everything from business deals to spiritual crises. It was best known for organizing an annual prayer breakfast attended by many officials in Washington and invited guests from around the globe.

Founded in 1942 by an anti-union, anti–New Deal, anti-Communist Methodist minister named Abraham Vereide, the Family promotes capitalism and Republican-leaning politics at home and what it considers to be American/Christian interests abroad. Vereide was, for example, opposed to the creation of Israel on the grounds that a Jewish state was inconsistent with the "divine plan as declared in the Bible." The organization's view on Israel changed as many evangelicals turned to a nineteenth-century theory that the Bible foretold the creation of the Jewish state as a condition of Christ's return to Earth. This view imagined that God planned the future as a series of events that would work, like tumblers in a lock, to eventually return Jesus to reign over Earth. The establishment of modern Israel was key to the plan and would be followed by the Rapture, during which believers would rise to heaven, leaving others to endure an agonizing period called the Great Tribulation. Under these conditions, Jews would have the opportunity to convert or be consigned to hell. Either way, Zionism would play an essential role in fulfilling Christianity's dream of paradise.[22]

The supernatural Christian view of events supplied an exciting narrative for understanding current events. It was popularized by a flood of books, which began with evangelist Hal Lindsey's *The Late, Great Planet Earth*. Lindsey cherry-picked current events, ignoring progress in science, medicine, and even the cause of peace to create the sense that a crisis was building. He expected the Rapture to come in the 1980s. Although it didn't, his book kept selling, eventually reaching twenty-eight million copies sold worldwide. The book would inspire hundreds of imitators and even a shelf full of apocalyptic books for children and young adults.

End-times fervor was, and is, common in the growing number of churches and organizations where the absence of a hierarchy encourages a freewheeling approach to belief. The Family falls into this larger trend, which finds Americans moving away from the structure of churches, denominations, and doctrine in favor of a spiritual commitment to the love of a supernatural Jesus. In this version of American Christianity, a supernatural relationship with Jesus is primary, and individuals choose their own moral codes. (Deep concern for common morals and ethics is, in this view, a negative practice called *legalism*. Legalism is bad because it promotes such behavior as humility or charity while ignoring the notion that a profession of belief, offered at any point, outweighs all the good or evil that a person ever does.)

Although faith is enough for any Christian to find eternal reward in heaven, the Family's leaders considered the Bible stories of Jesus and his early followers and concluded that even today, on a supernatural basis, some people are held closer to Him than others. It is this favored position, preordained by God, that explains their worldly success. As one of the Family's documents notes, Jesus has "levels of relationships much like concentric rings." His favorites are obviously those He enabled to be powerful, including high-ranking politicians and businesspeople.

Coe promoted the notion that God works through powerful "key men" who can create His dominion on Earth. With God's endorsement, key men have justification for violating social norms and common ethics, and their successes are more evidence of God's favor. And just as God's will should be obeyed, superior men and women deserved the obedience of their lessers. This self-reinforcing logic meant that insiders could be forgiven almost anything—past, present, or future—once they professed their faith. As a result, criminals, dictators, and mass murderers like Indonesia's Suharto have all been counted as members or friends who could be useful and may be God's tools for His work on Earth.

To reach key men and promote its view of Christian government, the Family funds trips abroad for members of Congress and others. Senators and House members travel on the group's dime but arrive in the Middle East, Asia, or elsewhere, with their status as American officials well understood. The difference is that their mission is devoted to the Family's Christian Right goals. On these missions, Americans meet and encourage locals who are friendly to the cause. In Africa, for example, Uganda's president, Yoweri Museveni, was identified as a key man despite documented human rights abuses of his regime. The Family worked through him—it sent members of Congress to Uganda—to promote antigay initiatives, including a call to institute the death penalty for some homosexual conduct.[23]

Although the Family uses members to promote its favored ideals, the exploitation is mutual, as members use the organization to cultivate friendship and business contacts. In this way, the Family functions like a fraternal organization on steroids, where wealth and power are displayed and celebrated and can be amplified through relationships. As Michael Cromartie of the Washington-based Ethics and Public Policy Center told *The New Yorker* in 2010, "You bring an oligarch over to the Cedars and he says, 'Ah, these are my kind of people. They have pictures on the wall of all these presidents, they seem to be in touch with power, they know people with money, this will help my business.'"

Among members and friends of the Family, Congressman Mike Pence would be a midlevel figure ranked below senators and better-known national Christian activists like his friend Charles Colson. However, he was ranked closer to God than most other mortals. And like so many whom the Family drew close, he was still on the rise. Pence became more visible as an outspoken critic of most of the policies Barack Obama proposed after Obama became president in 2008. At the same time, Pence aligned himself ever more closely with groups sponsored by the industry billionaires Charles and David Koch.

In April 2009, Pence signed a pledge, which had been distributed by the Koch-funded Americans for Prosperity, announcing he would vote against any program that would increase federal revenues in order to combat climate change. This meant he would oppose a so-called carbon tax on the pollutants that caused climate change, which Koch-owned facilities spewed at a rate of twenty-four million tons per year. Echoing the Kochs' false claim that a proposed carbon levy would be the largest tax increase in history, Pence was a leader of the effort that defeated a "cap and trade" plan that would have limited carbon emissions and created a market for credits that polluters could earn and trade for reducing their output.

Pence also became a leading promoter of the so-called Tea Party movement, which various powerful conservative organizations helped to create in response to Obama. Typical was an Americans for Prosperity spin-off called FreedomWorks, which was led by former congressman Dick Armey and helped organize protests that were intended to draw greater numbers of people to rally against Obama policies. A classic example of a practice called astroturfing, these efforts mimicked grassroots protest movements. In September 2009, Mike Pence joined Armey at a FreedomWorks rally at the United States Capitol. He stood in shirtsleeves and told the crowd, "I'm Mike Pence, and I'm from Indiana."

With the same clear, broadcaster's tone he offered at the 2000 Republican National Convention, the voice Pence used sounded cheerful, but his message was ominous. Squinting at the sun, he said that because of Obama's proposed health care plan, the nation risked "the abyss that has swallowed much of Europe in an avalanche of socialism." A year later, after the health care plan was enacted and no abyss swallowed the nation, Pence spoke at another rally organized by the same group on the same spot and made the upcoming congressional election a matter of existential concern. "If we do not succeed in November, all that once was good and great about this country could someday be gone."[24]

7

HIGHER AMBITIONS

I will instruct you and teach you in the way you should go; I will counsel you with my eye upon you.

—Psalm 32:8

The GOP and Pence succeeded in a big way in the 2010 elections. After three consecutive losing cycles, the party regained the House with the biggest shift in seats since the 1930s. Mike Pence took two-thirds of the votes cast in his race on November 2, 2010, against his Democratic challenger, Barry A. Welsh, whom he had also beaten soundly in 2006 and 2008. Welsh, a Methodist minister, might have been best known for getting punched in the face when he tried to stop an angry public official in Delaware County from assaulting a newspaper reporter. He suffered a black eye.[1]

Despite the fact that he hadn't faced a serious challenge since getting elected in 2000, Pence's campaign fund-raising had soared. He had more than $450,000 on hand as Election Day passed and was well positioned to simply occupy his seat, becoming more senior with every term, or reach for something bigger. A day after the election, Pence invited speculation about a presidential bid. He resigned as chairman of the House GOP conference—he had been fourth in the Republican hierarchy after Boehner, the House majority leader, and the majority whip. "I have fulfilled my commitment to the Republican Conference," Pence told fellow Republicans. "My family and I have begun to look to the future. As we consider new opportunities to serve Indiana and our nation in the years ahead, I have come to realize that it may not be possible to complete an entire term as conference chairman."

In Indiana, people in both parties recognized that Pence, who was in his early fifties, wanted much more. Political scientist Andrew Downs of Indiana University Fort Wayne considered his increasing outspokenness and his standing with the powerful Kochs, who had started to bring Pence to their private gatherings for big political donors, and wondered if he might be planning to run for president. With the Kochs and their tax-cut-and-deregulation conservatives in his corner, Pence focused on the religious Right, where he was already well known. In September 2010, he gave the most loudly cheered address heard at an annual Values Voter Summit sponsored by the Family Research Council (FRC).

Founded by Pence's friend and mentor James Dobson, the Council opposed equal rights for gay citizens and favored restrictions on divorce and a ban on legal abortion. The organization's leaders said, erroneously, that homosexuals were more prone to pedophilia than heterosexuals, and in early 2010, a spokesman had told a national TV audience watching the MSNBC network that homosexual behavior should be criminalized. The FRC began conducting its annual summits, which were one part revival meeting and one part political convention, in 2006. Fox News network hosts such as Sean Hannity and Bill O'Reilly were often asked to speak, and politicians with national ambitions used the meeting to impress important organizers who might become supporters.

In 2010, the big star of the event was Mike Pence, who mustered more energy than he showed in most of his speeches and hit every theme on the Christian Right agenda. None of the ideas he presented were new. He called for less government spending and policies to enforce his version of sexual morality. However, he did discuss these notions in a way that connected them all, saying, "To those who say that marriage is not relevant to our budget crisis, I say you would not be able to print enough money in a thousand years to pay for the government you would need if the traditional family continues to collapse." Pence was also a bit more strident than usual, saying, "We must demand, here and now, that the leaders of the Republican Party stand for life, traditional marriage, and religious liberty without apology!"

At the summit, Pence showed he could be fiery as well as smooth. He also left no doubt that he was as much preacher as politician—which, in this setting, served him well. "We must not remain silent when great moral battles are being waged," he said. "Those who would have us ignore the battle being fought over life, marriage, and religious liberty have forgotten the lessons of history. As in the days of a house divided, America's darkest moments have come when economic arguments trumped moral principles."[2]

The performance was rewarded when the attendees were polled on whom they preferred for president. Pence won 24 percent of the vote. Mike Huckabee, who was actually a preacher before he became governor of Arkansas, trailed him by two points. The showing won Pence some headlines in the news media but wasn't so impressive that it established him as a favorite in the field already jostling to win the GOP nomination for 2012. Weeks later, Pence would learn a bit more about his chances at a fund-raiser in Iowa. With its first-in-the-nation caucuses, Iowa was a key state for presidential hopefuls, and it was also being worked by eight different prominent Republicans, including Newt Gingrich and former Massachusetts governor Mitt Romney. Pence also visited New Hampshire, which holds the first presidential primary every four years, and South Carolina, which also selects delegates early.

All the exploration revealed to Pence that others eyeing the nomination were well ahead when it came to organization, money, endorsements, and name recognition. Also, the House of Representatives was hardly a reliable starting point for someone who wanted the presidency. In all of U.S. history, only one person, James Garfield, had made such a leap. Many others who had served in the House had become chief executive, but only after holding some other office, such as senator or governor. The Senate seat that would be contested in 2012 was held by Richard Lugar, who was a GOP institution. This meant that, for Pence, the logical next step would be to run for governor, as the popular sitting Republican,

Mitch Daniels, was barred by term limits from running in 2012. Daniels, moderate in both manner and policy, was highly popular and would have been a shoo-in if the state constitution hadn't made a third term impossible.

Daniels represented a potential problem, however; he also had been mulling a possible presidential run. If Daniels did run and failed in his presidential bid—he was not well known nationally—and if Pence ran for governor, it would be more difficult to say that Pence, another Indiana governor, was also seeking the presidency. Finally, Daniels, whose wife and daughters were strongly opposed to the idea of a presidential bid, decided to drop out. Then Daniels's lieutenant governor, Becky Skillman, represented another potential obstacle for Pence in Indiana. But Skillman also took herself out of contention for the governorship, claiming sudden health problems, which was convenient for Pence.

"My end-of-year physical exam revealed minor health issues," Skillman said in a television interview. "Nothing will interfere with my devotion to my duties as lieutenant governor, and I plan to continue the same pace as always. However, it is best to continue without the additional stress of a gubernatorial campaign."

During his last year in the House, Pence cemented his position with Christian conservatives by advocating two extreme antiabortion measures. One would have required that all women undergoing abortion be shown ultrasound images of the embryo or fetus and hear a description of its condition before the procedure. The other would have denied federal funding for abortion to rape victims if certain levels of force had been absent from their assault. (This was what some politicians called "legitimate rape.") Neither proposal passed, but cosponsors like Pence could point to the effort as a sign of their determination to do everything possible to prevent as many women as they could from having the procedure.[3]

Pence's advisors were split about whether he should pursue the presidency or needed to bolster his résumé with a term in the Indiana governor's residence. He ended the speculation at a private meeting with Karen and his closest advisors. The setting was rural Brown County, between Bloomington and his hometown of Columbus. "It was in the spirit of, 'Look, I'm making the decision to go for governor. Now what does that mean?'" recalled Van Smith, who had been working with Pence since serving in Pence's first successful bid for Congress.

Although everything was decided, Pence played a coy game, letting people guess and speculate as to whether he would be running for president or running for governor of Indiana. He scheduled a fund-raiser in the key presidential primary state of South Carolina in December. There he appeared with another GOP rising star, Governor-elect Nikki Haley. Pence aides said he was praying about his future and trying to determine how he could best serve others.

Conservative funders, above all the Koch brothers, were confident in his campaign abilities as well as his antitax and anti-Obamacare positions. Betsy and Richard DeVos were impressed by Pence's support for their pet project of developing and enhancing charter schools, often to the detriment of public education. Erik Prince, Betsy DeVos's brother and the founder of the security and private military contractor Blackwater USA, had long been his backer. Eventually, Pence also would receive support from Sheldon Adelson, the casino billionaire who was moving beyond his single-issue concentration on Israel to boost Republicans running for state-level offices. Superficially, Pence was a moralist on gambling and said he wanted to limit its spread, but as governor, after receiving donations from gambling-related donors, he would smooth the way for casino operators.[4]

The financial backers were not exactly grooming Pence for the presidency, but they supported the notion. However, Pence didn't think the moment was favorable. "I think he knew that he needed executive experience to run for president," said John Krull, a veteran journalist, university professor, and former executive director of the Indiana ACLU. The governor's slot "was the only path."

In an email to his supporters on January 27, 2011, Pence ended some of the speculation. "In the choice between seeking national office and serving Indiana in some capacity, we choose Indiana," Pence wrote. "We will not seek the Republican nomination for president in 2012."

The royal "We," which Pence used often, made it appear that he was speaking on behalf of Karen and his children, and that "They" were making these life decisions together. "I have learned to follow my heart, and my heart is in Indiana," Pence continued. "In the months ahead, as we attend to our duties in Congress, we will also be traveling across the state to listen and learn about how Hoosiers think we might best contribute in the years ahead." As he often did, Pence included a quote from the Bible in his statement. This one suggested that he had a sense that God had big plans for him, and yet he wanted to show humility. "In the wake of such encouragement," he wrote, referencing those who thought he should run for higher office, "we have often thought to ask, 'Who am I, Lord, and what is my family, that You have brought me this far?'"

It was evident to most politicians and reporters that Pence was going to run for governor, but he continued to delay a final announcement. Pence was straddling constituencies—with the Republican takeover in Washington, he had a national following among social conservatives, and he led the push toward challenging Obama and his programs to the point of being prepared to shut down the government by blocking a vote on the federal budget. At a Tea Party rally outside the Capitol on April 6, he blamed Democrats and liberals for overspending and declared, "It's time to pick a fight." Pence spoke to Tea Party principles; his personal target was an attempt to take away federal funding for Planned Parenthood, but the event was staged and promoted by Americans for Prosperity, David and Charles Koch's conservative-libertarian advocacy organization. Pence said this was a moment to fight for principle. "It's time to take a stand. We need to say to liberals, 'This far and no further.' To borrow a line from another Harry, we've got to say, 'The debt stops here.' And if liberals in the Senate would rather play political games and force a government shutdown instead of accepting a modest down payment on fiscal discipline and reform, I say, 'Shut it down.'"

A shutdown was averted through last-minute negotiations, but Pence and other Tea Party members bucked Speaker John Boehner by voting against the bill that prevented the crisis. Pence's performance won praise from his big-money backers, along with notoriety, new interviews on national television, and a chance to reiterate his insistence of standing up for principle. "Are you willing to hold up this entire budget over defunding Planned Parenthood?" Willie Geist asked Pence on MSNBC. "Well, well, of course I am," Pence replied.

"Planned Parenthood and its defenders will claim that the money that it's received from the government is not used to fund abortions. But that is only technically true," Pence said in a speech on the House floor. "There's no question that taxpayer dollars received by Planned Parenthood are used to cover allowed expenses like overhead operational cost, thus freeing up other money for the clinics that do provide abortions." This remark brought ridicule from Jon Stewart, who played a clip of Pence's speech on his satirical program *The Daily Show* and quipped, "It's like a shell game, except instead of a ball underneath a walnut shell, it's a womb."[5]

On Monday evening, April 11, 2011, fifty potential Pence supporters gathered to meet him in New York City at a secret dinner sponsored by the conservative magazine *The American Spectator*. Originally based in Indiana, *The Spectator* was founded by R. Emmett Tyrrell Jr., who published his first issue in 1967 when he was a student at Indiana University. The magazine sported the same title as one that had been published in the 1930s by George Jean Nathan and H. L. Mencken, which suggested the height of Tyrrell's ambition. His *Spectator* would make the libertarian critique of American liberals and mainstream Republicans. Ironically, for a venture promoting free enterprise, it was not very profitable and was supported in large part by grants from foundations.

The meeting took place at Brasserie 8½, a French restaurant on West Fifty-seventh Street. It brought together a journalists' roundtable known as "the Saturday Evening Club," but only a handful of those in attendance were actually journalists, and all of these were conservatives from such outlets as Fox News and *The Wall Street Journal* editorial page. Pence sat at the head table; to his left was Tyrrell, the publisher; to his right was David Koch, who must have been delighted that his anointed political prodigy had followed well along the road toward relevance and visibility. Also present were members of Pence's staff, pollster Kellyanne Conway, and Grover Norquist, the president of Americans for Tax Reform. (Norquist was forever gathering signatures among Republicans for his Taxpayer Protection pledge, a written promise to oppose all tax increases.) Other prominent attendees included Lisa Spies, a fund-raiser with Pence's political action committee; Mitzi Perdue, the widow of chicken magnate Frank Perdue; along with Steve Grasso, a Wall Street investment manager, and Thomas Lehrman of the consulting firm Gerson Lehrman Group, both of whom were being cultivated as future donors.

Technically, Pence was not permitted to raise money that evening for the governor's race. Indiana law barred such activity while the state legislature was in session. A spokesman for Pence said that any money raised that night would go to the Pence congressional campaign committee. Besides, the contacts Pence made when he attended Tyrrell's parties were more important than cash. Tyrrell, a voice of conservatism for half a century, was building an organization with legitimacy and power. Years later, Tyrrell mused, "Kellyanne Conway reminded me that, during those dark days, *The American Spectator* repeatedly invited Mike to address our supper club, the Saturday Evening Club. He was always very thoughtful and easily amused, something unheard of in Washington."[6]

In the spring of 2011, fund-raising seemed assured; Mike Pence and his staff were ready. Pence's travels around Indiana served to stage a slick infomercial, showing him talking with all the right people: farmers and family and old folks—Hoosiers all. The video would also include footage of casual Mike walking down a country road, hand in hand with Karen. The announcement was set for Monday, May 2. As they were ready to go, world news intervened: President Obama announced that the United States had tracked down and killed Osama bin Laden somewhere in Pakistan.

Upstaged by the killing of bin Laden, the Pence team decided to delay their announcement, but someone on the campaign staff sent out a blank message to supporters by mistake. It included a background logo that made it clear without saying so that Mike was running for governor. The mistake highlighted the difficulties of controlling events. With this in mind, the campaign decided to rely on a video announcement, rather than a news conference, to confirm what people already knew. In the film, Pence stood before a solid oak tree. He wore an open-necked shirt the color of the tree trunk behind him. Karen's blouse was the color of the sky.

"Hi, I'm Mike Pence," the new gubernatorial candidate said. He then turned to his left, nodded, and said, "And this is my wife, Karen."

Karen looked up at her husband, then turned to the camera with a pleasant gaze, her auburn hair fluttering slightly in the wind.

"As lifelong Hoosiers, we love Indiana . . . the small towns, court-house squares, big cities, and open fields; the strong and good people of Indiana make up the heart of the heartland."

With his gestures, especially the way he shook his head from left to right as he offered upbeat notes, Pence looked like he had studied and copied much of Ronald Reagan's style.

Karen, much like the ever-adoring Nancy Reagan, continued to look devotedly from Mike to the camera but said nothing throughout the two-minute statement.

As Pence continued, the video turned to B-roll, showing him driving his car down the road, then chatting with farmers with a tractor in the background. He described that his mission these past months was to ask Hoosiers how they thought he might serve their interests. In Pence's telling, the people were greater than he was; it was all an act of humility. "I've been humbled by the outpouring of encouragement we've received from people across this state," he said, the video now returning to Mike full frame in front of the oak, Karen gently cropped out of the frame. "I wanted you to be first to know I'm in this race. We think now is the time to move forward. And as any real Hoosier knows, any real race begins in May anyway." Mike Pence had mastered the art of speaking, and his staff had put together a winning, warm presentation that would be hard to beat. The medium was the message.

Technically, one more Republican would enter the race for the Re-publican primary for a time. Jim Wallace, a councilman from Hamilton County in central Indiana, was dropped from the ballot by the state elec-tion board when he failed to supply the required number of names on his petition to seek office.

On the Democratic side, luckily for Pence, Evan Bayh, who had served two terms as governor from 1989 to 1997 and then U.S. senator from 1999 to 2011, had decided he would not run for governor again. (It was possible to serve more than two terms as governor as long as the terms weren't consecutive.) Instead, Pence would be competing against John Gregg, an affable former Speaker of the Indiana House of Representatives when the chamber had been in Democratic hands. Despite the support and the evaporation of Republican challengers, Pence could not take the race against Gregg for granted. Gregg was charming, and his style was homespun. His campaign literature often featured a design of his trademark handlebar mustache. Gregg, as in the case of Bayh, had the reputation of being a moderate Democrat, even to the point of being considered a so-called Blue Dog conservative Democrat. This played well in a state that did not favor extremes.

One of Gregg's early problems in the campaign was that he actually liked his opponent personally. "He is a conservative, but unlike some conservatives he's not angry," Gregg said. "I don't find him shaking his finger at a moderate or liberal. He invites discussion and an exchange of ideas."

When Gregg finally began criticizing Pence he called attention to the fact that he and his family had been living in Arlington, Virginia, ever since his first term in Congress in 2001. Pence's congressional website said that he lived in Columbus, Indiana, his childhood home, and stayed in Arlington when Congress was in session. Confusing the matter more, Pence and family rented a house in McCordsville, a northeastern suburb of Indianapolis, after he announced his candidacy for the governor's race. Pence's heart might be with the Hoosiers, but Gregg suggested that he might really be out of touch.

"It's a touchy issue," said Jim Shella, a TV reporter in Indianapolis. Pence "will likely soon find himself explaining that 2000 decision to move to Virginia in ways he didn't consider twelve years ago." In fact, voters didn't seem to care.

In the meantime, Pence decided to run on a generic, moderate-sounding economic platform that he would call "Road Map for Indiana." Many of his top aides and supporters, such as Jim Kittle, the Indiana Republican Party chairman, and Fred Klipsch, a billionaire Indianapolis investor and supporter of charter schools, recommended that Pence play down social issues, which were likely to cause controversy and divisiveness. "Mike made the decision," Van Smith told *Indianapolis Monthly*, "that the major issues in the campaign for governor in 2012 should be and must be jobs and education."

"I'm running for governor for two reasons," Pence would say on the stump. "Number one is, I love this state. I love everything about it. The other reason I'm running is because this is no ordinary time in the life of our state. It's time to take Indiana from reform to results." Pence brought along one other proposal on the stump—lower taxes—that was the hallmark of the libertarian Koch brothers, who were central bankrollers of the gubernatorial campaign.

"The centerpiece for our Road Map for Indiana is to lower the personal income tax rate by 10 percent," Pence said. "That does a couple of things that I get excited about. It puts several hundred dollars in the pockets of every working Hoosier—which, as a family that's lived on a budget most of our lives, a couple hundred in the billfold is always a good thing. Truth is, the most effective way to lower taxes on job creators in the city and on the farms is to lower the income tax rate."[7]

Although Pence shied away from social themes when he could, Gregg portrayed him convincingly as a member of the extreme right. He attacked Pence's dismal record in passing legislation in Congress over six terms: "Zero for sixty-three," Gregg said on the failure rate of bills Pence authored in Congress. "He can't separate himself from the Tea Party because he is the Tea Party," Gregg added.

Throughout the campaign, Gregg had linked Pence's candidacy to another right-wing Republican, Indiana secretary of state Richard Mourdock, who had defeated longtime senator Richard Lugar in the Republican primary and was now running against Joe Donnelly, a three-term congressman.

"There came to be the so-called RINO idea—Republican in Name Only," recalled Lugar ruefully. "This has come to fracture the Republican Party." Opposing the RINOs were men such as Mourdock, members of the Tea Party, and Pence was on that side of the political equation. The Tea Party painted conservatives such as Lugar as being too moderate and too interested in bipartisanship.

"Mike has been very much involved with the Tea Party from the beginning and very supportive mutually back and forth," Lugar said. "And there are people in the Tea Party or Club for Growth or Freedom-Works . . . who just have their own scorecards. They're not affiliated with the Republican Party, they are affiliated with their own ideas of what needs to happen."

Pence did not go so far as to speak out against Lugar. "I think he was silent," Lugar said. "I don't recall him as a factor. He may have been behind the scenes, at least, I don't recall public expressions. But he was not supportive. When I was first campaigning for him in these two congressional defeats that he had, very clearly, I was supportive of him as a young Republican. I thought he had great promise. Subsequently, Mike was not involved in supporting any of my campaigns that I know of."

Mourdock, like Pence, was staunchly antiabortion but landed in the national news just before the Pence-Gregg debate with an outrageous antiabortion statement. In the case of a woman who became pregnant after rape, Mourdock said, "even when life begins in that horrible situation of rape, that's something God intended to happen."

In the final month of the campaign, Pence opted for a populist touch—a mature version of his first political campaign twenty-four years earlier. Instead of a bicycle tour, Pence launched a media campaign that had him driving around the state in a red Chevrolet Silverado pickup, highlighting that it was manufactured in Fort Wayne, Indiana. The populist effort didn't have much of an effect and Pence's eighteen-point lead over Gregg melted to six points.

Mourdock's extremism and Pence's red pickup gave Gregg an opportunity to cut even more into Pence's support as the men began a televised debate in Fort Wayne on October 25. Gregg attacked Pence as being part of a Mourdock-Pence ticket. Both were too extremist, he said, for Indiana. "As governor, I'll keep our state from being controlled by the Tea Party," Gregg said. When the questions turned to Mourdock's antiabortion statement, Pence dodged trouble by saying he disagreed with Mourdock. But then Gregg turned to the red Chevrolet pickup and the automobile industry. "The congressman uses that red pickup as a prop," said Gregg.

Pence had voted against the Obama administration's auto industry bailout in 2009 after the Bush-era financial meltdown, noted Gregg. Mourdock had sued the federal government to shut down a Chrysler plant in Indiana. "Congressman, that ain't a prop," Gregg charged. "That's

120,000 Hoosier jobs that the Pence-Mourdock ticket didn't lift one finger to help."[8]

Analysts said Gregg had roundly won the debate. GREGG PUMMELS PENCE, read one headline. In the waning days of October polls showed Pence's lead shrinking; the separation between the candidates was approaching 5 percent. Some of Pence's trouble was being attributed to a third-party candidate, Libertarian Rupert Boneham, who was more appealing to Republicans than Democrats and whose votes would mostly be taking away from Pence's total. Gregg, in a parting shot, said he was not surprised that he was doing so well. "I'm not painting him as an extremist," Gregg told *The Indianapolis Star* a few days before the election. "He painted himself that way."[9]

On November 6, Pence won the governorship by about 3 percentage points in a much weaker showing than early polling had indicated. Gregg fared well in traditional urban strongholds, notably Indianapolis itself, but more conservative suburbs and rural areas gave Pence a victory margin of around 70,000 votes out of 2.5 million cast. At the top of the ballot voters gave a much wider margin of victory to Mitt Romney, who defeated President Obama in the state by a 10 percent margin. Richard Mourdock could not overcome his extremist declarations on rape and abortion and was defeated by Joe Donnelly. After Gregg called Pence to congratulate him on the victory, Pence issued a statement with familiar wording; he said he and his running mate, Sue Ellspermann, were "profoundly humble and grateful for the confidence that has been placed in us."

In retrospect, Pence's supporters had been wise to downplay his social conservatism and evangelical fervor in what had been a mostly civilized campaign with only a few sparks generated in debates. Pence would go to the Indiana Statehouse facing suspicion from not only the Democratic minority but from many Republican legislators who also thought that Pence was more unyielding and right-wing than the GOP mainstream. They were wrong, however. The Republican Party was making a historic shift itself—to the extreme right.

8

HEAD HOOSIER

Defend the weak and the fatherless; uphold the cause of the poor
and the oppressed. Rescue the weak and the needy; deliver them
from the hand of the wicked.

—Psalm 82:3–4

On the clear but freezing-cold morning of January 14, 2013, Mike and
Karen Pence awoke for the last time in their controversial "professional"
residence in the McCordsville suburb of Indianapolis. As the couple and
their children got ready for an eventful day, close friends and family arrived for pastry and hot coffee and prayers. A reporter for Pence's hometown newspaper, *The Republic*, was on hand to chronicle the governor-elect's
movements as if it were a mission to the moon. It was nothing more than
the unremarkable inauguration of a new governor in a midwestern state
on a typically cold winter morning, but the newspaper breathlessly reported each step of the way with time-stamped entries.[1]

> *8:16 A.M. Mike, Karen, and their eldest child, Mike Jr., exited the
> McCordsville house. The governor-elect wore a gray wool coat and
> bright blue tie. Karen wore a bright red coat and black hat. They
> boarded a Black Chevy Tahoe and rode with a State Police escort to*

*Indianapolis' Union Station, the historic nineteenth-century termi-
nal that is one of the oldest railroad hubs in the world.*

*8:55 A.M. The Tahoe reached Union Station, where daughters
Audrey and Charlotte joined them among a throng of well-wishers.
A cheer went up with a standing ovation when Mike introduced
Karen to the crowd: "the love of my life," who "loves God, her family
and the people of Indiana."*

*10 A.M. The Pence family arrived at State House to receive
greetings and handshakes and then joined dignitaries on the steps of
the State House, a Neoclassical gem built to replace one that had been
so poorly constructed its roof collapsed.*

*11:04 A.M. Pence's long-time friend The Rev. Charles Lake,
offers an invocation, praying that Mike might stay true to conviction
over compromise.*

*11:26 A.M. Eastern Standard Time (10:26 in the Central
time zone counties) Pence, left hand on the Bible and right hand
raised, takes the oath of office.*

*11:30 A.M. He stepped to the lectern decorated with the state
seal which depicts a woodsman chopping down a tree, a buffalo jumping over a log and the sun setting in the distance.*

Fifteen hundred people had gathered to hear the governor's first address. To many, his specific policy plans, if they existed at all, were a
mystery. During the campaign, which had been mainly concerned with
signaling his identity as a Christian conservative, Pence had not said
much about specific actions he intended to take. Even fellow Republicans
were uninformed. They weren't going to learn much more in this moment,
as Pence said little about what he would do in office. Instead, he spoke
about values and the fact that the transition of power from one governor
to the next had been accomplished through peaceful means (as if this
hadn't always been true):

*Fellow Hoosiers, for the 50th time in our state's storied history, a
new administration has peaceably taken office as a living testa-*

ment to the strength of our constitution and the character of our people. Young and old, city and country, rich and poor. We are all Hoosiers.[2]

A homespun magic word, *Hoosier* was a term with no firmly established origin story or definition, but most agreed that it was a wholesome, perhaps even, in the way of salt-of-the-earth midwestern folks, a *superior* thing to be. Boosters and cheerleaders used the word often, as did headline writers and politicians. Abraham Lincoln grew up there; Eugene Debs and Booth Tarkington were born Hoosiers. More recent notables included David Letterman, Michael Jackson and his siblings, and Kurt Vonnegut. In *Cat's Cradle,* Vonnegut wrote that Hoosiers could be regarded as a *granfalloon,* which was a word he coined to describe "a proud and meaningless association of human beings." He wrote, "If you wish to examine a granfalloon, just remove the skin of a toy balloon."

A granfalloon could create an attachment or identity that made life seem more substantial and less random. Vonnegut, who was born and raised in Indianapolis, wrote about this quality in a way that was both teasing and warm. In one passage, his narrator encounters a woman from Indiana:

> *"My God," she said, "are you a Hoosier?"*
> *I admitted I was.*
> *"I'm a Hoosier, too," she crowed. "Nobody has to be ashamed of being a Hoosier."*
> *"I'm not," I said. "I never knew anybody who was."*[3]

Certainly without intending to do so, Pence echoed Vonnegut in an inaugural address that was heavy on greetings and expressions of gratitude—for everyone from his children to God—and included a recitation of the state's history. Aside from vague promises of progress, Pence didn't pledge himself to a single detailed proposal. However, he did use the word *Hoosier* seventeen times in thirteen minutes.

"Hoosiers are willing to do hard work," he said; "patriotism and individual responsibility exemplify Hoosier character"; "Hoosiers have strong opinions and stronger hearts"; "Hoosiers are the best people on earth."

In a gesture to numb fingers and frozen toes, the new governor noted, "the air is cold, so let's get back inside and get to work!" and retreated to his new office on the second floor. Appointed in wood with gilded details, the office occupied the south end of the statehouse building. Once he reached his teakwood desk—it had been fashioned from the deck of the World War II–era battleship USS *Indiana*—he turned to the reporters who had followed him inside. He pointed to a shiny red telephone, which had just been installed, and explained that it was a "hotline" connecting him to one person: Indiana's new First Lady, Karen Sue Batten Pence. Where others may have been satisfied with private cell phones, the Pences would be hardwired together.

The First Lady would have her own office in the statehouse. It was just down the hall from her husband's, equidistant from the rotunda at the center of the building, but on the north side. A substantial suite with a reception area and conference area, it previously had been home to the state budget director. Karen, too, had a red phone on her desk.

Other First Ladies had worked from a small office in the official governor's residence. Karen Pence would be the first to keep an office in the statehouse. The choice to make room for Karen at the capitol was like Bill Clinton's decision to devote prime space at the White House to his wife, Hillary. It said something important about the relationship. The Pences may have presented themselves to the world as conservative Christians with 1950s sentiments about gender roles, but they were modern enough to be comfortable showing themselves to be a team. They were both keenly interested in politics and power, and she was his most trusted advisor.

Unlike the Clintons, who were so wonky it seemed that their pillow talk must have been about government business, the Pences were hardly consumed with policy matters. As close friends and political allies came to see, the Pences were committed first to the idea that God had decided that Mike Pence was destined for greatness. The Lord's calling had been personal, not political, which meant Pence was a man of faith, not party. This was why he said so frequently that he was a Christian, a conservative, and a Republican in that order. How far did God want him to go? To place a limit on it would be to thwart His will, which explains why the governor sometimes prefaced a decision with a question: What would help me most to become president?

The first big decision made by Governor Pence involved turning down funding to expand Indiana's Medicaid program under the federal Affordable Care Act. Branded as "Obamacare" by Republicans who saw the president's name as a slur, the ACA provided nine federal dollars for every one that a state dedicated to expanding its health care program for the poor. Rejecting the money, and the care it provided citizens, became a way for Republican governors to demonstrate their disdain for Obamacare. In the end, however, many, including Pence, would find ways to tweak their state programs in order to take the money and increase Medicaid rolls while also appearing to push back against Obama.[4]

In his work with the state legislature, Pence focused on seeking a 10 percent cut in the state income tax and sought tougher penalties for people who were caught possessing marijuana. Such tax cuts were being pushed by the Koch-created advocacy group Americans for Prosperity, which had announced a nationwide campaign to get state lawmakers to reduce taxes. On the issue of pot legislation, Pence's fellow Republicans were actually determined to *reduce* punishments and went ahead with their plans but appeased Pence by taking a more gradual approach. On taxes, Pence got far less than he wanted—the rate was reduced from 3.4 percent to 3.3 percent. This would yield $1 per week for a person making $50,000 a year. However, other parts of the tax-cut plan reduced corporate levies more substantially and eliminated state taxes on inheritances. For the small number of wealthy people who would have paid the inheritance tax, the change produced a $150 million annual benefit.[5]

Although his own party controlled the legislature, Pence hadn't come close to getting what he wanted. Nevertheless, like George W. Bush on the deck of the aircraft carrier *Lincoln* during the Iraq War, he declared victory anyway. "At the end of the day," he said, "I think the tax relief that we crafted together is better than what I was proposing."[6] Lawmakers noticed the disconnect between the policy sausage produced by the political process and the way Pence regarded it as a prime fillet. However, the governor's sunny statement, simple and direct, established a record that he could return to again and again with pride. The tax cut, which was included in a state budget bill, would become part of the legend of Mike Pence, and only a patient study of actual events would refute his claim that it was a win. And anyone who challenged Pence's version of the story could be dismissed as a partisan or a nitpicker. Harsh criticism out in the open was not the Hoosier way, especially if the target seemed to be a nice guy.

For Pence, niceness wasn't passive. It was weaponized as a tool of persuasion and deflection. At the start of his term, he decided he would expose every legislator to his personal charm, and he managed in the first hundred days to have one-on-one meetings with 90 percent of them. He met twice with the capitol's black caucus, which was once more than Daniels had managed in eight years. This personal outreach was accomplished even as Pence (and his wife, Karen) adopted a work style that called for very few late nights or missed family dinners. Supporters, opponents, and neutral observers all said that Pence didn't seem to be very attentive. At one point, the governor and his entire staff departed Indianapolis for a leadership retreat and left a handwritten note saying, "Closed for the day." A charitable view would regard Pence's work habits as relaxed. A less charitable assessment would hold that he was more interested in the status of the job than the job itself.[7]

"He kept banker's hours while he was governor," recalled Ann DeLaney, who was once head of the Democratic Party in the state. "You didn't want to have a crisis on a weekend because there wouldn't be anybody in the office. I've worked in the governor's office. And that can be a twenty-four-hour-a-day job." DeLaney saw, in Pence, a combination of traits ill-suited to the executive branch of government. "This is going to sound pretty uncharitable. But my impression of Mike is that he does not like to work very hard, and he's not that intellectually curious. I mean, the Bible is nice. I'm happy for him that he reads the Bible. But he needs to read other things besides that. It's my impression that he doesn't."[8]

If Pence was diffident when it came to his job, he was much invested in his stylistic approach to *being* governor. He ordered up a collection of custom-embroidered clothes—dress shirts, polo shirts, and vests and jackets—decorated with his name and the words *Governor of Indiana*. Some of these garments also bore the state symbol, which included a gold torch and nineteen stars, indicating it was the nineteenth state admitted to the union. No previous Indiana governor had acquired an official wardrobe of this sort, but U.S. presidents going back to Dwight Eisenhower (who had designed his own military uniforms) had worn bomber-style jackets decorated with official seals. President Obama looked great in his bomber jacket, and Governor Pence would look fine in his specially designed wardrobe.[9]

The signs and symbols aligned with long-standing speculation about Pence's national ambitions. In the spring of 2013, Chris Cillizza of *The Washington Post* ranked him seventh in a list of top ten contenders for the GOP nomination in 2016. (Among the others were New Jersey governor Chris Christie and Florida's governor, Jeb Bush.) As a first-term governor of a midwestern state far from the spotlight, Pence started behind many other hopefuls when it came to visibility and experience. However, he had already consulted with and impressed national pollster Kellyanne Conway, and he was a favorite of the Koch brothers and all those who followed their lead. (In 2010 and 2012, David Koch alone donated $200,000 to Pence's campaigns.)[10]

National and even international contacts would be essential if Pence sought the presidency, and he began traveling overseas almost as soon as he took office. In 2013, he went to Japan, where Karen and his daughter Charlotte shopped the Ginza district and discovered Vera Bradley handbags (an Indiana-based brand) for sale. In the spring of 2014, he went to Germany, where, among other stops, he visited the U.S. Ramstein Air Base, where "on behalf of all Hoosiers," he praised the "Hoosier troops [who] play an integral role in the operations of our military forces in Europe." On this visit Pence criticized President Obama's foreign policy. This critique broke the rules of decorum that bar American officials from criticizing their government while abroad, and suggested that he was more interested in foreign policy than Hoosier matters. He also said this about Russia: "With Russian aggression on the rise again, it is clear that our policy of conciliatory diplomacy has failed." Pence continued, "Especially now, I believe it is imperative that we who believe in democracy and freedom, stand against the forces that would reshape Europe by aggression."

Six months later, Governor Pence would visit Israel, where he told Prime Minister Benjamin Netanyahu that the United States would be a strong security partner. In China, the United Kingdom, and Canada Pence's missions amounted to preparation for someone who might soon be asked about foreign policy and who could then answer with delight that he had just come back from a fact-finding mission abroad.

The trips, which were sometimes followed by announcements about foreign firms investing in Indiana, often included large delegations of state officials. (Dozens accompanied Pence to Japan.) It was not possible to say whether the business deals reached on these trips would have been achieved without the governor's efforts. However, critics couldn't complain about the cost to taxpayers. The nonprofit Indiana Economic Development Foundation paid for Pence's international forays. The money was donated by corporations that covered everything from the international flights to hotels and meals. Among the top-ten donors were five utilities, including Duke Energy and Indianapolis Power & Light. The same foundation, and thus these same firms, paid for Pence's domestic travel as well. One trip to New York City included a visit to Yankee Stadium that cost $24,000.[11]

At home, Pence refined his skills in news conferences at the Indiana Statehouse and interviews in which he demonstrated he could talk at length without really answering a question. Most galling, recalled long-time *Indianapolis Star* reporter Mary Beth Schneider, was the way Pence "would always preface his unclear answer by saying, 'Well, let me be clear.'" In one instance, she and her colleagues asked about a simple state budget item, and the governor drove the "entire press corps absolutely nuts. We kept asking him the same question over and over and over again. And even though he kept saying how he was being clear, we did not know what the answer was at all." In another instance, Brian Howey, dean of the political press corps, asked Pence what he thought of giving tax breaks to homeowners instead of businesses. Pence passed the question off to his aides. No answer ever came.[12]

Many in the Indiana press corps found Pence to be pleasant but standoffish, except for a strange habit: he was into shoulder rubs. John Krull, who had been with *The Indianapolis News* and later with the ACLU, had his run-ins with Pence, yet they got along well enough. "Why are you so tough on me?" Krull said Pence asked once in a while. Krull used the complaint as fodder for a column. Then one day, he stood chatting with a colleague when, "all of a sudden, somebody was grabbing my shoulders from behind and almost massaging them. I turned around and I was surprised—it was the governor, Mike Pence." Pence did this a number of times with Krull. "Grabbing," he said, "a real quick grasping thing." It made him uncomfortable. "I'm not a touchy-feely kind of guy," added Krull. "That's not something I would do with someone else without an engraved invitation."[13]

In the locker room subculture of political men, Pence's extra-warm physical greetings communicated volumes. On one level, it was a bonding move. On another, it indicated aggression. Watch older politicians when they are together and you will see that they shake hands, touch shoulders, and lean into each other in ways rarely seen in other settings. This is great ape dominance behavior indulged by men in suits and ties. For some, the move is a bicep grab. For others, it's invading a colleague's personal space. Pence had a thing about shoulders. Later, he would remark that "to be around Donald Trump is to be around a man with broad shoulders," or that "he's a man with broad shoulders, he's got a clear vision, he's strong."[14]

Friendly though he might be with reporters, Pence was resistant when it came to the public's right to know what was happening inside the government. Bureaucratic stalling is a time-honored tradition for politicians hoping to muffle bad news. However, as a veteran of the mass media, Pence wanted to take the game a bit further. He ordered his office to create a state-run news agency that would be called "JustIN" and was designed to provide state news to Indiana newspapers and broadcasters without the middleman—that is, without reporters gathering the information. The idea of a government news agency competing directly with the press while providing an official propagandistic slant was met with outrage and derision by publishers and reporters in Indiana and beyond. *The Atlantic* dubbed the project "Pravda on the Plains" and mocked Pence for the idea.

"Can you imagine, for example, that a Republican governor with a reputation as a small-government conservative would try to launch a government-run news service to disseminate information under the guise of journalism?" wrote David A. Graham. "What JustIN most resembles is a push by successive presidential administrations of both parties to marginalize the political press corps."[15]

Pravda on the Plains stuck. Even state Republicans mocked him. The speaker of Indiana's House of Representatives, Brian Bosma, said the idea was "horrible," then joked that he had ordered Russian translation software to deal with Pence's news service. The Democratic minority leader, Scott Pelath, said Pence's news service initiative provided "several days' worth of ridicule for our state from all sectors." Pence and his staff abandoned the news service idea within a week and tried to argue it had never been a serious notion. However, they already had hired a managing editor for the news service, who was discreetly sent packing.

Although he was mocked for his failed news service idea, Pence was still taken seriously enough to be an appealing potential presidential candidate. Of course, he would have to win Republican Party primaries and caucuses before he could even think about a general election, and that task would require appealing to hard-right conservatives who were more influential and invested in national Republican politics when it came to the candidate selection process than were Republican moderates. These voters expected Pence to talk like someone who was tough on crime, opposed to abortion rights, against unions, and in favor of private education. They also expected him to back his words with action.

On education, though, Pence was often stymied by Glenda Ritz, who was Indiana's state school superintendent, an elected position. Nationwide, only a few such elected state commission posts existed, and for Pence, this oddity meant that he was more constrained than most governors when it came to influencing public school policy. The challenge was even trickier given the fact that Ritz, a career teacher who had never run for office before, had received more votes than Pence had in the 2012 elections.

With Republicans controlling the legislature and governor's office, Ritz was the only Democrat who could wield real power in the state government, but her reach was limited to regulating some aspects of education and setting broad policy outlines. (One of her specific proposals involved lowering the age when all children were required to be enrolled in school from seven to five.) The governor did have authority to appoint members to a state education board that could place checks on the superintendent. Pence moved to further impede Ritz by creating a new agency, which he called the Center for Education and Career Innovation. This new bureaucracy was tasked with advancing Pence's education ideas, most notably an expansion of school vouchers and a new school evaluation system. Pence also wanted schools to focus more on training programs for employment in local industry. These measures echoed the interests of his major campaign supporters—Richard ("Dick") and Betsy DeVos, who spent millions on promoting school vouchers nationwide.

Publicly, the governor insisted he was only looking out for Indiana's children. Ritz "misunderstood my sincere desire" to help the state's students, Pence wrote in an opinion piece published in state newspapers. Ritz saw a power grab, and her view was confirmed when journalists uncovered an internal memo at Pence's new education center, recommending changes in state law to remove her as head of the state education board. Then came a conflict over staffing for the education board. Members appointed by Pence wanted to bring in aides working for the new education center. Ritz wanted to keep things as they had always been, with her department staff doing this work.[16]

The conflict between Ritz and the governor was, ultimately, a struggle over the status of traditional public schools, where children received academic training and came into contact with peers from different backgrounds. Ritz generally favored supporting community-based schools. Pence wanted to allow parents to use tax money to pay for private schools, charter schools, and homeschooling. This idea had created a boom in for-profit schools around the country, but the benefit for students was not clear. In fact, a 2016 Brookings Institution analysis of Indiana's program found that high-achieving students performed well in voucher programs, but lower-ranking students, who supposedly were the main beneficiaries of the policy, did not. "A student who had entered a private school with a math score at the 50th percentile," noted the Brookings Institution report, "declined to the 44th percentile after one year." However, the policy was clearly consistent with the governor's ideology, which followed the playbook of the American Legislative Exchange Council, a right-wing national political organization that promoted the privatization of American schools.[17]

ALEC, as the group was known, was yet another creation of the political activist Paul Weyrich and his usual funders, including the Koch brothers. It produced model proposals that were then introduced in state legislatures and often became law. The bills reliably favored corporations, from gun manufacturers to tobacco companies to for-profit prisons. ALEC opposed environmental regulations, sought to weaken labor unions, and favored privatization of schools. ALEC's political leanings were evident. In the 1980s, it opposed sanctions intended to end apartheid in South Africa and argued, against all scientific evidence, that pedophilia was "one of the more dominant practices within the homosexual world."[18]

ALEC promoted governmental forums and meetings to encourage state officials to adopt its policies. In education, this meant finding ways to take tax money out of public schools and put it into private hands. This happened early on in Wisconsin in 1990, under a program pushed by Republican governor Tommy Thompson. Thompson said he "loved" ALEC gatherings, "because I always found new ideas, and then I'd take them back to Wisconsin, disguise them a little bit, and declare [they were] mine."[19]

Mike Pence was a prominent figure at ALEC, which promoted antigay policies he favored. He spoke at ALEC events and contributed to its publications. During his battle with Glenda Ritz, he wrote the foreword to ALEC's annual education report and boasted that Indiana had a recent fivefold increase in the use of school vouchers. That statistic translated into just twenty thousand, or less than 2 percent, of the state's public school students, out of more than one million. Nevertheless, Pence promoted the fact that he was pushing Indiana in ALEC's direction. He continued to promote the ALEC agenda and to undermine Ritz, eventually persuading the legislature to remove the superintendent as chair of the board of education. The change would be delayed, however, until after the 2016 election. When he won this skirmish, Pence quickly dissolved the Center for Education and Career Innovation.[20]

Ironically, with the public focused on his political maneuvering, Pence didn't get all the attention and credit he deserved for his more effective education initiatives. For example, he worked with Ritz to make prekindergarten more widely available and eventually accepted federal funds—an idea he usually abhorred—in order to expand the program. The state's experience, and long-standing research, had shown the value of prekindergarten for later student development.[21]

Although Ritz surely annoyed the governor, her presence meant that he was forced to work with someone who was guided by a different philosophy, who possessed the power to oppose him, and who was willing to use that power. In every other area of Indiana governance, Pence could do almost as he pleased, and the legislature, where Republicans had a supermajority in the Senate and the House, was not inclined to get in his way. The result included projects that in the end turned out to be either poorly conceived or badly executed.

As Indiana approached the bicentennial of its statehood, Pence proposed more than $50 million worth of projects to mark the occasion, including the construction of an archives building and statehouse welcome center. He appointed Karen as the state's bicentennial ambassador, and she began to travel around the state promoting Indiana history. Since he was a self-proclaimed fiscal conservative, Pence faced a bit of a challenge when it came to paying for the commemoration. His answer involved an unconventional plan: leasing state-owned cell phone towers to an Ohio company—Agile Networks—that would make an up-front payment of $50 million and promise future payments of $260 million.

Experience elsewhere in such ventures, in which public assets were sold or rented to private entities that would turn a profit by charging users, was mixed at best. Politicians valued the idea of partnerships that allowed them to pursue new projects without raising taxes. However, some studies reported that once engaged in a government partnership, private operators used their monopoly positions—drivers usually have no choice about using a bridge to cross a river—to wring high profits from assets the public had created. For example, investors in a highway sold by the state of Indiana expected to recoup all their purchase cost in fifteen years but had a right to collect rising tolls for seventy-five years. In the first two years of the deal, made by Governor Daniels, the benefit reaped by the taxpayers fell $186 million short of expectations.[22]

Despite the problems with the toll road, Pence pushed his cell phone tower plan with the argument that privatization had worked well for the state. "Indiana is a national leader in partnerships that deliver sound financial returns and long-term benefits to Hoosiers," he said as he announced the deal. "This agreement, if approved, will put underused assets into full play, enhance Indiana's communication capabilities throughout the state, and fund the state's bicentennial projects."[23]

The cell phone tower plan met stiff resistance in the state legislature. "Everyone was skeptical that we could lease those cell towers for that amount of money," said Karen Tallian, the ranking Democrat on the state Senate Appropriations Committee. "Amongst the budget writers at the time was the general consensus, 'Oh, this is never gonna fly.'" It did not fly. After the Pence administration signed a tentative contract, a closer examination of the arrangement revealed it was not going to deliver what the governor had imagined. The plan was scaled back, and the legislature had to scramble to find revenue to support what was left of the celebration. There would be no new state archive. The construction of a $24 million hotel, imagined for a state park in northern Indiana, was also canceled.[24]

A second and more consequential Pence proposal envisioned a twenty-one-mile extension of Interstate 69 from Bloomington to Martinsville, Indiana, in a public-private partnership—an infrastructure plan known in government industry shorthand as "P3." Pence touted the project as the right way to build infrastructure, a marriage of private entrepreneurship and government. The interstate project was a telling precursor of what

Republicans in Washington—including Pence and Trump—foresaw: nationwide, a $1 trillion infrastructure agenda that would blend government and private enterprise.

Originally part of the federal interstate system, I-69 was mapped to cut across the state from its northeast corner to the southwest city of Evansville. The incomplete Martinsville-to-Bloomington stretch slowed travel and isolated part of the state. It was also a more dangerous roadway than the completed part of the interstate. Previous administrations' efforts to finish I-69 had been blocked by politics and funding problems. A private-public partnership would ease the way on both fronts, as federal law permitted a faster review process and outside investors might help finance the $325 million cost.

When the bids for the private portion were opened, Indiana officials were surprised to find that one, from a firm called Isolux, was a quarter below all the others. A European company with little experience in the United States, Isolux beat three American companies that each estimated the cost at around $400 million. The Isolux plan seemed too good to be true, and it was. Within weeks of winning the contract, top officials of Isolux were arrested in Spain on charges they had embezzled money and issued bribes in connection with construction of a high-speed rail project. An investigation by *The Indianapolis Star* reported that the European firm had been banished from other projects it had bid on in Brazil, Bolivia, and Chile. "The company is near insolvency," the newspaper reported. "The bonds it used to finance I-69 construction, to use the industry's term, are 'junk.'"

As Isolux commenced work the project was almost immediately mired in cost overruns. Officials reported slowdowns in construction. Commuters between Indianapolis and Bloomington—the Democratic-majority home of Indiana University—encountered constant traffic jams, and the state Department of Transportation reported a significant increase in the number of traffic accidents in the work zone. The mayor of Bloomington, John Hamilton, sought help from Pence to resolve the dangerous problem. "My first job as mayor is public safety," Hamilton told reporters. "The seemingly ever-delayed nature of this construction and the danger it poses [to] travelers are unacceptable."

Hamilton, a Democrat and nephew of longtime Indiana congress-man Lee Hamilton, said he had no philosophical issue with the concept of public-private partnerships. "I am not against experimenting in gov-ernment and trying new ways to get things done, but this is a debacle," Hamilton said. "My community and our neighbors are all suffering because state government hasn't kept up its end of the bargain."[25]

The estimated final cost of the twenty-one-mile stretch of road was raised to around $500 million. By 2016, with just 10 percent of the an-ticipated paving done, the project was in chaos and two years behind schedule. A private-public initiative that was intended to prove the concept was superior to government-built highways was proving the opposite. Even the libertarian Reason Foundation, funded by Pence's benefactors David and Charles Koch, criticized the project. "This is one of the worst failures that I've seen in state-level P3s," said Robert Poole, director of transpor-tation policy at the foundation, which also publishes the conservative-libertarian magazine *Reason*.

The I-69 problem was mostly one Pence made for himself, but others, including the Isolux execs, helped to make the mess. In other instances, Pence was the sole cause of his own trouble. A case in point in-volved a single citizen—Keith Cooper of Elkhart—whose conviction for an armed robbery and a shooting had been overturned by a state appeals court, but only after he had served ten years in prison. Some of the facts of Cooper's case can best be explained as he related them to the press: "One morning I decided to go to the store. And on my way returning from the store, I got caught by a train. And I was sitting there waiting on the train. And I see all these police cars with their sirens on—they're just coming from everywhere. And I'm like to myself, these cops gotta be crazy . . . not knowing they was coming for me."[26]

Two witnesses identified Keith Cooper as being the tall black man involved in the robbery and shooting. He was convicted after a brief trial. In prison, he was convicted of assaulting another inmate. He also earned a high school equivalency degree and two junior college degrees, and trained for hospice care. His conviction, which came with a forty-year sentence, was overturned when two witnesses recanted and suppressed

DNA evidence, which had not been shared with him at the time of the trial, showed someone else had been at the scene of the crime.

The Indiana Court of Appeals ordered Cooper's release in 2006, but the felony remained on the books. Because the law allowed for him to be charged and tried again Cooper was out of prison but still not fully free. Also, his prison time counted against him when he applied for jobs. A trucking company finally gave him a job as a forklift operator, but he always felt the weight of his record. Cooper said, "I didn't commit the crime. I feel as though I have the right to go and apply for a job without them looking at my background and seeing that hideous crime that's been placed on my record, for which I'm actually innocent."

In 2014, a young attorney named Elliot Slosar, who had taken on his case as he left law school, appeared on behalf of Cooper before the Indiana Department of Corrections Parole Board. Slosar asked the board to approve a pardon for Cooper, which would wipe his record clean. (Board approval is generally the first step in the pardon process in Indiana.) The board chairman at the time, Thor Miller, telegraphed his opinion during the hearing. "Basically, you were African-American and you were tall, and that was the only relationship you had toward the suspect, and the investigating detective was manipulating the witnesses with their identification," said the board chairman, "It's rather shocking."

The main witnesses in the case tearfully apologized for having wrongly identified Cooper as the assailant. An online campaign gathered at least one hundred thousand signatures in support of seeking something that never had been done before in state history: a gubernatorial pardon based on actual innocence. The parole board voted unanimously to recommend that Governor Pence grant the request.

Years passed without Pence making a decision on the Cooper case. Three others who had petitioned for pardons without claims of innocence received them. It was possible that Pence declined to act on the Cooper request because a pardon would have given Cooper some advantage in a civil claim against the government, but Pence never explained his inaction. In 2015, *The Indianapolis Star* published a series of articles on the case. The reports left little room for doubt about what happened. The

prosecutor who brought the case against Cooper asked for the pardon to
be granted, and still Pence refused. Finally, he left it to the general counsel in the governor's office to write a letter passing the buck to the court
system. "Although the judicial system may not be perfect," wrote Mark
Ahearn, "given the extraordinary nature of Mr. Cooper's request, we need
to be certain the judicial process is complete and has been given every
opportunity to address any error that may have occurred."

What chance did Cooper have in the court system? Experts disagreed
about what might happen if he found some way to petition for relief. Some
thought previous agreements made to secure his release from prison barred
further action. Others thought that a judge might show him mercy. However, no doubt could be raised about the fact that with his inaction, Pence
had added three years to the process and that a new effort would be costly
for a family that had already been financially ruined by Keith Cooper's
legal torment.

At best, Pence's inaction could be seen as cruel but thoughtless. At
worst, he was a powerful official willing to inflict pain on an innocent man
in order to show he was tough on crime. It was also impossible to overlook the fact that Cooper was a powerless black man who had lived in a
predominantly Democratic-voting, African American northern portion
of the state. The reality was, however, that Pence's staff treated the Cooper case not in human terms, but as a political problem. Aides were particularly cautious about dealing with the Cooper case once their boss had
been named as Trump's vice-presidential choice.

We have obtained emails sent by members of Pence's staff that reflected caution and concern about handling the case. On July 25, 2016,
Tim Harmon, an editorial writer at *The Journal Gazette* newspaper in
Fort Wayne, Indiana, asked Kara D. Brooks, Pence's press spokesperson,
in an email: "Is the governor considering granting Cooper's [pardon] request?" Harmon's query provoked an email exchange among Brooks,
Ahearn, the governor's general counsel; and Matt Lloyd, Pence's deputy
chief of staff. Brooks's idea was to tell the reporter that "the request for
Keith Cooper is still under consideration," and to ask the others if that
was acceptable. Ahearn answered soon afterward, saying, "I'm good with
it. Accurate and preserves all options. We just aren't talking about it." But

Lloyd asked for a revision: "I think in the future we should say there is no change rather than no comment. It is still under consideration." Brooks then settled on the following official reply: "The request for Keith Cooper is still under consideration."

This type of studied inaction was repeated in southern Indiana in late 2014 and early 2015, where doctors and public officials detected a sudden rise in drug overdoses along with a surge in cases of human immunodeficiency virus (HIV) infection. The overdoses and infections affected drug abusers who had shared hypodermic needles. This practice is a well-established pathway for HIV infection, and is often associated with inner-city heroin addicts. Some of those who were infected in Indiana worked as prostitutes at highway truck stops, which meant that their customers could be exposed to HIV during sexual encounters.

Officials across the country often treated drug-related HIV outbreaks with benign disinterest. They regarded addiction as a moral failing and, since the people affected often engaged in criminal behavior, they were seen as unsympathetic. (This was the same attitude expressed by certain evangelical Christians when HIV, spread by sexual contact, devastated gay communities.) In this case, however, the epidemic emerged in sparsely populated, almost all-white Scott County, where the victims were injecting the opioid Opana. The location, the cohort, and the drug, which was not heroin, all cast the outbreak in a different light.

In January 2015 the Centers for Disease Control reported eleven new cases of HIV in the Indiana outbreak. CDC officials said that the rural area, with twenty-four thousand residents—about 20 percent live below the poverty line—would have been expected to report only five such cases in an entire year. Local and state officials joined the CDC in asking the governor for permission to distribute clean needles to addicts. While there was no specific mention of hypodermic needles in state drug laws, needles could only be obtained by prescription and otherwise were considered illegal drug paraphernalia. For months, Pence refused to waive the rules.[27]

In the same way that opponents of sex education feared that knowledge about sex promoted promiscuity among teenagers, opponents of clean needle distribution—addicts exchanged used ones for new—argued without basis that this would encourage addiction. (Scientific studies were stacked against both notions.) Months passed and the number of HIV infections ticked upward. Pence began to reconsider and said that he was praying about the issue. Finally, on March 24, 2015, the governor telephoned the sheriff of Scott County. Dan McClain, a tough cop and a Navy veteran, said the scope of the epidemic had made him change his own view of the matter. He was certain that offering clean syringes to drug users would save lives and help fight the outbreak.

"If you had asked me six months ago if I approved of needle exchange programs, I probably would have told you no," McClain said. However, he had come to believe that needle exchange was "the only thing we can do to stop" the epidemic. Two days after speaking to the sheriff, Pence declared a state of emergency and issued a thirty-day waiver for the distribution of needles. "I am opposed to needle exchange as anti-drug policy," Pence said. "But this is a public health emergency and as governor of the State of Indiana, I'm going to put the lives of the people of Indiana first."

By the time Pence had completed his prayers and issued his proclamation many more lives were in jeopardy. Eleven new cases of HIV infection had grown to 77. A month later, the CDC reported 135 cases, and, as officials had warned, infections extended beyond intravenous drug users to sex workers in the county. Not included in the statistics was the likelihood that the drug users had been spreading hepatitis C, which often goes undetected. Shane Avery, a family doctor who treated some of the HIV patients, told reporters he was relieved that Pence had finally allowed the needle exchange, but he and other medical professionals said they doubted the spike in HIV cases was confined to one impoverished rural Indiana county. "There is no doubt in my mind that this has spread beyond the borders of Scott County," Avery said. "Scott County is not an island."

While the governor insisted his actions would be temporary and limited, the Republicans in the Indiana legislature stepped in. In April, they passed a bill that ended state regulation of local distribution of needles. Many who approved of the new law had previously supported the ban on needle exchanges. They said they were simply being pragmatic. The exchange program in Scott County was working.

The Scott County crisis had presented Governor Pence with an acute public health emergency and a direct way to confront it, but his ideology had delayed making a necessary decision. The second major public health challenge of his tenure, a lead poisoning problem in the city of East Chicago, had simmered for years only to boil over in 2016.

A city of twenty-nine thousand people in the northwest corner of the state, East Chicago was predominantly African American and poorer than the rest of Indiana. It was also one of the few Democratic Party strongholds in the state. Like many of the communities that hugged the lakeshore south of Chicago, it had been home to a succession of heavy industries. A lead smelter, last run by a company called USS Lead, had operated in the West Calumet section of the city for more than a century. In the early 1980s, parts of West Calumet were declared a federal Superfund cleanup site after arsenic and lead were discovered in the ground. Both are known to cause cancer, and lead is especially dangerous to children who, once exposed, may suffer from low IQ and developmental and behavioral issues.

For years, city and state officials had checked the health of people who lived in West Calumet, paying special attention to residents of a predominantly African American housing project. In 2016, they detected a rise in the levels of lead in some residents' blood, and officials provided funding to conduct further screening and assessment. Mayor Anthony Copeland, a Democrat, determined that the city had depleted most of the state and federal funding available to deal with the problem. He wrote a letter to Pence:

> I am asking that as Governor, you declare that a disaster emergency exists in the USS Lead Superfund zone . . . in order to make additional state resources available to the city of East Chicago and the residents of West Calumet which are necessary to cope with the disaster, including securing housing for the residents of West Calumet. By this letter I ask you to pardon formal requirements, and make all needed State of Indiana resources available to adequately respond to this crisis which is impacting Hoosier families.

Copeland sought help with the closing of an elementary school close to the lead site and asked for $5 million in disaster relief. This money would help with the cost of expenses such as providing clean drinking water to replace supplies found to be contaminated. In this way, East Chicago's troubles were similar to the infamous case of Flint, Michigan, where lead contamination in city water was blamed for a host of health problems. The Flint crisis, widely publicized, had been a political disaster for politicians in Michigan. Even though he used the magic word *Hoosier* in his pleadings, Mayor Copeland got nowhere with the governor. Pence refused to grant the petition, saying enough was already being done by local, state, and federal agencies.

As in the cases of Keith Cooper and the opioid users, Pence delayed, stayed far away, and took no action. All three cases involved the poorest segments of society: drug users, prostitutes, an African American man who was arrested for being black, a city to the north populated by black residents with muffled voices and little power. Pence was chastised locally for his inaction, but the controversy was contained. Once again, he managed to avoid broader scrutiny. Eventually, though, despite his efforts to maintain a low profile, Pence's commitment to a Christian Right social agenda soon would reverberate on a national stage.

For years, evangelical activists had argued that Democrats and liberals may have seemed devoted to expanding the rights of certain minorities but were, instead, intent on restricting religious liberty. In this analysis, protections for gays and lesbians, abortion rights, and even testing regimes in public schools were official attacks on Christian family life. In the broader society, those who said "Happy Holidays" rather than "Merry Christmas" were prosecuting a war on Christmas. Pence and his allies believed they had to fight against changing mores, especially when the shifts seemed to favor the rights of gays, lesbians, and transsexuals.

Pence and other social conservatives feared that equal rights for gay and transgendered people added up to an assault on their own freedom. A year into his term as governor, a case emerged in Indianapolis that raised the issue of equal rights, guaranteed by the Constitution, against Pence's own sense of religious freedom. This time, Mike Pence's story went nationwide, and he would now be recognized for his adherence to a strict religious code that would not bend easily to the majority. One day in March 2014, Randy McGath and his wife, Trish, the owners of a bakery,

111 Cakery, which happened to be located in a traditionally gay neighborhood of Indianapolis, received an order by phone. The callers, couple Shane Laney and Mike Stephens, wanted a custom cake for their upcoming gay commitment ceremony. Citing religious grounds, the McGaths refused to make a cake for them. "There was zero hate here," said Randy McGath. "We were just trying to be right with our God."[28]

As news of the McGaths' refusal spread, the 111 Cakery became the scene of protests and counterprotests. Pence landed squarely on the side of the McGaths, arguing that they had a right to discriminate against certain kinds of customers on the basis of religion. This position put Pence in a battle against the tide. With federal courts rapidly overturning both state and U.S. prohibitions on same-sex marriage, Indiana's ban was sure to be voided. In October 2014, it was. Within months and with solid support from the governor, conservatives in the Indiana state legislature offered up a proposed law—the Religious Freedom Restoration Act (RFRA)—that would prohibit "a governmental entity from substantially burdening a person's exercise of religion." Plainly, the law meant that if people with a god like the McGaths' wanted to deny service on the basis of a customer's sexual identity, they had a right to do so.

Pence signed the bill—it came to be known by its acronym and pronounced "RIFF-ra"—on March 26 at an odd signing ceremony closed to the news media. In an official photograph commemorating the moment, Pence was surrounded by a tableau of people apparently intended to represent religious diversity in favor of the bill. Pence was seated and smiling at his desk, pen in hand, surrounded by half a dozen nuns in black habits, a man in a priestly collar peeking over the backs of the nuns, Franciscan monks in full-length robes, and a bearded man with a broad-brimmed hat, who appeared to be an Orthodox Jew. The governor's aides refused to further identify those present.

The backlash was immediate and widespread. Business leaders, politicians, gay rights activists, and others declared that RFRA amounted to official sanctioning of illegal discrimination. Pence's longtime ally Curt Smith, a Christian right activist, sought to quell the controversy by explaining the context. His argument was shocking. Permitting conservative Christians to discriminate against gay customers, he said, was similar to letting "a Jewish printer forego printing signs claiming the Holocaust was a lie or that his ancient ancestors killed Christ. We might agree an Indiana Muslim restaurant owner need not serve pork tenderloins, a Hoosier State delicacy."[29]

Smith, a former campaign operative and Pence congressional aide, was so important to the governor's political identity that he enjoyed veto power over some of the governor's appointments. He also headed the conservative Christian Indiana Family Institute, which was influential with Pence's core supporters. He had written about threats to Christianity in stark and idiosyncratic terms in a self-published booklet called *Deicide—How Eliminating the Deity Is Destroying America*. (On the cover, he emphasized the word *Destroying* by having it displayed in red.) "The opponents of our political work are committing deicide," he wrote, "so their unbridled self-autonomy in all spheres, including human sexuality, will remain unchallenged." The result, as he saw it, was a nation in terrible decline and suffering all around.

Approved and signed at the same time that national public opinion was shifting quickly in favor of gay rights, RFRA was a powerful example of a policy approved to satisfy an extremist constituency. Within a day of the signing ceremony, students at Indiana University marched while chanting, "No hate in Indiana." Business leaders knew that angry reaction to similar laws in other states had led to travel bans and product boycotts. Fearing a similar backlash they flooded Pence's office with calls of protest. Among them, the managers of Cummins Engine, who cultivated diversity in Pence's hometown, said they didn't want to alienate workers or customers, especially sports leagues and tourists. In a sign of what could come, the University of Southern California announced it would no longer send sports teams to Indiana. The National Collegiate Athletic Association, which was about to host basketball's Final Four championship tournament in Indianapolis, issued a statement that criticized RFRA.

As in most states, major business leaders in Indiana leaned toward the GOP on most issues. However, some had expressed private concerns about Pence ever since he declared his candidacy for governor. He was, they feared, inexperienced as an executive and captive to extreme elements of the religious Right. Passage of RFRA confirmed this fear and provoked one of the state's top business leaders, Bill Oesterle, to break publicly with the governor. Oesterle ran the online home services company Angie's List, which is based in Indianapolis. Angie's List would postpone a $40 million expansion in the state, he announced. Mayors across the country, including New York and San Francisco, Portland and Washington, banned or curtailed official travel to Indianapolis. Even Greg Ballard, the Republican mayor of Indianapolis, protested and said the city council would be considering a resolution to denounce RFRA. A Protestant denomination announced it would cancel its plan to hold a convention in Indianapolis if RFRA stood. "Our perspective is that hate and bigotry wrapped in religious freedom is still hate and bigotry," said Todd Adams of the Christian Church (Disciples of Christ).

When the hosts of national TV talk shows chimed in, all was lost. David Letterman lashed out and dedicated a Top Ten List of "Guys who Mike Pence looks like." (Number eight: the guy whose wife has to tell him he's "getting a little loud"; number one: "The guy fishing in a Cialis commercial.") "This is not the Indiana I remember as a kid," said Letterman. "I lived there for twenty-seven years, and folks were folks, and that's all there was to it."[30]

Pence held out for several days, consulting with advisors and polling friends. His aides spoke with Curt Smith, who opposed compromise and urged Pence to hold tough. Smith had launched a press blitz in defense of RFRA, telling reporters that the Christian Right was an oppressed group deserving protection from laws that would require those who ran businesses to treat customers equally. "Why would you want to engage a bunch of hateful people," he said of the other side. "We're always accused of being bigots." In this way, he framed the right to discriminate in a secular setting—like a bakery—as a matter of religious freedom. The Christians were victims, not bigots, and Pence needed to stand firm. Nevertheless, Smith saw that something needed to be done on the public relations front. Privately, in talks with the governor's aides, Smith endorsed a plan for Pence to go on national television to defend himself as a reasonable man.

On March 29, 2015, three days after Pence signed the bill, he went to an Indianapolis TV studio where he was connected via satellite to the ABC TV network, where George Stephanopoulos, the host of a news program called *This Week*, would interview him.

Confident in his abilities—after all, he had been a TV host too—Pence sat in front of an image of the Indiana Statehouse. He knew the points he wanted to make; the press was distorting reality, RFRA was about religious freedom, and even Bill Clinton had signed a federal religious freedom act in 1993.

Stephanopoulos, who had been senior advisor to Clinton in his first term, was well aware of the details of the federal law. Pence raised the Clinton talking point and said the state law had not been written with the intent of discriminating against gay people in Indiana. Stephanopoulos pointed out that laws in other states specifically protected the civil rights of gay citizens, balancing religious freedom law with civil rights. Indiana's law had no such civil rights provision. He also noted that one of the proponents of the Indiana bill, Eric Miller of a group called Advance America, had said that RFRA was an anti-equality measure that "will protect those who oppose gay marriage." Stephanopoulos then quoted Miller as saying, "Christian bakers, florists, and photographers should not be punished for refusing to participate in a homosexual marriage."

When he finished with the quote, Stephanopoulos asked, "Is Advance America right when they say a florist in Indiana can now refuse to serve a gay couple without fear of punishment?"

Pence evaded the question, blaming misunderstandings, distortions, and the news media and complained that Stephanopoulos was playing into a false narrative. Four times, Stephanopoulos asked Pence to answer "yes or no," and four times Pence evaded the question. Each time, with increasing irritation, Pence reverted to his talking points.[31]

> PENCE: George . . . there's a lot of people in this country that are concerned about government overreach into their religious liberty, and I'm one of them, and I stand with them and we've defended them in Indiana. This is about protecting every Hoosier of every faith.

STEPHANOPOULOS: Do you think it should be legal in the state of Indiana to discriminate against gays or lesbians?

Pence took a breath and, sounding exasperated, said, "George . . ."

STEPHANOPOULOS: It's a yes-or-no question.

PENCE: Come on. Hoosiers don't believe in discrimination. I mean, the way I was raised in a small town in southern Indiana is you're kind, you're caring and respectful to everyone. Anyone who's been in Indiana for five minutes knows that Hoosier hospitality is not a slogan, it's a reality. . . . This is not about discrimination, this is about protecting the religious liberty of every Hoosier of every faith, and we're going to continue to work our hearts out to clarify that to the people of Indiana and the people of this country.

Not willing to let go, the TV host came back at Pence. "Yes or no," he said. "Should it be legal to discriminate against gays and lesbians?"

"George, you're following the mantra of the last week online and you're trying to make this issue about something else," Pence said. "What I am for is protecting with the highest standards in our courts the religious liberty of Hoosiers. . . . I stand by this law. It was an important step forward when Bill Clinton signed it in 1993. It's an important step forward of keeping the promises of our Bill of Rights and the First Amendment and our Indiana Constitution, and I'm proud that Indiana has adopted the Religious Freedom Restoration Act."

Pence's performance got negative reviews even in his home state. "If it seemed impossible to make things worse, Pence found a way in the course of those five minutes on Sunday," wrote Dave Bangert, a columnist at the Lafayette *Journal & Courier*. "He couldn't answer simple yes-or-no questions when given access to a national TV audience." Pence "only poured fuel on the fire for his critics," wrote Tom LoBianco in *The Indianapolis Star*. "But Pence's bona fides with his core base of supporters, on the religious right, cannot be questioned now. And maybe, if you're the Pence Team, that's worth the massive backlash."[32]

On April 2, four days after his national television appearance, Pence spoke to Curt Smith, who urged him to resist the pressure to change RFRA. He said that Pence shouldn't fear long-term repercussions because the NCAA tournament, about to start in Indianapolis, would eclipse the controversy in the minds of basketball-crazed Hoosiers. Pence did not agree and instead backed a revision to the bill, which specified that no one "may deny service to anyone on the basis of sexual orientation, race, religion or disability."

The change reversed the effect of the law. Business leaders who had pressed Pence for it were pleased. Curt Smith, who had been dismissed from his day job at a law firm because of his many public statements during the RFRA controversy, felt it as a betrayal. In *Deicide,* he would hold to his principles, writing that Pence's reversal would have "grave implications beyond our national borders." He wondered if Pence had acted first on the basis of his religious convictions and finally out of concern for his national political ambition.[33]

For his part, Pence could claim to have used every opportunity he could to push the Christian agenda. After the RFRA debacle, he signed a law making Indiana's restrictions on abortion, which were already among the tightest in the nation, even more intense. The new law required women to receive antiabortion counseling prior to having the procedure and then wait at least eighteen hours to have it performed. It also mandated funeral services for fetuses, required abortion providers to have admitting privileges at nearby hospitals, restricted the use of fetal tissue in medical research, and barred abortions based on fetal abnormalities. Although it was eventually struck down by federal courts, the abortion bill signaled that Pence was willing to use his power to do whatever he could to block women from exercising their rights. This position would assure him unwavering support from the Christian Right for whatever ambition he would chase next, including the office of president of the United States.[34]

The White House had occupied a place in Pence's imagination from his time as a boy in Columbus. In 2015, he was not openly seeking the presidency, but he was taking stands that might appeal to GOP primary voters. In foreign policy, this meant sounding and whenever possible *acting* tough when it came to America's enemies. And although Pence was not among the large field of Republicans about to run for the 2016 Republican presidential nomination, he stayed close to the Republican message: Barack Obama was not doing enough to protect the United States.

In 2015, with the Cold War against communism a distant memory, foreign terrorists linked to radical Islam were the replacement bogeyman, as they had been since the attacks of September 11, 2001. Nothing of the scale of 9/11 had happened in the United States since then, but whenever an incident occurred anywhere in the world, politicians in America sought public support by issuing dire warnings about doing enough to protect the homeland. Pence was ready to follow suit.[35]

On November 13, 2015, terrorists affiliated with a murderous group called ISIS (Islamic State in Iraq and Syria) launched six coordinated attacks around Paris, killing 130 people and injuring more than 400. President Obama led U.S. condemnation of the attacks, which followed many other ISIS attacks in Europe and in the Middle East that year. "This is an attack not just on Paris, it's an attack not just on the people of France, but this is an attack on all of humanity and the universal values that we share," President Obama said. "The American people draw strength from the French people's commitment to life, liberty, the pursuit of happiness. . . . We're going to do whatever it takes to work with the French people and with nations around the world to bring these terrorists to justice, and to go after any terrorist networks that go after our people."[36]

Pence sided with most of the seventeen GOP candidates running for president who used the Paris attack to justify claims that Obama's immigration and refugee policies were allowing potential terrorists to slip into the country. More than one thousand Syrian refugees had settled in the United States, and about ten thousand were scheduled to come in 2016. (They would be among eighty-five thousand refugees from around the world.) Florida governor Jeb Bush, whom many considered the front-runner in the race to be the Republican nominee for president, said he was most concerned about protecting Syrian Christian refugees. Ted

Cruz had already called the Obama administration's refugee policies "nothing short of crazy." He went further after the Paris attacks. Allowing Muslim refugees to enter the United States, he said, was "lunacy." Donald Trump, who was not widely considered a viable candidate, advocated a total ban. "We cannot let them into this country, period," Trump said. "We have no idea who these people are. This could be one of the great Trojan horses."[37]

In fact, the Obama administration had initiated a long, complicated vetting process for refugees, which included investigations that could last eighteen months or more. No one would be admitted before this screening was done. Included in the process were fingerprinting, retina scans, exhaustive interviews that determined prior job status, and the identification of relatives and friends in the United States. Investigators also tested refugee candidates' claims that they would face retribution if they returned to their countries of origin.

"The process for any citizen of a Middle Eastern or majority-Muslim country to get into the United States is tortuous and has become more so over the past 15 years, with additional screenings, interviews and other background checks," said Natasha Hall, a former Homeland Security immigration officer. "While the average wait time for refugee resettlement is 18 to 24 months, Iraqis and Syrians typically wait several years."[38]

As critics sought to halt the processing of Syrians, President Obama lashed out at the Republicans for playing politics with humanitarian concerns. He opposed the notion that only Middle Eastern Christians, not Muslims, be admitted. "That's shameful," Obama said. "That's not American. That's not who we are. We don't have religious tests to our compassion."[39]

On the Monday after the Paris attacks, Pence announced he would suspend settlement of Syrian refugees in the state. "Indiana has a long tradition of opening our arms and homes to refugees from around the world but, as governor, my first responsibility is to ensure the safety and security of all Hoosiers," Pence said.[40] Governors in more than a dozen other states took similar action, although legal analysts said neither Pence nor the other governors had the authority to do so. On that basis, the American Civil Liberties Union promptly filed suit against Pence. His actions violated "both equal protection and civil rights laws and intrude on authority that is exclusively federal," said Ken Falk, ACLU Indiana legal director.[41]

The ACLU legal challenge was accompanied by a moral challenge from the Roman Catholic Church. Joseph W. Tobin, the archbishop of Indianapolis, decided to bypass Pence's dictate and to allow the resettlement of a Syrian family in Indiana under the auspices of Catholic Charities. In early December, Pence met with Tobin at the statehouse for about an hour and directly asked that the Syrian family not be brought to the state. The governor cited concerns that the Obama administration had not done enough to check on the refugees, while Tobin reminded the governor that all refugees, including this particular family, had undergone an exhaustive screening process before entry. The archbishop politely refused Pence's request and thanked him for his time. Tobin made a more pointed statement when the Syrian family arrived the following week, focusing on Catholic mercy and tradition.

"Three years ago, this family fled the violence of terrorists in their homeland of Syria," Tobin said. "After two years of extensive security checks and personal interviews, the United States government approved them to enter our country. For forty years, the archdiocese's Refugee and Immigrant Services has welcomed people fleeing violence in various regions of the world. This is an essential part of our identity as Catholic Christians, and we will continue this life-saving tradition."[42]

Pence held to his position. A spokesman for the governor said that he held Catholic Charities "in the highest regard but respectfully disagrees with their decision to place a Syrian refugee family in Indiana at this time." At the agency coordinating the Syrians' settlement, staff scrambled to protect a family that was en route. "We didn't want anyone coming into a situation where they might be met with hostility, or even massive amounts of attention," recalled Cole Varga, director of the agency, Exodus. "They were diverted to Connecticut."

Noting that no refugee had been involved in a terror attack in America since 1980, Varga pointed out that in Indiana, employers eagerly competed for those who settled in the state because they were such good workers. "It's a population that has overcome torture, abuse, and long

waits to come to the United States. They do very well once they arrive."
Exodus aided their adjustment, and amid the controversy stirred by Pence,
it received a spike in donations, and more than four hundred people called
to volunteer. This support was sustained as one of the Republican presidential candidates spoke even more forcefully.

At a campaign rally in South Carolina, Donald Trump called for a
ban on the entry of all Muslims into the United States. "We have no
choice," Trump said. "Our country cannot be the victim of tremendous
attacks by people who believe only in jihad."[43]

Governor Pence was among those who thought Trump had gone too
far. He issued his response in a tweet on his official Twitter account the
following morning. He said: "Calls to ban Muslims from entering the U.S.
are offensive and unconstitutional."[44]

A year later, things would change. Pence would no longer object to
Trump's ban on Muslims entering the United States. By now, he had become Trump's most ardent supporter, no matter what the presidential
candidate and eventual president might say.

Tobin, however, had not changed. Neither had Pope Francis, who
was a constant advocate for mercy and for protecting the refugees. A
month before the presidential election, the pope took a step that seemed
to reward Tobin for his stand against Mike Pence's ban on Syrian refugees. On October 9, 2016, the pope named Tobin a cardinal and assigned
him to the Archdiocese of Newark, where he continued to speak out for
refugees and the poor. A headline writer at the *Detroit Free Press* in his
former diocese asked the question: CAN CARDINAL JOE, A NATIVE DETROI-
TER, RISE TO BECOME THE 1ST AMERICAN POPE?[45]

9

WHEN TRUMP CALLS

Let another man praise thee, and not thine own mouth; a stranger, and not thine own lips.

—Proverbs 27:2

On Wednesday, April 20, 2016, which was an unseasonably warm day in Indianapolis, Mike Pence stood at the front steps of the governor's mansion wearing a light gray suit, white shirt, and blue tie. Blooming pansies and violets filled two big planters to either side of him. His serene face betrayed no emotion as a pair of black SUVs slowly entered the curved driveway. When the car stopped, Donald J. Trump and New Jersey governor Chris Christie emerged from the back seat of one of the SUVs into the warmth of the day. The three stood and chatted for a moment before they entered the mansion, followed by their aides. Christie would come to rue this day. It was the start of a beautiful friendship, or at least a strategic alliance, between Trump and Pence.

Inside, Trump and Christie found a homey version of an official residence. Family photos were arranged on the stairway leading to the second floor. A beagle named Maverick and two cats—Oreo and Pickle—wandered the house, and somewhere a bunny named Marlon Bundo and a snake named Sapphira were safely put away. A notorious germophobe, Donald Trump had owned a dog early in his first marriage, but he generally considered pets to be déclassé.

As governor of New Jersey, Christie had come to know Pence through the Republican Governors Association. He had been acquainted with Trump much longer. Christie had endorsed Trump after ending his own presidential campaign, becoming one of the very first to pick him out of the big field of candidates. For weeks, Christie had campaigned for the front-running candidate, often appearing with Trump, where he had a tendency to let his face go blank. This invited observers to imagine he was more than a little ambivalent about his circumstance. Trump was a vulgar man with no government experience, and in the previous year, Christie had said, "I just don't think that he's suited to be president of the United States."[1] From this starting point, he had evolved into a key Trump surrogate and the broker for this meeting with Pence.

Trump, who claimed to have a great memory, should have remembered that he had met with Pence twice before. A few years prior, Pence had visited with Trump at his Mar-a-Lago estate in Florida. Before that, in November 2011, Pence had met with Trump to ask for his financial support as he prepared to run for governor. This time, it was Trump who wanted something. The Indiana presidential primary was two weeks away, and Trump was fresh off a resounding victory in his home state of New York. He was hoping for a decisive win that would end the chances of his only remaining competitor, Texas senator Ted Cruz. He knew that Pence was unlikely to give him an endorsement. Pence and Cruz were aligned as hard-right Christians, and Cruz had offered Pence public support in 2015 after Pence signed the Indiana religious freedom act. "Governor Pence is holding the line to protect religious liberty in the Hoosier State," Cruz had said at that time. "I'm proud to stand with Mike."[2] It was logical that Pence would now be expected to return the favor—by supporting Cruz in what could become a make-or-break primary on the march to the Republican convention.

Christie's job was to help convince Pence to tone down his expected primary endorsement. Endorse Cruz if you must, was his message, but avoid saying anything negative about Trump. Cruz had dismissed the outcome in New York as a matter of home-field advantage. However, he was desperate to win in Indiana, where a May 3 victory for Trump would lead to the nomination at the national convention. If Pence would temper his support for Cruz, Trump would return in the fall to help the governor, who faced a difficult reelection bid against Democrat John Gregg.

The meeting went well. Pence would still back Cruz, but in the mildest terms. Christie departed first, flying back to New Jersey, his mission accomplished.

Trump and Pence talked a bit more and hit it off. Afterward, Trump rode off to a campaign stop at the Indiana State Fairgrounds, where he railed against "Lyin' Ted" Cruz and his likely Democratic opponent, "Crooked" Hillary Clinton. He also made a point of expressing his support for the state's governor and even hinted that he had come to Indianapolis just for his meeting with Pence.

"You know I wasn't supposed to be here today," said Trump. "I'm supposed to be here in two weeks. You know that, but I had to come early," he added. "By the way, I have to tell you, you have a governor, Governor Pence is really fighting hard for you." He might have planned to say more, but a protester interrupted his monologue. "Get him out," Trump said, pointing at a man wearing a Trump mask. "Get him out, that's all right."

As Ted Cruz campaigned in Indiana, he understood he was the only one who stood between Trump and the Republican nomination. Governor John Kasich of Ohio was on the ballot, but he had no realistic chance to win. The key for Cruz could be a strong endorsement from Pence, which might shore up the conservative Christian vote. Trump was going for blue-collar workers by visiting industrial plants like a Carrier air-conditioning factory, where he promised to save jobs slated to be moved to a lower-cost facility in Mexico. (State aid facilitated by Pence would delay the move but not save the jobs.)

Pence finally made his move on April 29, a few days before the balloting. Then, rather than appearing with the Texas senator so Cruz could get photos with him, Pence booked an on-air visit with radio host Greg Garrison, who had replaced him years earlier as Indiana's conservative radio voice. In his statement, Pence used the word *clear* twice, which signaled the truth of the matter, which was that his endorsement was hardly ringing.[3]

It's clear, this is a time for choosing. I have met with all three candidates . . . and I want to say clearly I like and respect all three of the Republican candidates in the field. I particularly want to commend Donald Trump, who I think has given voice to the frustration of millions of working Americans with the lack of progress in Washington, D.C.

And I'm also particularly grateful that Donald Trump has taken a strong stand for Hoosier jobs when we saw jobs in the Carrier Company abruptly announce leaving Indiana—and not for another state but for Mexico. I'm grateful for his voice in the national debate. Let me say, I've come to my decision on whom I'm supporting, and I'm not against anybody, but I will be voting for Ted Cruz in the upcoming Republican primary. I see Ted Cruz as a principled conservative who has dedicated his career to advocating the Reagan agenda.

Governor Pence, who understood that Cruz could only slow and not stop Donald Trump's march to the nomination, had served himself well by recognizing what Trump needed and delivering it. The milquetoast quality of his endorsement made it clear that his loyalists could support Trump without reservation, and many did. On Election Day, the New Yorker grabbed 53 percent of the vote, swamping Cruz's 38 points. Kasich dropped out, and Reince Priebus, chairman of the GOP, announced that Trump was the presumptive nominee. This statement freed every Republican and the party's donors to focus on supporting one man and opposing Clinton.

As Indiana's Republican primary voters clinched things for Trump, Chris Christie could take some of the credit for the Pence maneuver. Surely he thought that Trump appreciated what he had done, and as he continued to travel around the country on Trump's behalf, speculation raged over whether he might be the nominee for vice president. Approaching the end of his second term as governor, Christie's approval rating was below 30 percent, which meant he was doing far worse than Pence was doing in Indiana. But superficially, at least, he seemed to have more in common with Trump. Both were tough-talking, brash and egotistical. This made it hard for him to play a supporting role in Trump's campaign.

Indeed, Christie was so much like Trump that his presence on the GOP ticket would do little to reassure voters who were concerned about the New Yorker's style. To make things worse, Trump had taken to teasing Christie in public.

When Christie was with Trump in Youngstown and the candidate intended to mock Ohio's own governor, Kasich, Trump couldn't resist bullying Christie too. Like Kasich, Christie had spent weeks looking for votes in New Hampshire, with little success.

"Where's Chris? Is Chris around?" said Trump as a campaign rally crowd looked on. "Even more than Chris Christie, he was there [in New Hampshire]," Trump said of Kasich. "I hated to do that, but I had to make my point," he said to Christie.

Christie was forced to roll with the punches when he was teased, especially about his weight. His answer to insults was always to play along. He even joked with Jimmy Fallon on *The Tonight Show* about the proper method of eating M&Ms. It was harder for Christie when Trump was the one taking shots at him. After Trump agreed to help out with Christie's estimated $250,000 presidential campaign debt, Trump made fun of him for it. This was the campaigning style of an insult comic, and yet it worked for Trump. At an appearance on Christie's home turf— Lawrence Township, New Jersey—Trump said, "There's nothing like New Jersey. Wise guys, so many wise guys. If you can make it in New Jersey, you can do just about anything you want in life." He then pivoted to the subject of jobs and joked he would stop eating Oreo cookies because the manufacturer, Nabisco, had moved one of its plants to Mexico.

"I'm not eating Oreos anymore—neither is Chris!" said Trump, pointing to Christie, seated to his right. "You're not eating Oreos anymore. No more Oreos. For either of us, Chris. Don't feel bad, for either of us."

Playing along with the joke was a small price to pay for the prize Christie sought, so even as commentators and comedians pointed to the indignity of it all, Christie continued to serve as comic target at his rallies and met with skeptical Republicans to persuade them that Trump was worthy of their support. After one report had Trump ordering Christie to personally bring him fast food, reporters corralled the New Jersey governor at a campaign appearance. Trump had just lashed out at U.S. District

Court judge Gonzalo P. Curiel, who was hearing a lawsuit in California against Trump University for allegedly deceptive practices. Trump called Curiel "a hater of Donald Trump" and claimed that the judge was Mexican and was biased against him. In fact, the judge was born in Indiana.

Assigned to clean up after Trump, Christie said that he didn't "know the judge" or the particulars of the Trump University case (Trump eventually settled for a $25 million payout to deceived customers), but "Donald Trump is not a racist," Christie said. "So, you know, the allegations that he is are absolutely contrary to every experience I've had with him over the last fourteen years, and so we're going to end it there."

As the Republican National Convention approached, news reports circulated that Christie was in line for the job he was angling for with Trump: vice president. The choice would be a bit unconventional, as it violated the usual practice of a presidential candidate seeking to "balance" the top of the ticket. Later, members of Pence's staff claimed that Christie himself was the source of the rumors that he was being strongly considered. "He was the one doing all the leaking about the decision," one said. A Trump-Christie combination would put two people from the same region and with the same personal style together. It would also run contrary to Trump's preference, whenever he hired someone, for a person whose good looks reflected well on the boss. Trump considered job-seekers in the way a casting director regarded a group of actors auditioning for a role. He preferred people who looked the part.

Presidential candidates select their own running mates, and some use the process to test the feelings of party leaders as well as voters. (It can also be a way to identify members of a cabinet.) On July 9, a week before the convention would begin, Christie was asked to meet with A. B. Culvahouse Jr., an attorney who had helped John McCain review his choices for vice president in 2008. This was considered the final step before Trump would make his decision. The press also reported that former Speaker of the House Newt Gingrich, Lieutenant General Michael Flynn, and Mike Pence were under consideration. Christie enjoyed front-runner status, in part because he had a good rapport with Trump and in part because he had shown himself to be a loyal and effective campaigner.

Although Christie could bring skills and a comfort level to the Trump campaign, he had two problems. First, despite Trump's claims of financial independence, his campaign was looking for funding support. Neither Christie nor Flynn would be a conduit for campaign contributions. Gingrich had some fund-raising strength, but Pence, who had broad support from right-wing donors like Charles and David Koch, was just as likely to be able to tap the wallets of skeptical donors. The more nagging, immediate problem for Christie, and one he could not escape, was the question of how much influence Jared Kushner, Trump's son-in-law, would have in the final decision. As U.S. attorney in New Jersey in 2005, Christie successfully prosecuted Kushner's father, Charles, in a sordid case that included charges of illegal campaign contributions, tax evasion, and witness tampering. The witness tampering story was particularly ugly. Charles Kushner, thinking that his sister, Esther, and her husband were providing information against him to Christie, had set up the brother-in-law with a prostitute, filmed their sexual encounter, and sent the tape to his sister. Kushner was convicted and sentenced to two years in federal prison.

Christie's secret meeting with Culvahouse had taken three hours and involved questions about personal issues and details surrounding the infamous "Bridgegate" scandal. (The governor's closest aides had been charged with organizing a traffic jam during rush hour at the George Washington Bridge to retaliate against a New Jersey mayor who had not supported Christie's reelection.) He had not even confirmed meeting with Culvahouse, but in a Facebook posting, Gingrich did describe his experience in the same process. Gingrich reported being grilled by Culvahouse and three other lawyers. He said Culvahouse told him, "If you run for president, the American people vet you, the news media vets you. But if you're picked to be vice president, there is no—you're not in a primary, you're not out in the open. You're not being investigated by the reporters. And so it's a much more rigorous process, actually, to be vetted for vice president than there is to be vetted for president."[4]

As the interviews proceeded, Trump highlighted the drama over his selection as if it were an episode of his reality TV show *The Apprentice*, where a winner is selected after grueling competitions. The Trump campaign leaked the fact that the four final candidates included Christie, Gingrich, Pence, and Flynn. Flynn's star seemed to dim on July 10, when on ABC TV, he said that he supported abortion rights. No matter that Trump had been glossing over the fact that he had also once supported abortion rights. Flynn then appeared on the Fox News network, saying that he was actually against abortion rights; waffling on such an important issue would not sit well with the voters in the base Trump had assembled. Trump immediately signaled the problem: "I do like the military, but I do very much like the political," Trump told *The Washington Post.* "I will make my mind up over the next three to four days. In my mind, I have someone that would be really good."[5]

On Monday morning, July 11, Christie went to a rally in Virginia Beach, Virginia, to introduce Trump as he had many times since he'd quit the presidential race himself. Trump said he had "always demanded the best from everyone who has worked for him and with him," Christie said. "He is someone who will give you confidence every night when you put your head on the pillow that his number-one priority will be the safety and security of your family."[6]

This time, however, Christie was not invited to stay on the platform when Trump spoke. It was a subtle but obvious sign, and Christie had reason to be worried. In the meantime, Pence backers fretted too. They claimed that the New Jersey governor was issuing leaks to the news media about the vice presidential contest in order to boost his own position. In fact, the momentum had shifted in Pence's direction. On Tuesday, July 12, Trump flew to Indianapolis for a campaign appearance with Pence. He was accompanied by Ivanka Trump, his daughter, and her husband, Kushner. Christie did not make the trip.

"I often joke, you'll be calling up Mike Pence," Trump said at the rally. "I don't know if he's going to be your governor or your vice president. Who the hell knows?"[7]

Rather than leave Indianapolis that night, Trump stayed in town. His aides said the cause was a flat tire on his airplane but mechanics can change a tire on a jetliner in about forty-five minutes. If Trump wanted to leave he could have, which meant he had a purpose in staying. This story would become a key element in the intrigue around the selection of Trump's running mate. It would later emerge that Trump's campaign manager, Paul Manafort, who thought Pence would bring doubters to

Trump's side, might have concocted the flat tire tale in order to keep the candidate in Indiana. As CBS News and others would report, Trump had offered the job to Christie, but Manafort and Pence's family hoped to change the candidate's mind.

The layover gave Pence, the governor with an uncertain future, more time with Trump at dinner, where he was able to make a hard sales pitch for himself. On the following morning, Trump, Ivanka, Kushner, and the candidate's son Donald Jr. were guests at the governor's mansion for a ninety-minute breakfast meeting. To all appearances, the family was passing judgment on the man who secretly had become front-runner as the vice presidential candidate.[8]

Whether it was the family or Manafort or someone else who had propelled Pence to the front of the line, the Indiana governor had his own decision to make. "He was going into this with his eyes open," said one source who was in close contact with Pence those days. "He knew exactly who Trump was and what he faced." Pence and Karen pulled aside to pray for clarity, this source said. Pence believed that his political life had been guided by miracles, and had previously prayed for a clear sense of God's purpose for him. Based on this perspective, the airplane's flat tire could be seen as a sign from heaven. Now his prayers gave him the guidance he sought. He would accept. "Once he got to that point, he never looked back."

After breakfast, Pence, wearing an open shirt, accompanied Trump to the candidate's SUV. Neither man said a word to reporters, who were kept at a distance. As cameras recorded the departure, they shook hands vigorously. Trump patted the governor on the shoulder and pointed at Pence as he told him something. Pence appeared to agree in single syllables to what Trump had said. The men then turned to photographers, and Trump flashed a smile. Then he was on his way.

Before they left Indianapolis, Trump and his family met with Newt Gingrich, who seemed to be making a last-ditch effort for his own candidacy. In the meantime, aides to Pence told reporters that meetings with Trump had gone very well.

After Trump left the capital, Pence put on one of the governor's signature polo shirts he had ordered for himself (it was emblazoned with his name) and went to the Indiana State Fair. His body language and words revealed little as he shook his head and shrugged at questions. Pence's replies combined his typical, very un-Trumpian aw-shucks humility and statements that showed how he might help the man at the top of the ticket win over skeptical Christian conservatives.

"I'm thinking he's giving it very careful consideration," said Pence, "and we're humbled to be a part of that. We were really honored to have not only Mr. Trump but a number of his children and son-in-law join us at the governor's residence. It's great to have them in Indiana and great to have a chance to break bread. Nothing was offered; nothing was accepted. . . . These are good people; this is a good family. He's a dedicated family man, a great dad. He's a builder, he's a fighter, and he's a patriot." Pence was already campaigning to normalize the man he sought to serve; and Pence knew that what he had said about Trump that day was not "clear" at all—or true.[9]

Later, Pence would say that Trump called him one evening soon after the family visit and made the formal offer. "It was eleven o'clock at night," Pence recalled, speaking to a gathering of Christian religious leaders. "We heard the call might be coming. We prayed all the way through it as a family, we talked it over with our kids, and we knew that we would answer the call if it came. I picked up the phone at eleven o'clock with Karen at my side in the governor's residence, and I heard that familiar voice, and he said, 'Mike, it's going to be great.'"[10]

Trump delayed announcing his choice when a terrorist driving a truck in Nice, France, on July 14, killed 86 people and injured 458. Pence and his team, however, circulated word that he was the choice. Among themselves, aides and friends debated whether Pence should accept. Two of Pence's closest political friends, Ryan Streeter and Al Hubbard, decried Trump's lack of principles and mean-spirited style and advised against joining the ticket. Pence, sensing his big chance was at hand, rejected their counsel. Finally, on Saturday, July 16, Trump made the announcement during an event at the New York Hilton Hotel. "I found the leader who will help deliver a safe society and a prosperous, really prosperous society for all Americans. Indiana governor Mike Pence was my first choice."[11]

That phrasing—*first choice*—must have especially galled Christie, who admitted to disappointment. "Of course," he told reporters a few days later at the Republican National Convention. "I don't get into anything that I don't want to win. So when you're not picked, of course it's disappointing. You know, I've been through this parade before, and I realize that it's like getting hit by lightning. . . . So it didn't happen, that's fine . . . you get disappointed, you take a deep breath and you get ready for tomorrow."[12]

For consolation, everyone figured—especially Christie—that if Trump won the election, Christie would be given an important post in the administration. The same was true for Michael Flynn, who vigorously supported Trump and would campaign for him throughout the summer and fall. Flynn became a highly controversial figure as he continued to make appearances on Trump's behalf, crossing a political divide usually respected by members of the military.

Flynn was an accomplished, veteran intelligence officer. He had served with distinction in Iraq and Afghanistan for a decade and had been appointed director of the Defense Intelligence Agency (DIA) in 2012. It was in this job where his chaotic, confrontational management style became a serious problem. In 2014, two years into his tenure at the DIA, President Obama considered complaints from the director of national intelligence, James Clapper, and other professionals and decided that Flynn had to go.

Untethered, Flynn began advocating his own solution to geopolitical problems. He paid special attention to Syria, where he wanted the United States and Russia to cooperate in fighting the Islamic State. His willingness to speak openly won invitations to appear on the Qatar-based Al Jazeera Network and on RT—Russia Today, a Russian government-owned, English-language television network. In these appearances, Flynn avoided criticizing President Obama directly, focusing instead on issuing warnings about "radical Islam." He came across as the kind of tough guy who appealed to Donald Trump. However, Flynn suffered from certain deficiencies as a public advocate. Steve Coll, Pulitzer Prize–winning author and chronicler of U.S. troubles in Afghanistan, said Flynn's skills on the battlefield did not translate well into politics. "He was promoted above the level he was suited for when he was promoted to head the Defense Intelligence Agency, which is a big bureaucracy and really a Washington insider's job. He had spent years on the battlefield; he was trained as a tactical intelligence leader, a door-kicker," said Coll. "When he got fired at DIA during the Obama administration, I think it really infuriated him, and it set him off on a course which I can't explain entirely, which is very different from who he was in the military."[13]

Flynn's overarching concern was the growth of ISIS, which he was ready to fight with methods others rejected, including torture and the killing of terrorists' families. At the same time, Flynn criticized the Bush and Obama administrations for weakness in dealing with terrorism: "I think the narrative was that al Qaeda was on the run, and [Osama] bin Laden was dead. . . . They're dead and these guys are, we've beaten them," Flynn said—but the problem was that no matter how many terrorist leaders they killed, they "continue to just multiply."[14]

When it came to domestic affairs, the newly minted angry private citizen Michael Flynn frequently criticized Hillary Clinton for the use of a private email server and said she should quit the presidential race. "If it were me," said Flynn on CNN, "I would have been out the door and probably in jail." He also criticized President Obama and his administration for not recognizing the danger represented by ISIS.

By mid-2016, Flynn had perfected his positions and his speaking style, and appeared regularly on television. At the GOP national convention in Cleveland, where he acted as a surrogate for Donald Trump, Flynn agreed to a live video interview with Michael Isikoff, the chief investigative correspondent for Yahoo News. Isikoff focused less on Trump than on the general's life as a private citizen and asked him about his travel to Moscow in 2015 to deliver a speech about U.S.-Russian relations. During the visit, Flynn sat next to Russian president Vladimir Putin at a dinner celebrating the creation of RT.

With the convention floor in the background, Isikoff asked why Flynn had agreed to sit with Putin at an event honoring a propaganda arm of the Russian government. Flynn had been caught off guard, and his angry response was unconvincing.

"Because I wanted to tell Russia to get Iran the hell out of the four proxy wars they're involved in in the Middle East in order for us to settle the situation down," he said, rambling on about a situation with which he had no official status—more than a year after he had left the Defense Intelligence Agency.

"Were you paid for that event?" Isikoff asked.

Flynn's eyes drifted for an instant before he tried to answer.

"I . . . You'd have to my, uh . . . the folks I went over there to, to . . ." Flynn said, waving his hand in Isikoff's direction.

"I'm asking you, you'd know if you were paid."

"Yeah, I went over there. It was a speaking event, it was a speaking event."

"And . . ."

"What difference does that make?"

"Well . . ."

"Is somebody gonna go, 'Ooh, he's paid by the Russians . . .'"

"Well, Donald Trump has made a lot of the fact that Hillary Clinton has taken a lot of money from Wall Street, Goldman Sachs—"

Flynn interrupted Isikoff, shaking his head, leaning back in his chair overlooking the convention floor.

"I didn't take any money from Russia, if that's what you're asking me."

"Then who paid you?"

"My . . . my speakers' bureau. Ask them."

"OK."

"So I was given a great opportunity and I took it."[15]

Eventually, it was disclosed that Flynn received $45,000 for the Russia trip and did not declare the funds on his government financial disclosure form. Flynn could only hope that the interview, which was conducted for the Yahoo website, would not be widely circulated.

When Flynn finally addressed the convention delegates, he assailed President Obama. "We are tired of Obama's empty speeches and his misguided rhetoric," he said. "This, this has caused the world to have no respect for America's word, nor does it fear our might." He then launched into a familiar attack on Hillary Clinton as all things evil in the world. At the mention of her name, Flynn joined in with the chants of the ardent convention-goers.

"Lock her up. Lock her up," chanted the crowd.

"Damn right," said Flynn. "Exactly right. There's nothing wrong with that."

Flynn continued, adding, "You know why we're saying that? We're saying that because if I, a guy who knows this business, if I did a tenth, a tenth of what she did, I would be in jail today."

A week after the convention, Flynn blamed Clinton's campaign and Democrats in general for charges that Russians were hacking U.S. political sites. On the social media platform Twitter, he wrote, "The corrupt Democratic machine will do and say anything to get #NeverHillary into power. This is a new low." He appended an anti-Semitic comment from a user named Sait Bibiana (@30PiecesofAG_): "Cnn implicated. 'The USSR is to blame!' . . . Not anymore, Jews. Not anymore."

After his tweet, Flynn quickly apologized and said his message was a mistake. Nevertheless, the incident supported the notion floated by Flynn's critics that he was an impulsive figure. In August, he would show this trait again when he visited a synagogue in Massachusetts and said Islam "is a vicious cancer inside the body of 1.7 billion people on this planet and it has to be excised." Flynn's words signaled to extremist white supremacists known online as the "alt-right" that he was with them. It was also perfect material for radical Muslim propagandists who sought to recruit support and even would-be terrorists by claiming the United States was hostile to Islam and committed to a modern version of the Crusades.[16]

Compared with the fire-breathing Flynn, whom GOP stalwart and retired general Colin Powell called "right-wing nutty," Mike Pence was the campaign's voice of tempered reason. When he spoke at the convention, he fell into the role he had been assigned, praising the presidential candidate while reassuring conservative Christians that it was all right for them to put a foulmouthed, twice-divorced, political bomb-thrower into the Oval Office. After beginning with the trusty refrain that "I'm a Christian, a conservative, and a Republican, in that order," Pence reminded people of his long (and only) marriage to his wife, Karen, and described his children, Charlotte, Audrey, and Michael J. Pence, as "the three greatest kids in the world." The state of Indiana and its Hoosiers came in for eight mentions, and he made the expected attacks on the opposition. But Pence's main duty was to vouch for Trump, and he did, saying, "I've seen this good man up close, his utter lack of pretense, his respect for the people who work for him, and his devotion to his family."

The GOP campaign would combine attacks on Hillary Clinton and her running mate, Virginia senator Tim Kaine, with declarations of support for various constituencies assumed to have suffered in recent years. Coal miners, factory workers, and others in the white working class were symbolic representatives of the Trump-Pence target voter, and they would be regarded as forgotten victims of Washington policies. "We have but one choice, and that man is ready," said Pence. "This team is ready, our party is ready. And when we elect Donald Trump the forty-fifth president of the United States, together we will make America great again!"

Pence's speech got rave reviews from the conservative press, and when the convention ended, he embarked on a fast-paced tour of the states where conservative Christians were key to the election. In the entire month of August, he visited only one Northeastern city, Manchester, New Hampshire, and never touched down on the West Coast. Instead, his itinerary took him to Iowa (five stops), Pennsylvania (five), and Ohio (four). Most of his events were in small- to medium-size cities. Compared with Trump's raucous, stream-of-consciousness appearances where he lurched from the ridiculous to the profane but riveted both voters and the press, Pence was a conventional campaigner. He was so bland that when he appeared outside Toledo, Ohio, the local paper's headline read, VP CANDIDATE PENCE GIVES CAMPAIGN SPEECH.[17]

Dutiful and patient, Pence offered nothing but support for Trump even when he suggested a President Hillary Clinton might be shot if she limited gun rights and encouraged Russian operatives to hack into his opponents' computers. Pence held firm even when a videotape emerged with Donald Trump telling the host of a TV show called *Access Hollywood* that as a celebrity, he, Trump, could sexually harass and even grope women. "Grab 'em by the pussy," he said. "You can do anything."

The tape, which the Trump campaign initially dismissed as "locker room talk," disgusted many Americans, including, according to *Newsweek*, Karen Pence. Quoting an unnamed former Pence aide, the magazine said Karen Pence considered Trump "reprehensible—just totally vile," but a

Pence spokeswoman denied that she had ever said such a thing.[18] *The New Yorker* reported that the Pences refused to take Trump's telephone calls and told him they needed to assess whether Mike would remain on the ticket. Pence issued a statement saying he was "offended" by what he heard on the tape. "I do not condone his remarks," he said, "and cannot defend them."

In private, Pence and GOP chairman Reince Priebus were said to have considered ways to force Trump to resign as the presidential candidate, leaving Pence to take his place. Such a move would have pleased those Republicans who identified themselves as "Never Trumpers," but no workable mechanism existed to accomplish such a coup. People close to Pence denied that he ever had it in mind. "Once he signed on to the ticket with Trump, Mike knew what he was getting into," one insider said. "He knew and he had to accept the way it was. Above all, he was loyal, and the talk of a deal with Reince was not true."

Trump's response to the revelation suggested that the reaction, whether it came from Pence or others, got to him. In a video message to the country, he said, "I've never said I'm a perfect person, nor pretended to be someone that I'm not. I've said and done things I regret, and the words released today on this more-than-a-decade-old video are one of them. Anyone who knows me knows these words don't reflect who I am. I said it, I was wrong, and I apologize." Trump ended this uncharacteristic statement—he almost never apologized—with a promise. "I pledge to be a better man tomorrow and will never, ever let you down."

In the conservative Christian culture that Mike Pence knew, second chances were always available to repentant sinners, especially if they support the values and policies prized by members of the community. Pence had already anointed Trump in the eyes of this segment of the electorate, which meant there was almost nothing he couldn't get away with just as long as he said he was sorry. Just to make sure, Pence went on television to vouch for him, telling CBS News, "What he's made clear is that was talk, regrettable talk on his part, but that there were no actions, and he's categorically denied these latest unsubstantiated allegations. The Donald Trump that I've come to know, that my family has come to know and spent a considerable amount of time with, is someone who has a long record of not only loving his family, lifting his family up, but employing and promoting women in positions of authority in his company," he said.[19]

Whatever they themselves thought, Pence's statement tied his wife and children to Trump. As the husband and father in a conservative Christian family, he was privileged to make such a choice and could expect that he would not be challenged once he did. In the meantime, a huge controversy erupted over the FBI's revelation that emails mentioning Hillary Clinton were discovered on a computer belonging to disgraced former congressman Anthony Weiner, who was being investigated for sending lewd images to a minor. Weiner's wife, Huma Abedin, was a top Clinton aide.

Ultimately, Pence's vice presidential campaign would be recalled for his deft ability to stand with and for a presidential candidate whose life amounted to one long repudiation of the morals Pence promoted. The high point was the one debate he had with the Democratic Party's candidate for vice president, Tim Kaine. Wisconsin Republican governor Scott Walker helped Pence prepare for the debate by playing Kaine in rehearsals and Pence mastered the ability to deflect even the most difficult questions. For example, when asked in the debate why Trump had reneged on a promise to release his tax returns, Pence said, "He hasn't broken his promise . . . Look, Donald Trump has filed *over one hundred pages of financial disclosure*, which is what the law requires. The American people can review that. And he's going—Senator, he's going to release his tax returns when the audit is over." (Even two years later, Trump still had not released his tax returns.) Pence glossed over one of Trump's most outrageous claims—that Mexico was sending drug dealers and rapists across the border—to justify building a wall along the boundary. Other debate distortions offered by Pence included his denial that Trump had called for the expansion of nuclear weapons to Saudi Arabia and Japan (he had) and the false claim that "less than ten cents on the dollar in the Clinton Foundation" went to charity (eighty-seven cents did); Pence also denied that Trump had praised Russia's Vladimir Putin as a great leader. (Trump had said Putin was "a leader far more than our president [Obama] has been.")

From a fact-checker's perspective, Pence's performance was spotty at best, but people watching the debate were not equipped to test everything he said, and his calm demeanor reassured viewers that he might be a steady-ing influence on Trump. Watching at his home in Washington, Phil Sharp, the long-retired congressman who had soundly defeated Pence in Indiana, concluded that Kaine had lost within the first thirty minutes. "Pence had come a long way," explained Sharp after the debate. "He wasn't being truthful, but he looked and sounded calm and trustworthy. Kaine was too eager, too aggressive, and too wonky to connect with voters."[20]

Late in the campaign, on October 24, Pence appeared before a group of right-wing Christian organizations called the Faith and Freedom Co-alition, founded by Ralph Reed. After excoriating Hillary Clinton, Barack Obama, and liberalism in general, Pence turned to the justification for voting for Trump. "I've got to tell you," he said, shaking his head. "This man, he's a good father. He loves his family. And he loves this country. And he has a boundless faith in the American people, and I know he'll be a great president of the United States of America. I've seen it up close. I've seen it up close."

There was more: Pence had an intimate anecdote to share with the audience, as if he were standing at a backyard fence, chatting with decent folks who shared the same traditional values that those "others"—the Democrats—did not share. The time was the night after the Republican National Convention, said Pence. He then turned to his right in a bit of theater and gestured to Karen so that she could nod and acknowledge and recall the moment.

"Donald and I talked about the importance of prayer in our family life," Pence began. "We talked with them warmly and personally about that. And that night, he just happened to say to me as he walked by, he said, 'Before we break up tomorrow, could we have a little time for prayer?' And I said, 'Sure.' And the next morning, we were on the plane. And we did one stop and we were getting ready to go, and sure enough, he came out from the back of the plane where he'd gone to freshen up and he said, 'Can we pray?' And we grabbed hands and bowed heads, and I asked Karen to pray on our departure as we both begin to go and make our way on this cause to the American people—it was a precious moment, but a tender moment."

Notorious for his sins of the flesh, Trump the politician had tried to demonstrate some Christian bona fides before. Early in the campaign, when asked if he sought God's forgiveness, he had clumsily referenced Communion, saying, "When I drink my little wine—which is about the only wine I drink—and have my little cracker, I guess that is a form of asking for forgiveness, and I do that as often as possible because I feel cleansed." With Pence at his side, Trump could leap to the head of the Sunday school class.

After the audience applauded, Pence said he was certain of victory. "I truly do believe that at particular moments in the life of this nation, the American people have risen up to demand government as good as our people, and this is such a time. The American people are rising up, and they will elect this good man, and we will make America great again together."

On Election Day, November 8, 2016, Mike Pence awoke in Indianapolis at the governor's mansion and went for a bike ride with Karen. They wore gym clothes and helmets. After the ride, they spent time in the mansion, emerging just before noon to cross the street to vote at St. Thomas Aquinas Church, where Karen joked, "You got my vote." Mike said he felt "humbled" by the experience of voting. Later in the day, he, Karen, and some family members flew to New York to await the election returns at the Hilton Midtown Hotel. The tide turned in favor of the Republicans early in the evening, but Trump waited to speak until Hillary Clinton's concession and phone call well after midnight. He stood before supporters at around 3:00 A.M. and delivered a speech designed to sound duly presidential. "Now it's time to bind the wounds of division," Trump read. "To all Republicans and Democrats and independents across this nation, I say it is time for us to come together as one united people."

Pence and his family entourage cheered, and Mike went around to embrace each of them. Pence and family left the celebration before dawn on November 9. In the hours to come, he would appear to be much calmer and more confident than the president-elect. Chris Christie, previously named chairman of the transition, had been gathering names and résumés for several months. Now that the dream was a reality, Trump would have to work quickly to assemble a government, but neither he nor Christie seemed ready to make many decisions.

10

RUSSIANS, WHAT RUSSIANS?

The Lord detests lying lips, but he delights in people who are
trustworthy.

—*Proverbs 12:22*

Two days after the election, two elected officials of special note sepa-
rately warned President-elect Donald J. Trump against bringing Lieutenant General Michael Flynn into the new administration. The lesser of
them was New Jersey governor Chris Christie, the head of Trump's transition team, who assumed he was in line for a plum position. Christie had
been suspicious of Flynn's emotionally charged behavior during the campaign. When he met with Trump for ninety minutes on November 10 at
Trump Tower, he had committed the cardinal sin of telling Trump what
Trump didn't want to hear. "If I were president-elect of the United States,
I wouldn't let General Flynn into the White House, let alone give him a
job," Christie said.[1]

Flynn and Christie had a history of conflict. In August, both men
had attended one of the first intelligence briefings held for Trump after
he was nominated as the Republican presidential candidate. NBC News
reported, citing six sources, that after Flynn repeatedly interrupted the
intelligence briefers, Christie told him to shut up and "calm down." Pub-

licly, Christie and Flynn denied that had ever happened, but Christie said
he made it clear that "General Flynn and I didn't see eye to eye. I didn't
think that he was someone who would bring benefit to the president or to
the administration."[2]

The other government official who warned the president-elect about
Flynn was President Barack Obama, who had been shocked by Trump's
victory but who sought, in his last weeks in office, to respond to foreign
intervention in the election. On November 10, Obama warned President-
elect Trump against bringing Flynn into the administration, citing,
among other things, his divisive performance as director of the Defense
Intelligence Agency.

Unlike Trump, Obama actually read his daily intelligence briefs and
would have had additional information about Flynn, his work on behalf
of the Turkish government, and his contact with Russia. Mike Pence also
should have seen intelligence reports about Flynn's activities. There is no
record, however, that he expressed any concern about Flynn to Trump or
anyone else.

Pence's attitude had been consistent from the moment Trump had
chosen him as his running mate. "He was all in." This attitude shone
during the transition and in the early days of the Trump administration
as Trump veered from lie to lie and crisis to crisis and Pence remained
loyal. Pence seemed willing to do anything to maintain his position and
stay in the good graces of this new president, Donald J. Trump. But he
also maneuvered himself out of the line of fire at key moments. Was it
good fortune that he happened to be in Indiana or traveling abroad when
controversy arose? Or was he trying to avoid getting dirtied by Trump so
he could assume the role of president if necessary? Was this God's plan?
Had he been chosen to serve as president-in-waiting?

In the matter of Michael Flynn, Trump heard both Obama and
Christie and disregarded their advice. Trump loved having top military
men around him and had admired Flynn ever since they met in 2015. Flynn
had been advising several other Republican candidates during the primary
season but settled happily with Trump. "I think his view of the world and
his view of where America was and where it needed to be," Flynn said in
recalling his first meeting with Trump. "I got the impression this was not

a guy who was worried about Donald Trump but a guy worried about the country. I don't think people can BS me that easily, and I was sort of looking for that. I found him to be in line with what I believed."[3]

Within a day of the warnings, on Armistice Day, Christie was fired from the transition team. With no prospects for the future, all that was left was to return to New Jersey for the last few weeks of his term as governor. Most galling of all for Christie, who had such high hopes for himself after the election, was that he was replaced by Mike Pence. Trump announced Pence was taking over the role of transition chairman with Flynn remaining as one of the transition deputies. Trump's choice was an early sign of Pence's future status in the administration. He was now tasked with putting together a cabinet and recommending other top officials in the new government.

In Washington, as well as New Jersey, Christie's departure was blamed, in part, on his other mighty antagonist in the incoming administration: Jared Kushner. Neither Christie nor Pence ever talked about how the transfer of responsibilities was handled. However, reporters would learn that the new transition team erased almost everything Christie had done. They disposed of his files on potential job candidates and, in a foreshadowing of White House chaos to come, summarily fired Christie's top transition aides. Their departure meant that no one could pass along certain concerns about Flynn. If Christie had warned Pence about Flynn during the campaign or on his way out the door at the transition office, Pence gave no sign that he was concerned. At this stage in their relationship, he was not going to challenge Trump.

On November 17, one week after he heard Obama's warning about Flynn, Trump appointed him national security advisor. Flynn, said Trump, "is one of the country's foremost experts on military and intelligence matters." With Flynn "by my side," Trump pledged they would "work to defeat radical Islamic terrorism, navigate geopolitical challenges, and keep Americans safe at home and abroad."

Despite Trump's praise of Flynn, the general's record during the campaign had been mixed at best. Flynn had been charged with anti-Semitism, criticized as an Islamophobe, outed as having hidden ties to Russia and Turkey, to name a few, and he had a penchant for espousing

and retweeting wing-nut conspiracy theories. Unless he had been seques-
tered by his staff throughout the campaign and transition, Pence must
have noticed the controversies. However he did not appear to care much
about the danger Flynn posed to the new administration. This attitude
aligned with Pence's behavior throughout the campaign, when he serenely
looked past one controversy after another. If Trump issued an offensive
tweet or off-the-cuff slur, Pence responded with a shrug, said his boss was
joking, or insisted that Trump had not made the statement in the first
place. For example, he flatly denied that Trump had called for shutting
down the North Atlantic Treaty Organization (he had) and argued that
Trump had not said more nations should obtain nuclear weapons (he did).
Pence was either playing to an audience of one (Trump himself) or had
drunk the same Kool-Aid that gave him the temerity to deny the very
Trump statements that had been broadcast around the world and were easily available on the internet. Both declarations had shocked many Republicans, let alone Democrats and foreign allies, who were not yet accustomed
to Trump's unhinged tweet storms.[4]

A day after Flynn's designation as national security advisor, Congressman
Elijah Cummings, the ranking member of the House Committee on
Oversight and Government Reform, wrote to Pence as head of the Trump
transition about an obvious conflict of interest for Flynn, whose attorney
had acknowledged by now that Flynn was a paid lobbyist for the Turkish
government. Cummings wrote:

> Recent reports have revealed that Lt. Gen. Flynn was receiving
> classified briefings during the presidential campaign while his
> consulting firm, Flynn Intel Group, Inc. was being paid to lobby the
> U.S. Government on behalf of a foreign government's interests.

Flynn had not registered as a foreign agent as required under the Foreign Agents Registration Act and could be subject to criminal charges.
Responding to the reported breach, Flynn's attorney, Robert Kelley, had
a concise answer when asked whether Flynn's work for Turkey was based
on his close connection to Trump. "I hope so."

In his letter, Cummings cited information related to Michael Isikoff's interview with Flynn at the Republican National Convention about his 2015 speech in Moscow and Flynn's attendance at the celebratory dinner seated next to Vladimir Putin. During the visit, Cummings wrote to Pence, "Lt. Gen. Flynn gave a speech that was highly critical of the United States." Pence would say later that he didn't remember the letter from Cummings and maintained he had no knowledge of Flynn's connections to Russia or Turkey. Yet the warning had been received at his office. Cummings made public a reply from the transition office that said, "We will review your letter carefully."

Days later, Pence could not avoid dealing with another Flynn-related problem. The controversy began when Michael G. Flynn, Flynn's son, reiterated his interest in a conspiracy theory that apparently originated within a white supremacy organization. The conspiracy nuts believed that Hillary Clinton, her campaign manager, John Podesta, and other Democrats were running a Satanic child abduction, pedophilia, and sex ring, based on the nonexistent basement of the Comet Ping Pong pizza restaurant in northwest Washington. Although fringe media figures like Alex Jones of InfoWars spread the conspiracy theory around the world, reporters at *The New York Times* and other media outlets debunked the story as a baseless hoax. The debunking did not stop Flynn Jr. when working with his father on the Trump transition effort from promoting the fakery, which was now dubbed "Pizzagate." Remarkably, the senior Flynn helped spread the bizarre conspiracy theory by tweeting inferences about Hillary Clinton and the other unfounded claims linking her to the sexual abuse of children. Flynn wrote:

> *U decide – NYPD Blows Whistle on New Hillary Emails: Money Laundering, Sex Crimes w Children, etc . . . MUST READ!*

The Flynns' actions came as sober men and women of all political stripes were calling for restraint when it came to online commentary and inflammatory rhetoric. But here were key members of the Trump team—

the future national security advisor and his son—transmitting unhinged, divisive, and libelous stories. Viewed by some as merely provocative speech, this rumormongering led to threats against the pizza restaurant and its owner, James Alefantis, who had been besieged by threatening messages and web postings. Finally, on December 4, Edgar Maddison Welch, a deluded twenty-eight-year-old man from North Carolina, drove to the Comet Ping Pong restaurant on what he considered a divine mission to "rescue" the reported sex slaves. He entered the restaurant and fired three shots with an automatic rifle. No one was injured; Welch surrendered to police and was arrested. Eventually, he pleaded guilty, apologized for being reckless—and gullible—and was sentenced to four years in prison. Alefantis was relieved that no one was hurt, but the nightmare was not over. "This guy's going to jail," he said, but "InfoWars [Alex Jones's online radio outlet] continues to push this conspiracy, as do many others."[5]

Two days after the shooting incident at Comet Ping Pong, the vice president elect appeared on the MSNBC television program *Morning Joe* and was questioned about the younger Flynn's relationship to the transition. All he would say was that the young man was no longer employed by the Trump transition team. "Well, General Flynn's son has no involvement in the transition whatsoever," he said. For emphasis, he repeated himself: "He has no involvement in the transition whatsoever."

Later in the day on CNN, Pence struggled to respond to new information about previous efforts to obtain a security clearance for the younger Flynn, which would have authorized his access to classified information. CNN's Jake Tapper asked whether Pence knew that the Trump team had sought the clearance. Pence did not answer directly and tried again to minimize the younger Flynn's role in the transition, saying he had only pitched in with some scheduling and administrative work for his father. Pence's exchange with Tapper was one more case of a Pence promise to be clear, followed by a fog of words.

> PENCE: Look, all—all of our families want to be helpful. And four weeks to the day from Election Day, there's been an awful lot of work to do. But—but—but Mike

Flynn Jr. is no longer associated with General Flynn's efforts or with the transition team.

TAPPER: You're downplaying his role, but you must be aware that the transition team put in for a security clearance. For Michael G. Flynn, the son . . .

PENCE: I think that's the appropriate decision for us to move forward, avoid any further distraction and I'm very confident as we continue to build this team . . .

Instead of rejecting the conspiracy-mongering of Flynn and his son, Pence brushed off the entire matter and took up the age-old practice of media-bashing. However, he made one telling admission. He said he worked "very closely" with General Flynn as one would have imagined, since they were directing the transition together. If this were true, however, why had Pence not condemned the conspiracy hoax or replied fully to the questions sent by Cummings on November 18 about Flynn's lobbying contract with Turkey and Russia contacts? Weeks later, once Flynn had been outed for further contacts with Russians, Pence changed his characterization of his relationship with Flynn. His staff said Flynn and Pence had only occasional contact during the campaign and transition and did not work closely.

The Comet Ping Pong story was only one of the controversies that contributed to the growing sense that social media and the internet had played an outsized role in the presidential campaign. By early December, it was clear that Russia had meddled in the election, though not yet clear how much and with whom. Michael McFaul, the U.S. ambassador to Moscow from 2012 to 2014, raised an early alarm. "Stories also have circulated about Russian and other foreign actors involved in the production of fake news, as well as collaboration between Russian (and other foreign) and American leaders and movements regarding common political agendas," he wrote. "What was the full scope of these activities? Did any of these actions influence the election outcome? I don't know, but we need to know."[6] News outlets reported, meanwhile, that RT had more viewers on YouTube than did CNN's YouTube channel. A *Washington Post* report, among others, reminded that Flynn was paid by Russia's RT network a year earlier and had compared the Russian government broadcaster to CNN.

Pence showed no concern or anxiety about such matters. As Christmas 2016 approached, he prepared for a two-week vacation back home in Indiana. From the outside, the break appeared to be ill-timed. By all accounts, the transition—which essentially started over after Christie left—was far behind schedule in naming the hundreds of men and women who would be needed to staff the top echelon of the incoming Trump administration. The inauguration was less than a month away. Concern about Russian interference was growing. Yet Mike Pence opted to leave town; he and Karen went home with their family to Indiana. Flynn, meanwhile, also left town for a Caribbean vacation.

Happy to be back, Pence returned to his duties as governor of Indiana. On December 21, he went to the Wheeler Mission Ministries, a shelter for the homeless in Indianapolis. With cameras recording the action, he donned an apron and a blue Wheeler baseball cap and stepped behind the steel table where workers filled trays with holiday foods. Pence put trays into the hands of the men and patted shoulders. When one addressed him as "Mr. Vice President," Pence replied, "It's Mike to you."

After the meal was served, Pence walked along on the periphery of the lunch tables as Secret Service agents, aides, and even a chef looked on. Pence shook hands and spoke with a few of the men who men stood up. He then approached the camera. "I thought it was important to continue the tradition I've had throughout my life of stopping by and giving encouragement to ministries like this," Pence said. "I know that Hoosiers in big cities and small towns are taking time to reach out this week to the less fortunate."

As for the larger task ahead of him, Pence said there was much work to do. "I'm very humbled by the opportunity we've been presented to serve our nation."

The Pences sent out a general Christmas message on social media that said he planned a "tender Indiana Christmas. We'll be with Karen's family on Christmas Eve; we'll be sitting around the Christmas tree at the governor's residence on Christmas Day; and then, the really special event is that our son, Michael, who is a second lieutenant in the Marine Corps will be getting married at the governor's residence . . . we'll have a small, little intimate ceremony just for immediate families. So it's going to be a very special time as it is for every Hoosier family."

As the Pences celebrated, the transition team in Washington labored to fill six hundred executive positions at the White House, about half of which needed Senate confirmation. That confirmation process could have begun anytime after the November 8 election, but the task of matching people to jobs was proceeding very slowly. As 2016 came to an end, the Partnership for Public Service, a nonpartisan Washington group, said that the incoming administration would be lucky to have a cabinet selected by the time Trump and Pence were sworn in. Prior administrations had averaged one hundred key jobs confirmed by the Senate on Inauguration Day.[7]

The difficulties Trump confronted staffing his administration were not evident in Pence's schedule. True to the laid-back style of his first days as governor, he took time to relax and hardly seemed focused on the job at hand. Then, in the last days of the year, events unfolding in Washington would draw him into a controversy that would plague the new administration every day for the foreseeable future.

On December 29, President Barack Obama issued an executive order from his Christmas retreat in Kailua, outside Honolulu, where he was spending his final vacation as president. It read:

> *Today, I have ordered a number of actions in response to the Russian government's aggressive harassment of U.S. officials and cyber operations aimed at the U.S. election. These actions follow repeated private and public warnings that we have issued to the Russian government, and are a necessary and appropriate response to efforts to harm U.S. interests in violation of established international norms of behavior.*
>
> *All Americans should be alarmed by Russia's actions. In October, my Administration publicized our assessment that Russia took actions*

*intended to interfere with the U.S. election process. These data theft
and disclosure activities could only have been directed by the highest
levels of the Russian government. Moreover, our diplomats have experienced an unacceptable level of harassment in Moscow by Russian
security services and police over the last year. Such activities have consequences. Today, I have ordered a number of actions in response.*[8]

Some of the actions Obama ordered were classified and, no doubt,
were taken in the murky realm of cyber defense. The visible actions included the expulsion of thirty-five Russian diplomats and the closure of
two Russian annexes in the United States. Obama said that other actions
would be taken, some of which could be clandestine. Both Democrats and
Republicans in Congress generally supported the sanctions, although, pre-
dictably, Speaker of the House Paul Ryan, among other Republicans, said
the measures were overdue and said Obama was showing weakness.

Trump, spending the holiday at his Mar-a-Lago resort in Florida,
had learned of Obama's impending action a day ahead of time. On that
day, Pence and his family had celebrated as planned the wedding of his
son, Michael, to Sarah Whiteside at the governor's mansion. The couple
had met while attending Purdue University. The bride was a mental health
coordinator with the Indiana State Division of Mental Health and Addiction and was said to be a former aide to the Indiana Democratic Party.

The next day, as Obama's actions were revealed, Trump practically
yawned in response. "I think we ought to get on with our lives," he said.
"I think that computers have complicated lives very greatly. The whole age
of computer has made it where nobody knows exactly what is going on.
We have speed, we have a lot of other things, but I'm not sure we have
the kind, the security we need." This passive and incomprehensible statement tracked with the larger point he had expressed many times before.
He doubted reports of Russian hacking, insisting despite ample evidence
to the contrary that he wasn't helped in the election by their interference.

Whether by design or good fortune, Mike Pence was out of view as
Trump offered his very unpresidential response to the sanctions. Mary
Matalin, a popular conservative pundit and former aide to former vice
president Dick Cheney, noted sarcastically that Pence always managed to

be away from Trump at moments when it was better to be at a remove. "He is always in the right place at the right time, discreet, dedicated, and freakishly absent from tumultuous events," she said.[9]

Members of the transition team, including people who should have been very close to Pence, reacted quickly to President Obama's announcement of Russian sanctions. Within hours, General Flynn's deputy, K. T. McFarland, wrote a series of emails that included warnings that Obama's actions could be a problem for relations between Trump and Russia, "which has just thrown the U.S.A. election to him." When it became known, McFarland would say that rather than indicating she knew such a thing had taken place, she was simply repeating the language used by Democrats. This may or may not have been true. What was incontestable, though, was the fact that rather than demonstrating concern about the sanctity of U.S. elections, the transition officials worried that a focus on Russian hacking would be a tool to delegitimize Trump's victory.[10]

The concern held by intelligence officials, however, went to the heart of American democracy. By now, wrote then FBI director James Comey, the FBI, CIA, National Security Agency, and Office of the Director of National Intelligence had reached a clear consensus:

> *Russian president Vladimir Putin ordered an extensive effort to influence the 2016 presidential election. That effort, which came through cyber activity, social media, and Russian state media, had a variety of goals: undermining public faith in the American democratic process, denigrating Hillary Clinton and harming her electability and potential presidency, and helping Donald Trump get elected.*[11]

In her emails, McFarland said that her boss, Flynn, was scheduled to speak with Sergey Kislyak, the Russian ambassador to the United States. Flynn already had a relationship with Kislyak, and, in fact, some transition aides had warned Flynn previously about such contacts because they were almost certain to be intercepted by U.S. intelligence. Pence did not publicly say whether he was in touch with Flynn or anyone else during the Christmas holiday, nor whether he was aware of McFarland's message or the subsequent chain of emails. However, they were so widely distributed that any claim that Pence was bypassed is hard to believe. He was the top transition official and the president's second. If incoming presidential advisors Reince Priebus, Stephen Bannon, and Sean Spicer were informed—and they were—then Pence almost surely received notice.

As the Trump team digested Obama's sanctions, Thomas P. Bossert, another transition official, distributed an email to top officials in the transition and said their task should be to "defend election legitimacy now." He sent copies of his message—and one from McFarland—to a host of top Trump players, including Steve Bannon, Reince Priebus, Sean Spicer, and Flynn. The only key transition player—other than Trump— not mentioned as a recipient was Mike Pence.

On December 30, McFarland spoke with Flynn, who was on vacation in the Dominican Republic. Soon afterward, Flynn phoned Kislyak. It was later reported that Flynn called the Russian ambassador on orders from a "very senior transition official."

Following the chain of command, Pence was Flynn's superior and in charge of the transition. If Pence had not issued the order to call Kislyak and that report is true, the chain of command would have extra links. Trump himself, of course, would be the ultimate "senior transition official." Others could have included Kushner or Bannon. Flynn eventually testified to the FBI that his chat with Kislyak was a social call. He said he wished Kislyak happy holidays and may have expressed condolences for the plane crash that killed the members of the Russian Army Choir en route to entertain troops in Syria.

One of the most confounding elements of Flynn's contacts with Kislyak was that, as an intelligence officer, he should have known that telephone communications with Russian officials in the United States would be monitored by security officials. It would be equally odd that these contacts on a matter so concerning to the president-elect would have been kept secret from Pence, who was both the incoming vice president and the head of the transition.

On the day Flynn and Kislyak spoke, December 30, Russian president Vladimir Putin offered a mild response to Obama's sanctions. "We regard the recent unfriendly steps taken by the outgoing U.S. administration as provocative and aimed at further weakening the Russia-U.S.

relationship. This runs contrary to the fundamental interests of both the Russian and American people," he said. "Although we have the right to retaliate, we will not resort to irresponsible 'kitchen' diplomacy but will plan our further steps to restore Russian-U.S. relations based on the policies of the Trump Administration."[12]

Delighted by Putin's reaction, Trump took to Twitter, which would become his main mode for communicating with the world: "Great move on delay (by V. Putin) - I always knew he was very smart!"

While Trump tweeted, Pence left Indianapolis to headline a $2,700-per-ticket Illinois fund-raiser at the venerable Chicago Club. With the help of a security cordon, he was able to bypass about 150 protesters who had gathered to draw attention to the Russia hacking controversy. No mention was made of the demonstration at the private event. Pence "was very upbeat," said Jim Dirken, Republican leader in the Illinois House. "We raised a lot of money for the Republican National Committee."

Pence returned to Washington after the new year, where he finally did react to the warning about Russian hacking by saying that, as always, he agreed with Trump. The president-elect had often responded to the issue by casting doubt on the American intelligence community, charging that President Bush had gone to war in Iraq on the basis of faulty intelligence. (In fact, U.S. intelligence got the facts right: Saddam Hussein was not building a bomb. But Bush acted on cooked-up raw intelligence with pressure from his vice president, Dick Cheney.)[13]

Although this claim was not the view shared by most Republicans, Trump's argument made for a nice sound bite. Pence echoed it, saying, "Given some of the intelligence failures of recent years, the President-elect made it clear to the American people that he's skeptical about conclusions from the bureaucracy," Pence said. "I think the American people hear him loud and clear."[14]

Perhaps Trump *had* been loud and clear, but Pence recently had heard evidence that the intelligence community had gathered on Russian influence in the election. The information had been provided by the directors of the top four U.S. intelligence agencies, including James Clapper, the director of national intelligence; Admiral Mike Rogers of the National Security Agency; John Brennan of the CIA; and James Comey, the FBI director. At a meeting that Pence attended at Trump Tower in New York, they presented classified and categorical evidence that Russia had hacked into the U.S. election and that Vladimir Putin was personally responsible for authorizing this activity.

In addition to Pence, the Trump briefing was attended by the president-elect, Michael Flynn, and K. T. McFarland, Flynn's designated deputy as the new national security advisor. Long after the meeting, Clapper made two observations about the ninety-minute Trump Tower meeting: "Pence very astutely prompted us to clarify points on several occasions; I was impressed by the way he actively consumed the intelligence we were providing." He said that Trump also asked questions, and when they were done, he went on to say, "I believe everyone in the room realized that the evidence—particularly from signals intelligence and cyber forensics—to attribute the influence operation to Vladimir Putin and the Russian government was overwhelming."[15]

Clapper told Trump and the others that the intelligence community "had neither the authority nor capabilities to assess what impact—if any—the Russian operation had" on the outcome of the election.[16] Despite Clapper's clear position, Trump would continue to call the Russian investigation a witch hunt, and Pence would claim falsely, despite Clapper's denial and analysis of Pence's astuteness, that the intelligence community *had* determined that the Russian activity did not affect the election outcome. Pence could have seen himself merely as supporting the president, not as evading the truth, which in fact he was doing. Clapper later concluded that Russian interference *did* affect the presidential election. He wrote in his 2018 memoir, *Facts and Fears: Hard Truths from a Life in Intelligence,* that "of course the Russian efforts affected the outcome. Surprising even themselves, they swung the election to a Trump win. To conclude otherwise stretches logic, common sense, and credulity to the breaking point." Whether or not Pence thought or understood this was true at any point, neither he nor Trump pushed for an investigation or promoted efforts to prevent the Russian government from continuing to interfere in future U.S. elections.

After a few days of meetings, Pence made one more trip to Indianapolis, on January 9, for the inauguration of his successor as governor.

Eric Holcomb had been a congressional and United States Senate staffer but had not held office until Pence picked him to replace the retiring lieutenant governor, Sue Ellspermann. Once in office, Holcomb would move quickly to reverse some of his predecessor's decisions and to take action where Pence had done nothing. Citing his belief that Keith Cooper had been wrongfully convicted, Holcomb would grant the pardon Cooper requested. The new governor visited East Chicago and declared the state of emergency that Pence had rejected. And he opened up the limited needle exchange program so that local officials across the state could fight the spread of HIV among intravenous drug users. In the same time period, the Republican-dominated legislature would overturn a series of vetoes Pence had issued in the final months of his governorship. The lawmakers didn't explain themselves, but Scott Pelath, the Democratic House minority leader, said, "The Mike Pence legacy came to a very quick end today, probably the shortest one in Indiana gubernatorial history."[17] Legislatively, Pence was disappeared by his own party.

In private, many Republicans said that Pence had been a middling governor who accomplished little. That would hardly matter to a man who had been lucky enough to be selected by Donald Trump, who then, in turn, was lucky enough to win the presidential election. However, in the moment, Indiana was in a swoon over its new favorite son, so there was nothing to be gained by criticizing him. Pence was, himself, so busy he would have been hard-pressed to focus on what folks in Indiana thought of him. By the time Pence returned to Washington once more, his close associate Michael Flynn had told Donald F. McGahn II, attorney for the transition organization (and eventually White House counsel), that he was being investigated by the FBI. (They were probing, at the very least, his lobbying on behalf of the Turkish government without properly notifying American authorities.)

On January 12, the truth of Flynn's contacts with Russian authorities emerged as David Ignatius of *The Washington Post* reported that Flynn had spoken to Russian Ambassador Sergey Kislyak several times on December 29, the day when he supposedly extended a single holiday greeting from the Dominican Republic. Noting the time line in connection to Obama's sanctions announcement, Ignatius, a veteran analyst on intelligence matters, had a basic question: "What did Flynn say, and did it undercut the U.S. sanctions?"

Ignatius noted that the Logan Act of 1799 bars U.S. citizens from correspondence intending to influence a foreign government about "disputes" with the United States. Though two people had been indicted under the act in the nineteenth century, no one had ever been prosecuted under its provisions. However, in this case, Ignatius raised the possibility that the spirit of the law had been violated. He had contacted the Trump transition team but had not received an answer to his request for comment.[18]

Future White House press secretary Sean Spicer, already serving as spokesman for Trump, confirmed that Kislyak and Flynn had spoken but said that it was an innocuous phone call. "They exchanged logistical information," Spicer said. "That was all." Abandoning the holiday greetings scenario, Spicer indicated that the chats might have centered on a proposed conversation between Trump and Putin. He did not indicate who had been his source for this notion or who else knew about the communications between Flynn and Kislyak.

Only after Spicer's declarations did Mike Pence emerge as the Trump team's pinch hitter. With this mission in mind, he agreed to appear on the January 15, 2017, edition of CBS's *Face the Nation* with John Dickerson. Pence marked the occasion by dressing in a white shirt, blue suit, and plain red tie. Not content to let the colors signal his patriotism, he fixed a little American flag pin, the ubiquitous accessory of politicians nationwide, to his lapel.

With his motorcade gliding toward the CBS News studio on M Street in northwest Washington, Pence could reflect on the fact that members of the incoming Trump administration—and almost certainly Trump himself—would be watching and evaluating his performance. *Face the Nation,* first aired in 1954, had helped to set the American political agenda ever since. It might have lost some of its power in an era when cable channels and the internet gave people hundreds if not thousands of news options. However, it was the kind of program Donald Trump had grown up watching, and as the most media-savvy presidential candidate in history, he surely cared about Pence's performance.

As Pence waited in a chair across the table from Dickerson, CBS aired a video of Trump talking about the Russia issue. On tape, Trump said, "I think it was disgraceful, disgraceful that the intelligence agencies allowed any information that turned out to be so false and fake out. I think it is a disgrace. And that is something that Nazi Germany would have done and did do."

Dickerson turned to Pence and welcomed him to the program. Pence flashed a smile. The crow's-feet that framed his eyes added extra twinkle to his face. The host then noted that the Republican senator who chaired the foreign relations committee was going to conduct an investigation of Russian interference in the 2016 election. Pence, as he had when he became governor, hailed the peaceful transition of power that was about to take place and then declared that authorities had discovered "no evidence of any impact on voting machines" from the Russian effort. Pence's comment was not particularly relevant; voting machines are decentralized, and hacking would be difficult to effect a difference in the outcome of the U.S. election. Pence knew, however, that the U.S. intelligence community had reported a week earlier that Russian intelligence did hack into state and local electoral systems and that "Putin and the Russian Government developed a clear preference for President-elect Trump."[19]

Dickerson then asked whether, given the Senate inquiry that had been announced by a member of the president's own party, Trump still considered the concern over the issue a "witch hunt." Here was Pence's chance to agree that a legitimate controversy existed. He looked down at the table in front of him and then offered, along with some sighs and shakes of his head, a condemnation of the president's favorite enemy, the news media.

"I think that"—sigh—"there frankly has just been an effort by many in the national media, present company excepted, since this election to essentially demean and question the legitimacy of this incoming administration. And talk of that—sources within the intelligence community have been attributed with sharing that information, public officials—I think has been a real disservice to our democracy." Pence went on to say that Trump, who fell 2.9 million votes short in the popular balloting and gained office through the quirks of the electoral college, had won the election by a "landslide."

It was, in its clumsy syntax as well as its argument, the kind of statement Trump would have made himself: Reporters and the intelligence officials who were warning of trouble were bad actors. They didn't respect the president-elect's sweeping victory. These were the people, and not the Russians, who bombarded the country with propaganda and constituted the real threat to democracy. For good measure, Pence even threw in a comment about how soon he and Trump would start to "make America great again": very soon.

Not satisfied, Dickerson asked, "Did any advisor or anyone in the Trump campaign have any contact with the Russians, who were trying to meddle in the election?"

"No, of course not, and I think to suggest that is to give credence to some of these bizarre rumors trafficked in a memo produced as opposition research." He was referring of course to files handed to U.S. intelligence officials by Christopher Steele, a former British MI6 officer who specialized in Russia and who had been commissioned first during the 2016 GOP presidential primaries by Paul Singer, a hedge fund billionaire and "Never Trump" Republican. Singer dropped the research effort after Trump won the Republican presidential nomination, and Steele then began to work on behalf of the Democrats. Steele's dossier, which included startling raw material indicating that Russians had information about Trump that could be used to blackmail him, had been leaked to the press. Steele was well known and respected by U.S. intelligence officials, and his reporting was a valuable addition to ongoing U.S. investigations of Russian attacks on the election campaign. President Obama had authorized briefing Trump about Steele's dossier.

Trump, who told lie after lie during the campaign, had refused to acknowledge charges of Russian meddling and denigrated the intelligence community for even raising such suspicions. Defending Trump before this national audience, Pence insisted that Trump's mere presence in the White House would improve America's standing in the world. The vice president elect glowed with admiration as he spoke about how happy he was "to literally be sitting side by side with him. He's done hundreds of interviews and attracted men and women of extraordinary caliber to this cabinet."

As for General Flynn and the Russian ambassador, Pence said, "What

I can confirm, having spoken to him about it, is that those conversations that happened to occur around the time that the United States took action to expel diplomats had nothing whatsoever to do with those sanctions."

"But that still leaves open the possibility that there might have been other conversations about the sanctions," said Dickinson.

"I don't believe there were more conversations," replied Pence.[20]

With his practiced calm demeanor and steady voice, Pence had followed Trump's lead and would keep going in this direction for more than a year. As far as the Trump team and Russia were concerned, there was nothing to worry about.

Pence repeated these claims later in the day in a Fox News interview, in which reporter Chris Wallace asked if anyone in the Trump campaign had been in contact with Russians. "Of course not," said Pence. "Why would there be any contacts between the campaign and Russia?"

"Did members of the Trump campaign meet with Russian officials?" asked Wallace.

"All the contacts by the Trump campaign and associates were with the American people," Pence said. "We were fully engaged with taking his message to 'Make America Great Again' all across the country."

A day before the inauguration, Pence called a news conference to praise and take credit for the transition process of the incoming Trump administration. "Seventy-one days ago, Donald Trump set an ambitious schedule prior to this inauguration, and he asked me to chair the transition effort," Pence said. And as usual, he added, "I was grateful and honored to be given the opportunity to do just that."

While he said that hundreds of "beachhead" officials would be "reporting for duty" the following day, the Trump administration—and the transition under Pence—was running far behind previous administrations in filling key posts. Pence's other main claim about the transition effort was false. He said that $1.2 million of $6 million allocated in the federal budget for the presidential transition would be returned to the U.S. Treasury. The General Services Administration told the nonpartisan Center for Public Integrity that in addition to the $6 million provided from tax-payer funds, the Trump transition raised private money as well. Any amount left over went to rental costs for the Trump transition offices, according to the GSA.[21]

Late on the morning of Friday, January 20, 2017, Mike Pence was sworn in as the forty-eighth vice president of the United States. The ceremony took place on the West Front of the Capitol, which was not his favorite side—he preferred the natural lighting cast on the East Front of the Capitol. But then again, were he to become president one day, he might have another shot, in which he could change the venue. At noon, Donald Trump took the oath of office, with now former president Obama, George W. Bush, Bill Clinton, and Jimmy Carter looking on. Trump's inaugural address included ominous notes about "American carnage," and a bleak assessment of recent history that provoked George W. Bush's purported reaction: "Weird shit." Trump would spend subsequent days arguing that the crowd in attendance was far bigger than the photographic evidence clearly showed.

Retired lieutenant general Michael Flynn was also on the inauguration stand and was seen sending text messages from his phone *during the ceremony*. A confidential source told House Intelligence investigators that one message went to a colleague, saying that Russia sanctions were about to be dropped, and a private business deal he was promoting on a Middle East nuclear power project was "good to go." Two days after the inauguration Flynn was sworn in as Trump's national security advisor. That same day, a news report said that U.S. intelligence had reported more substantial contact between Flynn and Kislyak than Mike Pence had claimed. Faced with questioning from reporters at his first regular White House news briefing two days after the inauguration, Sean Spicer repeated what Pence had said a week earlier: whatever Flynn and the Russian ambassador had discussed, they did not talk about the sanctions.

Officials in the Justice Department and at U.S. intelligence agencies heard the White House denial with considerable distress. They had been debating what they should tell Trump and officials of his incoming administration about intercepted communications between Flynn and Kislyak. These proved that Flynn was lying. FBI director James Comey had argued before the inauguration that the briefing could wait. Now that Trump was president, Comey relented, and a plan of action developed.

First, on Tuesday, January 24, FBI agents went to the White House to question Flynn, who repeated that he had not discussed the Obama sanctions with Kislyak. Flynn should have realized the Justice Department already had a recording, captured by surveillance technology, of their conversation.

The next day, January 25, the FBI agents reported their interview findings to Sally Yates, the deputy attorney general who was running the Justice Department following the departure of Attorney General Loretta Lynch.

On Thursday, January 26, 2017, Yates took a ride up Pennsylvania Avenue from the Department of Justice to the White House, where she provided White House counsel Donald McGahn with information about Flynn's FBI interview and the available facts from intelligence intercepts. Yates said that this was a matter of national security—Flynn could be blackmailed by the Russians because of the discrepancy between his answers to FBI queries and the actual content of his talks with Kislyak. McGahn immediately told Trump about the proof of Flynn's lies and of a specific warning from the highest law enforcement officer in the land that the United States was in danger of a security breach. Trump did nothing. Flynn remained at the job with full access to U.S. intelligence.

Although vice presidents routinely receive the highest-level briefings on security issues, no one in the White House—neither Trump aides nor people close to Pence—reported what Pence had or had not heard. Leaks were rampant and regular from the people closest to Trump, but Pence's staff prided itself on maintaining a unified front and avoiding leaks to the news media. Even this early in the administration, the argument was that Pence needed to be protected and isolated from information that could be damaging to the Trump presidency. Should Trump be impeached or resign, Pence would be well served by having the ability to plausibly deny knowledge of problems like Michael Flynn.

For his part, Flynn continued to deny that he ever had discussed sanctions with the Russian ambassador. Finally, on February 9, an official told reporters that Flynn was changing his story. Flynn, the spokesman said, "indicated that while he had no recollection of discussing sanctions, he couldn't be certain that the topic never came up."

On February 10, Pence and Flynn were seen chatting and shaking hands at the White House. Flynn was amiable and looking straight ahead; Pence was serious and looked away from Flynn, but there was no hint of acrimony. Later on the same day, Trump fielded questions during an Air Force One flight to Florida, where he would spend the weekend at Mar-a-Lago. *The New York Times* and *Washington Post* were reporting that Flynn had lied about his contacts with Kislyak.

"I don't know about that," Trump told reporters. "I haven't seen it. What report is that? I haven't seen that. I'll look into that."

After the weekend, Trump came back to Washington. On the night of February 12, Flynn resigned, which, in Washingtonspeak, meant he was fired. His letter of resignation revealed for the first time that the vice president had been involved in the whole Kislyak mess from the start. The letter read:

> *Unfortunately, because of the fast pace of events, I inadvertently briefed the vice president-elect and others with incomplete information regarding my phone calls with the Russian ambassador. I have sincerely apologized to the president and the vice president, and they have accepted my apology.*

For a general who had tried to build a ramrod reputation for toughness and competence, Flynn's resignation letter was notable for its excuses and shading. Deceptions were painted as "incomplete information," and the "fast pace of events" was blamed for Flynn's decision to pass off these deceptions as truth. He closed his letter in Trumpian fashion, praising himself. "I am tendering my resignation," he wrote, "honored to have served our nation and the American people in such a distinguished way." Trump let him get away with it all, saying that Flynn had to depart because news of his Kislyak contacts had leaked out to the public.

Eighteen days had passed from Sally Yates's warning to the White House and Michael Flynn's firing as national security advisor. His letter absolved the vice president of any responsibility. "I was disappointed to learn that the facts that had been conveyed to me by General Flynn were inaccurate," Pence said a few days later. "But we honor General Flynn's long service to the United States of America, and I fully support the president's decision to ask for his resignation. It was the proper decision. It was handled properly and in a timely way."

Chris Christie was back in New Jersey, a former governor fulminating about the mistakes made by the Trump administration, but still holding out for a job and calling Donald Trump his friend. If Christie felt vindicated on the day Michael Flynn was fired or when he pleaded guilty to lying to the FBI, he mostly kept it to himself. Months later, after Flynn admitted to breaking the law, Christie would say he had "no need to feel vindicated." Christie added, "Suffice to say, I had serious misgivings, which I think have been confirmed by the fact that he pled guilty to a felony in federal court."

For Mike Pence, the Flynn scandal was a burden on top of what was already an overstuffed portfolio. Traditionally, vice presidents are asked to oversee a few policy areas at most, and they may be expected to work closely with members of Congress. But presidents typically come to office knowing what they want to do, whom they want to hire, and how they will proceed. Donald Trump was not typical in this way or any other way, which meant that Pence would be asked to do much more. This fact had been noted by the president's son Donald Jr., who had declared that Trump's vice president (when he offered the job to John Kasich) would be "the most powerful vice president in history." That was coming to be true. Indeed, while Trump chose Rex Tillerson to be secretary of state and rewarded Senator Jeff Sessions with the top post at the Department of Justice, he looked to Pence to recommend people to fill many top posts. The list was comprised of Pence supporters and cronies over the years, and a distinct number of them were Pence's very own Hoosiers:

- Seema Verma, who had worked in Indiana state government for Pence, became administrator of the Centers for Medicare & Medicaid Services (CMS), which together account for more than $1 trillion, or more than 25 percent of the government budget. Verma was a designer of the state Healthy Indiana medical program under Pence and his predecessor as governor, Mitch Daniels. Two other former Indiana staff members joined Verma at the CMS office. Brady Brooks became deputy chief of staff. Matt Lloyd, Pence's former spokesman and close aide, was placed in charge of public affairs for Verma. Lloyd had returned to the government after a stint working as director of communications at Koch Industries.

- Dr. Jerome Adams, his former Indiana state health commissioner, became United States surgeon general. Adams, an anesthesiologist, had defended Pence against complaints about his slow response to the HIV outbreak among drug users in Indiana.
- Tom Price, who was Pence's friend when they served together in Congress, became secretary of the Department of Health and Human Services. A conservative antiabortion, anti-Medicare physician from Georgia, Price would be forced to resign for having spent at least $400,000 on excess travel.
- Alex Azar, the president of Eli Lilly, based in Indianapolis, would be named to replace Price. Lilly was one of Pence's major corporate campaign contributors.
- Sonny Perdue, the former governor of Georgia, who became Trump's secretary of agriculture, was related to the wife of Pence's chief of staff, Nick Ayers.
- Dan Coats, Pence's friend and former United States senator from Indiana, was named director of national intelligence.
- Betsy DeVos of Michigan, the Amway billionaire and Pence's longtime political benefactor (DeVos and her family gave thousands of dollars to Pence's earlier political campaigns and more than $1 million to the Trump-Pence presidential campaign) became secretary of education.

Health care policy and the billions of dollars involved could easily fall to Pence's sphere of influence by default. Donald Trump was not interested in the details of governance and here Pence could coordinate his longstanding ideas on privatization of Medicare, Medicaid, and Social Security, much in line with his former Republican colleagues in Congress.

"The Trump people really didn't have much to say about how we deal with Medicare or Medicaid or people who have no medical help," said former senator Richard Lugar, a conservative stalwart who left the Senate in 2013. "So Pence had an opportunity here to come into the void and set up a program (similar to the Healthy Indiana program when he was governor) in Indiana that worked pretty well," Lugar said. "It's an area where the president really didn't have strong views. He didn't say: 'Mike stay out of that.' He may be indebted to Mike for getting into it, to offer at least a Republican solution or an alternative to what otherwise was a vacant part of public policy."

The same was the case with the choice of DeVos as education secretary.

DeVos and her family were well known to Republicans in Congress. Among the GOP senators who would be required to vote on her nomination were twenty who had received a total of more than $800,000 in campaign contributions from DeVos and members of her family. However, she had no previous experience running a large bureaucracy, and her involvement with education had been limited to her advocacy for vouchers and other policies that would steer tax dollars away from public schools and into private ones.

During DeVos's confirmation hearing, Senator Bernie Sanders asked her how much she and her family had donated to Republican campaigns over time. Devos said she didn't know. "I have heard the number was $200 million. Does that sound in the ballpark?" the senator asked. "Collectively." "My entire family? That's possible," she answered with a bemused expression, not blinking an eye. This would be a fantastic sum in the eyes of some ordinary Americans, but as major benefactors for the GOP, the DeVoses could have easily contributed more.

DeVos's comments on education were troubling to many of the senators. She did not seem to understand questions about determining student proficiency (measuring performance based on standardized tests) versus growth (the progress of a student over the course of a year). She also had no knowledge of the federal civil rights law that protects students with disabilities. Most memorable was her answer to a question from Connecticut Democrat Chris Murphy about whether she supported the presence of guns in schools. She said it depended on specifics, referring to a Wyoming school surrounded by a fence to keep bears out. "I would imagine there's probably a gun in the school to protect from potential grizzlies," she said.[22]

On the night before they voted on DeVos, the Democrats in the Senate kept the chamber open so they could air their objections to her nomination. "Betsy DeVos doesn't believe in public schools," said Elizabeth Warren of Massachusetts during the all-night proceedings. "Her only knowledge of student loans seems to come from her own financial investments connected to debt collectors who hound people struggling with student loans, and despite being a billionaire, she wants the chance to keep making money on shady investments while she runs the Department of Education."

All forty-eight Senate Democrats voted against DeVos. They were joined by two Republicans, Lisa Murkowski of Alaska and Susan Collins of Maine, who agreed that DeVos had no qualifications and was just a lobbyist for charter schools and right-wing causes. Republicans, regardless of what they said privately, were not going to buck the president. Neither would Mike Pence. In fact, as vice president, he possessed the tie-breaking vote in the Senate, and he would use it for the first time to help his friend.

Pence was ushered to the Senate rostrum as the votes were being cast. He received a quick primer on procedures required to preside over the Senate, then spoke from a script held before him by an aide. Some Senate members stood by, others were streaming out of the chamber, already having voted.

"On this vote," Pence read, "the yeas are fifty, the nays are fifty. The Senate being equally divided, the vice president votes in the affirmative, and the nomination is confirmed."

Pence's vote was the first tiebreaker of any kind in the Senate since Vice President Richard B. Cheney had broken a tie in 2008. It marked the first time in the 227-year history of the U.S. Senate that a vice president cast the deciding vote for a cabinet appointment. Some hours later, Pence administered the oath of office to DeVos, who stood alongside family members, and praised his longtime friend and benefactor. The tie-breaking vote, he said, "was also casting a vote for America's children. And I can tell you, my vote for Betsy DeVos was the easiest vote I ever cast."

Pence would handle the ceremonial swearing in for most of the

Trump cabinet members, not unprecedented for vice presidents in history. Vice presidents, in their positions as president of the Senate, also typically preside in swearing in new senators in their roles. Trump, who could if he chose, but did not, administer the oath himself, sometimes stood by as Pence administered the oath—he was there for Secretary of State Rex Tillerson but not in the case of DeVos. In each ceremony, Pence followed the same process. He welcomed each of the newcomers warmly and greeted their spouses and children. Family values were paramount for Pence, and it was on this basis that he regularly defended Trump after he said something outrageous. Trump and his family embraced Pence for such loyalty.

"I bring greetings from the president," he would say at many of his early public appearances as vice president. "This is a good man—a man with values, who loves his family."

In the spring of 2017, such reminders were often needed. Trump faced frequent charges of racial and ethnic insensitivity, and the issue of sexual harassment, raised frequently during the campaign, still hung over him. Pence stood by as the calm, moral voice, reminding Trump's more religious supporters that Trump was a good man at heart and they could trust him. When he was with Trump, Pence flattered him, but this effort couldn't always soothe the president's temper. As the months passed and the FBI as well as committees investigated the Russia controversy, Trump seethed.

In May, President Trump's eldest son, Donald Jr., traveled to Indianapolis to deliver the keynote address at the annual dinner of the Indiana Republican Party. About a year earlier, Indiana had voted solidly for his father and made the improbable a reality as Trump captured the GOP presidential nomination. In his remarks, he said the Indiana primary had been his family's introduction to Mike Pence. Since then, the families had become very close, both politically and on a personal level. Pence, he said, genuinely "cares about what's going on."

To illustrate the Trump family's connection to Pence, Donald Trump Jr. told a story about his younger brother Eric, who had called him a month earlier. Eric and his wife, Lara, were having their first child. "He goes, 'Don, you know who the first call was?' I go, 'Dad?' He goes, 'Nope . . . It was Mike Pence.'"

"It's not only a testament to the man," Trump Jr. said of Pence, but also "to the type of people I got to know, have become friends with, and will continue to spend a lot of time with from this great state." Trump Jr. did not mention, however, whether Trump Sr. eventually called as well.

Trump Jr.'s political message included a warning to Republicans about the future. The 2018 congressional elections were looming. Holding on to the GOP's majorities in the House and Senate would be essential to the fulfillment of the Trump agenda. Unsaid, but also true, was the danger that Trump could face if the other party won control of either body. Committee chairmanships, which would empower them to investigate the administration and subpoena both documents and witnesses. A Democratic Congress could also start impeachment proceedings.

The reality of the danger to the presidency was palpable in Washington. The Russia scandal had not let up since the inauguration. President Trump was angry about the investigation into Michael Flynn and with news media attention being given to the eighteen-day gap between Sally Yates's visit to the White House and Flynn's departure. The FBI investigation was in the hands of Director James Comey, who had won Trump's admiration in the waning days of the presidential campaign by announcing he was investigating Hillary Clinton's emails.

Trump and Clinton might have agreed on only one thing in life—that Comey's announcement in October had tipped the scales toward Trump. But now Comey was pursuing all Russia leads. Trump had called in Comey in January for a private dinner and asked him to go easy on Flynn. "He's a good guy," said Trump. Comey was noncommittal. Trump repeatedly asked Comey to state publicly what he had implied strongly in private to the president: that Trump was not a target of the Russia investigation. Comey did not comply.

Days before Donald Jr.'s appearance in Indiana, Comey had testified in an open hearing before Congress about Flynn and the Russia investigation. He said he was concerned that his announcement about the Hillary Clinton investigation had affected the election. "Look, this is terrible. It makes me mildly nauseous to think that we might have had some impact on the election." When asked if he was concerned that Trump, as he had hinted, possessed tape recordings of their conversations, Comey said, "Lordy, I hope there are tapes."

Trump spent the weekend of May 6 and 7 at his golf resort in Bedminster, New Jersey. He was enraged by Comey's testimony, especially the parts that seemed to impugn the legitimacy of the election. Comey had to go, he insisted, and he directed his aide Stephen Miller to write a draft letter that outlined why Comey should be fired. Back in Washington on Monday, Trump summoned Mike Pence, Reince Priebus, Steve Bannon, and White House counsel Donald McGahn to tell them he was ready to fire Comey. He showed them copies of the letter Miller had written for him.

For once, Pence was in Washington for a major development and could not say later that he did not attend the meeting. He did claim, however, that he had arrived late. Perhaps he hoped tardiness would serve as an excuse should trouble arise. None of those present—certainly not Pence himself—reported what, if anything, the vice president had said during the Comey meeting. However, McGahn urged Trump not to send the letter Miller had written.

On that same day, the question of what Pence knew about Michael Flynn—and when—was raised on Capitol Hill as Sally Yates was questioned by the Senate Judiciary Committee. Yates said she had gone to warn Donald McGahn on January 26 about Flynn, partly because Flynn had apparently lied to Pence about his contacts with Russian ambassador Kislyak. "We felt like the vice president was entitled to know that the information he had been given and he was relaying to the American public wasn't true."

Senator Dianne Feinstein of California, the ranking member on the Judiciary Committee, asked a follow-up question. "So what you're saying is that General Flynn lied to the vice president?"

Yates replied, "That's certainly how it appeared, yes, because the vice president went out and made statements about General Flynn's conduct, which he said were based on what General Flynn had told him. And we knew that [what Pence said] just flat wasn't true."

As Washington buzzed with talk of the Trump team and Russia, the president summoned Attorney General Jeff Sessions and his deputy, Rod Rosenstein, who had been placed in charge of the Russia investigation after Sessions recused himself. (His recusal was based on his previous service to the Trump presidential campaign.) The president ordered that they produce a document that would outline reasons for firing Comey. The document was produced, under Rosenstein's signature, as a memo to Sessions.

Rosenstein's memo criticized not Comey's work on the Russia scandal, which preoccupied Trump, but instead focused improbably on Comey's handling of the Hillary Clinton investigation. He wrote that because of it, Comey had lost the trust of Congress and the American people.

> *The current FBI Director is an articulate and persuasive speaker about leadership and the immutable principles of the Department of Justice. He deserves our appreciation for his public service. As you and I have discussed, however, I cannot defend the Director's handling of the conclusion of the investigation of Secretary Clinton's emails, and I do not understand his refusal to accept the nearly universal judgment that he was mistaken. Almost everyone agrees that the Director made serious mistakes; it is one of the few issues that unites people of diverse perspectives.*

Rosenstein suggested that Comey's departure was the only viable option for the president, but he did not explicitly recommend the FBI director's dismissal. "Although the President has the power to remove an FBI director," he cautioned, "the decision should not be taken lightly."

Rather than calling Comey himself, the president sent the FBI director notice he was fired in the form of a terse letter, which was delivered to the Justice Department by Trump's security chief, Keith Schiller. "I have accepted their recommendation," said Trump in reference to Rosenstein and Sessions, "and you are hereby terminated and removed from office, effective immediately."

White House strategists developed talking points to answer anticipated questions. Their main argument was that the president's decision to fire Comey had come in response to Rosenstein, who was a man of great integrity. Pence was quick to use those talking points on the morning of Wednesday, May 10, at the Capitol as he emerged from a gathering of jittery Republican leaders.

"President Trump made the right decision at the right time to accept the recommendation of the deputy attorney general. . . . Let me be perfectly clear . . . the president has been told repeatedly he's not under investigation, there is no evidence of collusion between the campaign and any Russians . . . let me be clear, that's not what this is about . . . the president took strong and decisive leadership here to restore the confidence of the American people . . . strong and decisive leadership. Director Comey had lost the confidence of the American people . . . [Trump] took decisive action . . . I am grateful."

Pence offered a bit of misdirection when asked if Trump had asked Rosenstein to write the memo.

"The new deputy attorney general," Pence said with a chuckle, "he came to work two weeks ago; he is a man of extraordinary independence and integrity and a reputation in both political parties came to work . . . sat down and made the recommendation. I personally am grateful that we have a president who is willing to provide the kind of decisive leadership to take the recommendation" of Rosenstein, he added, finding his way back to the talking points.

It was not a surprise that Pence said repeatedly that he wanted to be "clear." Of course, this was his unintended signal, like a bad poker player's tell, that he was about to obfuscate. His performance did nothing to clear up any point about the real reasons behind Comey's firing. In time, it would be revealed that Rosenstein was furious about how his memo was used as a pretext for firing Comey. This experience may well have motivated his choice of Robert Mueller, Comey's mentor and predecessor at the FBI, to serve as the counsel who would take up the investigation.

Shortly after Pence spoke to reporters at the Capitol on May 10, the president welcomed Sergey Kislyak and Russian foreign minister Sergey Lavrov to the White House. Earlier in the morning, an American reporter had called out to Lavrov at the State Department, arriving for a scheduled meeting with Rex Tillerson. Had the firing of Comey "cast a shadow" on the Washington visit? he asked. Lavrov responded with mock surprise. "Was he fired?" he asked. "You are kidding. You are kidding."

At the White House, in an unprecedented act, American journalists were barred from the Oval Office for the Kislyak-Lavrov-Trump tête-à-tête, but the Russian government news agency, TASS, was allowed in to film the encounter. A White House summary of the meeting, issued afterward, included quotes from the president's remarks to the Russians. "I just fired the head of the FBI," said Trump. "He was crazy, a real nut job, I faced great pressure because of Russia. That's taken off." So much for Mike Pence's statement about the reason for Comey's dismissal.

Trump further undermined Pence's false narrative in an interview on May 11 with Lester Holt on NBC. Comey, Trump said, "is a showboat, he's a grandstander, the FBI has been in turmoil, you know that, I know that, everybody knows that."

> HOLT: Monday you met with the Deputy Attorney General Rod Rosenstein.
>
> TRUMP: Right.
>
> HOLT: Did you ask for a recommendation?
>
> TRUMP: What I did is I was going to fire Comey. My decision. It was not . . .
>
> HOLT: You had made the decision before they came into your office [to make their recommendation].
>
> TRUMP: I—I was going to fire Comey. I—there's no good time to do it, by the way. They . . .
>
> HOLT: Because in your letter, you said . . .
>
> TRUMP: They—they were . . .
>
> HOLT: I—I accepted—accepted their recommendations.
>
> TRUMP: Yeah, well, they also . . .
>
> HOLT: So you had already made the decision.
>
> TRUMP: Oh, I was going to fire regardless of recommendation.
>
> HOLT: So there was . . .
>
> TRUMP: They—he made a recommendation. He's highly respected. Very good guy, very smart guy. And the Demo-

crats like him. The Republicans like him. He had made a recommendation. But regardless of recommendation, I was going to fire Comey knowing there was no good time to do it. And in fact, when I decided to just do it, I said to myself—I said, you know, this Russia thing with Trump and Russia is a made-up story. It's an excuse by the Democrats for having lost an election that they should've won.

Mike Pence said nothing about how he was contradicted by the president. In the months to come, he would maintain his status as the most loyal member of the president's inner circle, supporting virtually everything Trump said and did.

11

SHADOW PRESIDENT

And I heard the voice of the Lord saying, "Whom shall I send, and who will go for us?" Then I said, "Here am I! Send me."
—*Isaiah 6:8*

Like all vice presidents, who are elected mainly to ensure continuity should the president be unable to serve, Mike Pence was concerned about his role. Uncertain about the influence and power he would hold, he cast about for an interest to nurture. He had always been interested in space, and Trump had pledged during the campaign that he would "revive" America's space program. Allergic to anything done by his predecessor, Trump was not about to accept or endorse plans designed during the Obama administration for human missions to an asteroid in the 2020s and a manned Mars journey in the 2030s. However, he had no ideas of his own, save for Buck Rogers fantasies like the creation of a "Space Command" at the Defense Department. (The Pentagon had a well-established system for managing its space resources, and exploration was not part of its mission.)

Sensing an opening, Pence jumped the gun on Trump's plan in March 2017 by saying that he would be the chairman of the long-dormant National Space Council, an advisory group that Pence's fellow

Hoosier, Vice President Dan Quayle, had led during the George H. W. Bush administration. The idea of having such a council was better on paper than in reality. In the past, members who were political appointees had clashed with officials at the National Aeronautics and Space Administration, who were actual experts. Nevertheless, Trump did sign an order reestablishing the council and put Pence in charge. "Today's announcement sends a clear signal to the world that we are restoring America's proud legacy of leadership in space," Trump said at a ceremony where he was surrounded by NASA officials and retired astronauts. "Our vice president cares very deeply about space policy, and for good reason. Space exploration is not only essential to our character as a nation but also our economy and our great nation's security."

The vice president now set out to make his role a prominent one. Here was an outlet for his energy that came with the chance to rub elbows with the titans of the aerospace industry who were also potential campaign donors. As an extra bonus, Pence would get the chance to go behind the scenes where astronauts, scientists, and engineers did their work. An opportunity for this kind of fun came at Cape Canaveral in early July 2017. On a tour of the Kennedy Space Center, Pence approached the ten-ton Orion multiuse spacecraft, which is designed to replace the retired space shuttle. Accompanied by Florida Republican senator Marco Rubio, Pence solemnly reached out and placed his palm on the craft's titanium forward bay door. A sign in bold was affixed inches from his hand: CRITICAL SPACE FLIGHT HARDWARE. Below it was a large warning in red capital letters: DO NOT TOUCH.

A photograph captured the moment; memes and endless jokes flew across the internet. "Pence looked left. Then right," tweeted writer Jason Miller. "Mother wasn't anywhere around. He smiled to himself. He would touch." Some people combined the picture with an image of Chris Christie on the beach; others manipulated it to show Pence touching the butt of a male stripper, or stroking the belly of a crocodile.

Pence retreated to Washington. His staff, knowing the power of ridicule, went into full damage control mode. A coterie of communications aides came in and out of the vice president's office with drafts of tweets—they had to do something, but what? Pence was exasperated and didn't see a problem. What was the big deal? His aides laughed and realized the best option was to get in on the joke. They sent out their own tweets, blurring the warning sign with the message: "Sorry @NASA . . . @Marco-Rubio dared me to do it!" Next, they distributed a photo of Pence reaching out to touch a porcupine with the caption: "OK, so this isn't exactly the first time this has happened."

The self-deprecation, something the president couldn't do, inoculated Pence against more ridicule. It also pointed out the great difference between the VP's social media profile and the president's. The tweeter in chief was a sputtering font of anger and ridicule, and his social media blasts revealed him to be stuck in old conflicts. Irritated by the fact that Hillary Clinton had bested him in the popular vote by nearly three million, Trump repeatedly alleged, without providing a scintilla of evidence, that most of those votes were illegally cast.

Trump's obsession gave Pence another opening. On the extreme right, voter fraud had been a kind of MacGuffin—a plot device with no meaning—for many years. Time and again, claims of double-voting, noncitizens at the polls, and even ballots cast by the deceased were lodged and then disproved. Multiple nonpartisan studies have shown that voter fraud is exceedingly rare. One researcher found only 31 possible cases of fraud in one billion ballots cast between 2000 and 2014, with no sign of a change since then.[1]

Despite the evidence that fraud was not a problem, Republicans had pushed for laws that required state identification at the polls. This practice ran counter to long-established practices and put a burden on poorer citizens, who were known to vote for Democrats in greater numbers. (The head of the Republican Party in Pennsylvania had admitted the purpose was to suppress votes for Democrats.) The issue also played into anti-immigrant sentiment that politicians like Trump encouraged to energize supporters. Once Trump was elected, it became a cause that could be pursued with the might of the federal government. Encouraged by his most aggressive aide, Steve Bannon, Trump created a commission that would investigate this nonproblem and presumably prove he was right. Mike Pence, who knew how to please people in general and the president in particular, became the ideal choice to lead it. The mission not only fit his personality, but also aligned with his increasing interest in representing Trump to the world at large as a most commanding and popular leader.

Before the new administration had taken office, Pence had shown he was willing to indulge Trump's voter fraud fantasy. When asked by interviewer George Stephanopoulos about the voter fraud charge, Pence wouldn't deal with the substance of Trump's claims. Instead, he chose to talk about how it was okay for him to make them. "It's his right to express his opinion as president-elect of the United States," Pence told Stephanopoulos. "I think one of the things that's refreshing about our president-elect and one of the reasons why I think he made such an incredible connection with people all across this country is because he tells you what's on his mind."

"But why is it refreshing to make false statements?" Stephanopoulos asked.

"I don't know that that is a false statement, George, and neither do you," Pence said.

"I know there's no evidence for it," Stephanopoulos replied.

Pence had prior history with the issue. When he was governor of Indiana, the state police charged canvassers for the Indiana Voter Registration Project, which was supported by a liberal Washington funder, with attempting to register nonexistent voters. Indiana secretary of state Connie Lawson even went so far as to declare, "Nefarious actors are operating here in Indiana. A group by the name of the Indiana Voter Registration Project has forged voter registrations."

The "nefarious" activity prompted Lawson and Pence to sound an alarm in the news media and launch an investigation that covered most of the state. It all turned out to be a minor incident, inflated in good part because the Republican state government recognized that the voter registrations were likely to bring mostly Democratic voters onto the rolls. Officials at the Indiana Voter Registration Project had gathered about 45,000 voter registrations, mostly in a predominantly African American neighborhood of Marion County, in the Indianapolis suburbs. After officials at the Voter Project office fired several canvassers for turning in questionable voter cards, they segregated and flagged those registration forms and handed them over to local election clerks, as they were required to do by law. Project officials said the bad forms might have amounted to less than 10 percent of the 45,000 voter registrations they had gathered. Ultimately, a prosecutor would determine "that these are not allegations of voter fraud nor is there any evidence to suggest that voter fraud was the alleged motivation." For his part, Pence honored Lawson with a prestigious state award naming her a Sagamore of the Wabash. It was one of his last acts as governor.[2]

On the federal commission, Pence would be aided by Kris Kobach, the Kansas secretary of state, who had campaigned for the office on the unfounded charge that "the illegal registration of alien voters has become pervasive." After winning, he began an intense effort to scrutinize registrations, which led to about 15 percent of newcomers being blocked in their attempts to get on the rolls. As he oversaw this effort, Kobach crisscrossed the nation speaking to conservatives about his successes. His cause would eventually fail, as a federal judge found he had violated the rights of roughly thirty-five thousand people, mostly young college students. In the meantime, however, Kobach had won the short-term victory of preventing people who were more likely to vote for Democrats from exercising their franchise.

As Trump announced the creation of his Presidential Advisory Commission on Election Integrity, he mentioned the "sacred integrity of the ballot box and the principle of one citizen one vote." Pence was willing to promote a fake issue that didn't exist instead of dealing with the real problem, which Trump refused to address—Russia's meddling in the 2016 election and the prospects for more of the same in 2018.

On the same week when commission members convened, Kobach was fined by a federal judge, who said he had misled his court in a voter fraud case.[3] Concurrently, state and local officials who handled elections around the country were refusing to hand over documents requested by Kobach and Pence. The sweeping request would have put every voter's name and contact information into a single database that would have been under federal control. As many Republican secretaries of state noted,

Connie Lawson of Indiana included, this collection would trample on the states' constitutional obligation to maintain the records themselves. Almost all of them refused to comply.

At the first meeting of the voter fraud commission, Pence sought to paint a dire picture. "President Trump knows that the integrity of our electoral system transcends party lines," Pence said unabashedly with no sense of the irony his statement represented. "I'm grateful this commission has brought together a bipartisan group from the federal, state, and local level. Together, this bipartisan group will perform a truly nonpartisan service to the American people."[4] The panel heard from a few academic experts, who noted that fraud was rare to nonexistent in American elections. Kobach issued a dramatic claim that the results of a Senate election in New Hampshire had been decided by five thousand out-of-state nonresidents who had voted illegally. "Now there's proof," Kobach said. "It is highly likely that voting by nonresidents changed the result." The problem with Kobach's claim was that the so-called ineligible voters were college students who, though possessing out-of-state driver's licenses, merely had to declare themselves residents in order to register and vote legally.

The commission would soon be disbanded by a frustrated President Trump. Mike Pence would attend only its first meeting. He had lent his credibility to the effort, however, and added to the problem of the distortion of reality in American political life. As the commission was shut down, more than half of Trump voters told pollsters they thought that Trump had actually won the popular vote but fraud had blocked a true result. In fact, as *The Washington Post* reported, the 2016 election saw only four documented cases of voter fraud: "Two of those fraud cases involved Trump voters trying to vote twice, one involved a Republican election judge trying to fill out a ballot on behalf of her dead husband, and the last involved a poll worker filling in bubbles for a mayoral candidate in absentee ballots in Florida."[5]

Thus, Mike Pence was willing to say on national television—before the always skeptical George Stephanopoulos—that Trump's crusade against voter fraud was legitimate. During and after the election, Pence had established himself as a reliable supporter of Trump's most unreliable claims.

Pence was so resolute in his commitment that even when he wasn't speaking, his body language and his facial expressions showed that he felt Trump could do no wrong. Time and again, Pence stood beside or behind Trump and beamed with such adoration that pundits likened the look on his face to the wide-eyed gaze that Nancy Reagan fixed on her husband when they were together. The smile and the bright-eyed focus made Pence look almost as if he were in love, and then, when he spoke, he seemed to affirm this feeling.

Always careful to subsume his ego and glorify Trump, he followed a formula. "I bring you greetings from the president of the United States," he told people at campaign rallies around the United States. "I can tell you firsthand, our president is a man with broad shoulders and a big heart. His vision, his energy, his optimism are boundless, and I know that he will make America great again."[6]

At the administration's first full cabinet meeting, an unctuous Pence spoke as if he had forgotten his marriage and three children: "It is the greatest privilege of my life," he said, "to serve as vice president to a president who's keeping his word to the American people."

Pence had set the tone, and the other cabinet members followed through with equally obsequious words of praise. Attorney General Jeff Sessions, who had angered Trump by recusing himself from the Russian matter, said, "It's an honor to be able to serve you, to set the exact right message, and the response is fabulous around the country." Reince Priebus, chief of staff, said, "We thank you for the opportunity and the blessing that you've given us to serve your agenda."

Trump worked his way around the table, nodding at each member of the cabinet and gazing at them as they introduced themselves like attendees at a seminar and spoke their words of praise. It was a display that would have seemed absurd in the context of any government setting, but in the seat of the American democracy, which was founded on the rejection of the British monarchy, it was grotesque in every way. When the love-fest-on-command was over, Trump said, "Thank you, thank you, thank you," a cue for his staff to shoo reporters out of the room. That evening, the video of the ego-stroking was played over and over on talk and comedy shows as commentators struggled to understand how grown men and women, purportedly some of the most accomplished people in the country, could debase themselves in such a craven way.

In Indiana, people who knew Pence and had observed him for years considered the performance and wondered if he really did respect the chaotic Trump or if he was playacting in order to be of service to his country. Supporters said that Pence backed Trump, despite his flaws, out of a sense of patriotic duty. Critics, like Ann DeLaney, an Indiana Democrat, said that, given Trump's scandals, it looked to her like hypocrisy. "Mike is enabling him," DeLaney said. "I mean, he's standing up in front of the evangelicals and those that are religious in this country and saying, 'This is a good man, despite all of that.'"

Not so, said Sherman Johnson, his onetime congressional campaign manager and a conservative Republican. Pence's prime role is to serve Trump, he said. "I really think if you're a good vice president," said Johnson, "your name was not at the top of the ballot, this other guy's was, and you pretty much knew what you were getting into when you accepted the offer. And your job is to . . . is to counsel the president in . . . in private, not take your laundry out in public and don't create friction where it's not necessary."

If what Johnson said was true for all U.S. vice presidents, it was more so the case than ever with Trump. The president was such a temperamental and sensitive person that those who dealt with him often struggled to figure out a way to both avoid his wrath and manipulate him toward moderation. No one in the administration did a better job than Mike Pence of understanding the moment and responding to what was required, much like the child who intuits how to mollify an unpredictable and frightening parent. Whatever his motivation, Pence would not cease to gaze and praise and back Trump's claims no matter the facts.

Nowhere was Pence's backing more steadfast than in the matter of Russia. In defending the president on Russia, Pence could be seen as also protecting himself. Obvious questions about Pence's own role in the Russia story had circulated all along despite his attempts to stand at a distance and appear isolated. Pence had to know that he was not immune to fallout from the Russia probe. Within weeks of Mueller's appointment, Pence hired Richard Cullen, a former U.S. attorney and onetime Virginia attorney general, as his criminal defense lawyer representing him in the Russia probe. Coincidentally, Cullen was a friend and colleague of James Comey, whose firing was the impetus for establishing a special prosecutor. Pence had lawyered up at least one other time in his elective career. At the end of his gubernatorial career, he was embroiled in a battle over whether emails concerning state business he sent using a private America Online account should be released to the public. Some of the emails involved Pence's controversial Religious Freedom Restoration Act, the HIV outbreak in southern Indiana, and interaction with and about then presidential candidate Trump. Pence aides said he had paid legal fees in that case from gubernatorial campaign funds. In the Russia dispute, a Pence spokesman said the legal fees might be covered by a political action committee. Pence's own possible engagement with Russians became a subject of interest when, in September 2017, his press spokesman Marc Lotter would not answer a clear question about the subject on national television.

Bill Hemmer, an anchor on the Trump-friendly channel Fox News, asked Lotter in a live interview, "Did the vice president ever meet with representatives from Russia?" Inexplicably, Lotter did not offer a simple "no." Instead, he said, "Uh, the vice president isn't, is . . . is, is not focused on the areas where, you know, where on this campaign, especially things that happened before he was, uh, even on the ticket. As he has said, that when he joined the campaign his entire focus was on talking to the American people, taking the case that President Trump was going to make to the American people."

Hemmer, who seemed surprised, repeated his question, saying, "Just come back to this question. If it wasn't a private citizen from Russia, did he ever meet with representatives from the Russian government during the campaign?"[7]

Lotter waffled again: "You know, that stuff would be what the special prosecutor and the counsels are looking at . . ."

Hemmer tried one last time: "Just to nail this down, so it's clear: Is that a yes or no? Did he or did he not, and, and was it relevant in fact?"

Lotter, hemmed in, still evaded the issue defensively: "Um, I'm not aware of anything that I have seen . . ."

Following that performance, rumors about Pence and Russia receded with the chaotic daily diet of news and news leaks emerging from the Trump White House. Lotter would soon leave the vice president's office. Friends insisted that his TV performance was not the cause of his departure. However, they immediately tightened up their defense of the vice president. When the topic arose, they would say that Pence had been too busy campaigning during the run-up to the election to be aware of what was going on. Whatever Russian involvement there was, another staffer said, "it was run out of New York City."

Much as the White House wanted to put campaign controversies aside, they continued to create crises. Beginning with Flynn and then Comey, firings and resignations came at an unprecedented rate. Press secretary Sean Spicer resigned on July 21. A week later, Reince Priebus, chief of staff, also was dumped; Anthony Scaramucci, who had replaced Spicer, lasted eleven days and left on July 31; Steve Bannon, Trump's chief strategist, left on August 18 amid reports Trump thought Bannon was taking too much credit for the president's own success; Sebastian Gorka, a controversial right-wing ideologue, left a week after that, partly in reaction to Bannon's departure; security man Keith Schiller went next, followed by Health and Human Services secretary Tom Price. Eventually, more than twenty senior people would leave in the first year of the administration, a pace that far exceeded any presidency in modern times.

Some of the departures were Trump's doing, and some came as members of his team simply reached the limit of what they could stand. Economic advisor Gary Cohn approached his breaking point in the summer of 2017, when Trump remarked "fine people" were among the neo-Nazis who marched in Charlottesville, Virginia. Cohn, who is Jewish, faced what he later acknowledged was a "frenzy of criticism" when he did not speak out immediately. Finally, he said this: "Citizens standing up for equality and freedom can never be equated with white supremacists, neo-Nazis, and the KKK." He remained on board with Trump when the president pushed his ban against Muslims coming to the United States. But Cohn, the former chairman of the Goldman Sachs investment bank, reached the tipping point in March 2018 and resigned when Trump called for broad import tariffs on steel and aluminum, anathema to free-trade Republicans.

The Wall Street Journal reported a 34 percent turnover of staff at the White House, compared to the previous record in the first year of an administration—17 percent in Ronald Reagan's first year in 1981. Many more departures would come in 2018. Pence had an unusual number of departures among his own top-level staff, though none were described as firings. Among those who left was Pence's longtime chief of staff, Josh Pitcock, who went to work as a lobbyist for the technology company Oracle.

A longtime loyalist, Pitcock had served Pence for years. His departure was a sign of a new regime taking over. He was admired by the rest of the staff for his steady, gentle demeanor and his solid focus on policy. Pitcock was replaced by Nick Ayers, a thirty-five-year-old, high-powered Republican campaign strategist who was close to David and Charles Koch. Staff members said the arrival of Ayers marked a new reality, that Pence would now graduate to a different political level. He had the connections and the "sharp elbows"—everybody used the term as his nickname—to help Pence in an arena that called for the toughest political style. It was not, however, a style that matched the Pence brand as many understood it. After Pitcock left, others followed him out the door, concerned that Pence had sold himself to ambition at the expense of ideals.

Among others who served Pence for just a brief time were the vice president's counsel, Mark Paoletta; the associate counsel, Andrew Kossack; press secretary Lotter; and Daris Meeks, Pence's director of domestic policy. One of the strangest departures from Pence's staff was the resignation of Dr. Jennifer Peña, a U.S. Army physician who had complained about the comportment of the White House medical director, U.S. Navy rear admiral Ronny Jackson. Jackson had been nominated to run the Department of Veterans Affairs but withdrew amid charges of misconduct.

The vice president's aides did their utmost to steer clear of the Trump turmoil. When they did talk, insiders denied strife in their ranks. One made a special point of saying that Ayers, the new chief of staff, was not a source of friction. "He's great. I got along very well with him," said this source, not willing to be identified in any way. There was a tinge of fear in the way he dismissed any problem with Ayers, a power broker who everyone knew could be a dangerous antagonist. Staffers willing to speak at all drew the line on discussing any controversy, especially questions about Trump and concerns that the chaos he created could bleed into the vice president's office. "I don't want to be involved with [special counsel Robert] Mueller," said one, hastening to add that this was not to indicate there was a problem.

The touchiness raised obvious questions about Pence's strategy for dealing with Trump. Staffers worried that they and Pence could be tainted by further revelations of wrongdoing. In this case, the vice president's flattery of Trump and loyalty could backfire. This danger was noted by Joel Goldstein, a law professor and specialist on the vice presidency at Saint Louis University.

"All vice presidents, and not just Pence, work to develop and preserve rapport with that special constituency of one," wrote Goldstein. The difference was that "most recent vice presidents have largely demonstrated their loyalty without seeming servile." Pence's behavior was risky. "It potentially undermines Pence's credibility to hitch his star to such an unpopular and controversial president."[8]

Through all the turmoil, Pence, the one person in the administration who could not be fired, did not publicly object to anything the president said or did. In the case of Charlottesville, he said, "I stand with the president," even though one of the neo-Nazis had driven his car into the crowd and killed Heather Heyer, thirty-two, as she participated in a peaceful counterprotest. In a pastoral tone, he said, "Our hearts are in Charlottesville. Because just a few short hours ago, family and friends gathered to say farewell to a remarkable young woman, Heather Heyer, and we've been praying. We've been praying for God's peace and comfort for her family and her friends and her loved ones." On the same day, Heyer's mother rejected the idea that sympathy for her would serve a purpose. "You can't wash this one away," said Susan Bro, "by shaking my hand and saying, 'I'm sorry.'"

The vice president had offered his condolences during a visit to Chile, where he met with President Michelle Bachelet, and he encouraged the Chilean leader to join an international effort to isolate North Korea. President Trump was in the middle of a war of words with North Korean leader Kim Jong-un over Kim's rapid development and testing to both nuclear weapons and rockets to deliver them. Adding trade sanctions to bellicose rhetoric—threatening "fire and fury"—that rattled the world, Trump needed someone to play good cop to his bad—or rather, crazy—cop, and Pence was the logical choice. Beginning in the summer of 2017, the vice president would be dispatched to not only reassure nations but also rally them to the American cause.

Pence seemed to enjoy moving around the world in ways that Trump did not. Notoriously committed to his habits, Trump did not like to travel abroad, and as his early performances in the Middle East and Europe would show, he wasn't very effective in global gatherings. Images of Trump riding a golf cart while other leaders walked in Sicily and his daughter Ivanka occupying his chair at a summit in Germany sent the wrong kind of message for a president who wanted the world to see him as a vigorous man ever in command. In this atmosphere, Pence's ability to project calm and smile benignly proved to be a reliable asset. Trump was an outsized personality who drew protests and would not hold reliably to a script prepared for him by his aides. Pence could travel with a smaller retinue and with a smaller security contingent. He could perform in a quiet way that was not possible for Trump and was also more normal in the diplomatic world.

In the meantime, Americans were tossed by the mood swings of Donald Trump, which were displayed in his Twitter comments and then dissected on cable news. Day after day, it was Trump against the Justice Department, Trump against a porn actress, Trump and his worst instincts. Then, on October 8, Trump decided to dive into a controversy involving players in the National Football League, who were making a political point about the treatment of African Americans by police by sometimes kneeling during the national anthem. True to form, Trump made the issue into a weapon in his political culture war, declaring, "If a player wants the privilege of making millions of dollars in the NFL, or other leagues, he or she should not be allowed to disrespect our Great American Flag (or Country) and should stand for the National Anthem. If not, YOU'RE FIRED. Find something else to do!"

No one could be mistaken about the racial implications of a president who had praised neo-Nazis in Charlottesville going after athletes protesting the treatment of black men. The vice president dutifully followed a script prepared for him by attending a game in Indianapolis between the Colts and the San Francisco 49ers. Colin Kaepernick, the 49ers quarterback until 2016 who had quietly begun the kneeling protests, had found himself out of a job after it spread around the league. Trump railed against Kaepernick and any player who emulated him, and he deputized Pence to make the point. Just before the start of the game, Pence, wearing a suit jacket emblazoned with an American flag pin, stood with hand over his heart. Karen, also hand over heart, wore a blue number 18 Colts jersey, in honor of Peyton Manning, who had played in Indianapolis and whose number was being retired. After they saw that several 49ers had in fact knelt during the anthem, Pence and Karen gathered up their retinue and left the stadium.

Trump soon revealed that Pence's stunt was preplanned, tweeting, "I asked @VP Pence to leave stadium if any players kneeled, disrespecting our country. I am proud of him and @SecondLady Karen."

Pence's participation in Trump's drama cost around $250,000 in public funds. Others noted details of the staging. One reporter was warned ahead of time to avoid going into Lucas Oil Stadium, where the game was played, because Pence and Karen likely would be leaving early.

The football game stunt suggested Pence was little more than a prop in the president's drama. Pence rarely failed to support Trump, but he would in the case of GOP Senate candidate Roy Moore in Alabama. Nominated to fill the seat vacated by Attorney General Jeff Sessions, Moore was the subject of multiple allegations of sexual misconduct with teenage girls. A few days before the December 12 election, Trump went down to Pensacola, Florida, the media market just a few miles from the Alabama border, and spoke for him at a big rally. "We need a Republican in the House, we need a Republican in the Senate. We need more of them," he said.

Initially, Trump, Pence, and the Republican hierarchy saw no alternative but to support Moore, who was a shoo-in against Democrat Doug Jones. (No Alabama Democrat had represented the state in the U.S. Senate for twenty years.) However, when a series of women began providing details about their liaisons with Moore when he was a young prosecutor, many in the GOP, including Pence, refused to show support for him. Pence's spokesperson, Alyssa Farah, said, "The vice president found the allegations in the story disturbing and believes, if true, this would disqualify anyone from serving in office."[9]

When the ballots were cast, Doug Jones eked out a victory over Moore. Given GOP dominance in the state and the president's active campaign on Moore's behalf, Jones's win was widely regarded as a repudiation of Trump. On January 3, 2018, Pence performed his ceremonial duty of swearing in Jones at the Capitol. News reports made much of the image of Jones's gay son, Carson, who knew of Pence's judgmental regard for anyone who is not heterosexual, casting a withering gaze at Pence during the ceremony.

Days after the swearing in, Mike and Karen Pence left Washington for a rescheduled Middle East trip to Egypt, Jordan, and Israel. The visit had been postponed when Trump suddenly announced his decision to move the U.S. embassy in Israel from Tel Aviv to Jerusalem. The decision sparked criticism from Democrats and many European leaders who thought it was an ill-timed, even amateurish diplomatic move. When the criticism faded, Pence embarked with the public intention of making foreign policy points in all three countries and the private goal of expressing his religious fervor in the Holy Land.

12

GOOD COP/CRAZY COP

Let us build these cities and surround them with walls and
towers, gates and bars.

—*2 Chronicles 14:7*

Mike Pence moved so stiffly, his face frozen in a half smile, that he seemed like a wax museum version of himself. The occasion was a speech at the Israeli Knesset, and he had dressed for the occasion with a tie that matched the sky-blue color of the Star of David on the Israeli flag that hung nearby. His white hair and dusty pink complexion echoed the hue of the off-white limestone walls of the parliament hall. His placid gaze was as unyielding as stone. This moment, which came in January 2018, mattered to Pence on many levels—religious, political, personal—and he played it as if it represented the destiny God had chosen for him.

The context for Pence's appearance at the Knesset was astoundingly complex. First of all, the Middle East trip was a clear sign that the vice president would have an outsized role as the soft voice in the Trump administration. Where Trump's bombastic outbursts brought fear of miscues and diplomatic embarrassment, Pence knew how to stay within the bounds of civility, while always paying tribute to the ego-driven president. Meanwhile, a visit to Israel had deep religious meaning for Pence.

Conservative evangelicals considered Israel essential to the fulfillment of Bible prophecy and the return of Jesus to rule the Earth. Disagreement raged over just how events would unfold but no doubt attended the idea that the establishment of Jerusalem as a Jewish capital was part of the story.

In America, conservative Christians had also elevated concern about the treatment of the faithful in the Middle East. In October, Pence had met in Washington with a group called In Defense of Christians for a discussion of the prejudice and discrimination suffered by their brethren in the region. Pence had embraced their cause in terms that left no doubt that he was one of them.

"Nearly two thousand years ago, the disciples of Jesus left their home country," he said to the Israelis. "They left their land, radiating outward from Israel in every direction, bringing with them the Good News that is proclaimed to this day. But sadly today, Christianity is under unprecedented assault in those ancient lands where it first grew. . . . President Trump and I see these crimes for what they are—vile acts of persecution animated by hatred for Christians and the Gospel of Christ. And so too does this president know who and what has perpetrated these crimes, and he calls them by name—radical Islamic terrorists."[1]

Pence had originally planned to visit the Middle East at Christmas so he could draw attention to the plight of Christians in the region. However, Trump had announced that the United States officially recognized Jerusalem as the capital of Israel and would soon move its embassy there from Tel Aviv. Previous administrations had not made this move out of respect for the fact that Muslims also regarded Jerusalem as a spiritual home. Daniel Kurtzer, who had served as U.S. ambassador to Egypt during the Clinton administration and as ambassador to Israel during the Bush administration, said that Trump's announcement had diminished the U.S. role in peace talks. It also encouraged the creation of more Israeli settlements in the West Bank, on previously Palestinian land, which was a practice that had long angered Palestinians and their allies.

Pence and his brain trust had worked hard on a game plan for the trip. One of his key advisors on this matter was Tom Rose, a former Indiana radio host and ardent conservative. His family, prominent in the

Jewish community, had donated to Pence's political campaigns. Rose had proven his loyalty by defending Pence when he was chosen to be vice president. In that moment, Indianapolis rabbi Dennis C. Sasso of Congregation Beth-El Zedeck published an article saying that "Indiana Jews have long been repelled by Mike Pence's anti-LGBT, anti-immigrant, anti-choice stances." Sasso wrote that while he presented himself as a "pleasant and amiable person," Pence had "countered the very foundations of religious and moral values he purports to advance." Rose, who described himself as Pence's "closest personal friend for over 25 years," publicly defended Pence by accusing Sasso of trying to "smear and defame one of the best friends the State of Israel and the Jewish people have ever had. This is an attempt to rob a good and decent man of his most valuable possession, an attempt to rob him of his good name," Rose said. "A world in which good people are called bad and bad people are called good."[2]

Rose was not just a fierce loyalist. Before being ousted amid charges of having an abusive management style, Rose had been publisher of *The Jerusalem Post*.[3] This position had given him access to Israeli experts and officials and permitted him to build a base of knowledge about Middle East politics. He was, himself, a controversial figure and aided Pence in a low-profile way. His profile was so low that colleagues on the vice president's staff wondered how he spent his time. However, his influence was substantial, and Pence relied on him so much that he was added to the entourage that boarded Air Force Two at Andrews Air Force Base and took off for Cairo, which would be the first of Pence's three stops.

Egyptian president Abdel Fattah al-Sisi had warned Trump directly on the Jerusalem move to no avail. Once the announcement had been made, Sisi promoted the UN resolution to condemn the United States. However, he had to balance politics with economic reality. Egypt received more than $1 billion in U.S. foreign aid yearly, a result of the 1979 U.S.-brokered peace between Egypt and Israel. When he met with Pence, the Egyptian president said that the embassy move would complicate and possibly unravel peace efforts that had been undertaken by the current U.S. point man on this issue, Jared Kushner.

(In typical fashion, Trump relied on Kushner not because he was experienced or expert—he wasn't either—but because he was a loyal family member. Unsurprisingly, the thirty-six-year-old Kushner became embroiled in a series of problems, which prevented him from doing much of anything. Special Prosecutor Robert Mueller was investigating Kushner's role in the Russian influence scandal, and he was dogged by conflicts of interest. One of these conflicts involved his role as director of his parents' foundation—the Charles and Seryl Kushner Foundation—which had funded an Israeli settlement on land Palestinians claimed.)

Publicly, Pence tried to reassure the world that the United States was still committed to a two-state solution—one Israeli, one Palestinian—that would ease tensions. He also tried to calm fears that Muslims would lose access to Jerusalem, saying the United States was "absolutely committed to preserving the status quo with regard to holy sites in Jerusalem, that we have come to no final resolution about boundaries or other issues that will be negotiated." However, in his time with Sisi, reassurances about holy sites only went so far. "We heard President al-Sisi out," Pence said after their meeting. "He said to me about what he said publicly about a disagreement between friends over our decision to recognize Jerusalem as the capital of Israel."[4]

At Pence's next stop, in Jordan, a most reliable U.S. ally, King Abdullah, also warned that Trump's decision on Jerusalem was simply a mistake. Seated across the table from Pence, the king argued that Trump may have damaged the chances for a two-state solution and that the tinderbox of the Palestinian-Israeli conflict was a source of further radicalization in Arab countries. A decision on Jerusalem was intended to be a final step in a successful negotiation, not a preemptive move to support Israel. "The U.S. decision on Jerusalem . . . does not come as a result of a comprehensive settlement of the Palestinian-Israeli conflict," Abdullah told Pence. At the end of the visit, Pence said, "We had agreed to disagree."[5]

Jordan and Egypt had been placed on Pence's itinerary so the U.S. could be seen as operating in consultation with many actors on the Middle East policy; however, the real action had always involved just three parties—Israel, the Trump administration, and its hard-right political base. After a short flight from Amman, Air Force Two landed at Ben Gurion International Airport in Tel Aviv, where the weather was mild and clear. First to greet Mike and Karen on the tarmac was Israel's tourism minister, Yariv Levin, a Knesset member in Prime Minister Netanyahu's Likud Party. The bespectacled minister bowed excitedly from the waist as he pumped the vice president's hand and continued to bow even after Pence moved down the reception line to Ron Dermer, the American-born Israeli ambassador to the United States, and then David Friedman, the right-wing New York attorney who had worked for Trump and family on real estate deals before his controversial appointment as U.S. ambassador.

Friedman was a law partner of Trump's personal lawyer in the Russia investigation, Marc Kasowitz, and had known the president for more than twenty years. Ambassadors Dermer and Friedman had much in common; they were both born in the United States and were supporters of Trump and virulent critics of Barack Obama. Dermer, born in Miami Beach, had renounced his American citizenship in 2005. He said early in 2016 that Obama had colluded with dark forces at the United Nations, and he had been outraged when the Obama administration had not vetoed a UN Security Council resolution that criticized the Israeli occupation of the Gaza Strip and the West Bank.

Minister Levin, quite hawkish himself, was the embodiment of Israel's internationally condemned policies on occupation. He lived in the town of Mod'in-Maccabim-Re'ut, about eighteen miles west of Jerusalem, portions of which are along the 1967 West Bank border and are not recognized by the European Union as being part of Israel. When the handshakes were completed, he spoke words that became the theme of Pence's two-day visit. "Thank you for your important part in the president's declaration and in the recognition of Jerusalem as our capital," he said. "I am convinced that your wife, Karen, and you will feel at home here." Pence had every reason to feel at home among the people of the Holy Land, the land of Israel and where evangelicals believe the second coming of the Messiah will be staged.[6]

Mike and Karen Pence camped in a suite at the King David Hotel, where the three top floors had been designated for their entourage. The eighty-six-year-old hotel was in the heart of Jerusalem, overlooking the Old City and Mount Zion. Hotel staff had been bustling in preparation for the vice president's twice-postponed trip. As Mike and Karen had settled in for the night, the staff was content they had satisfied their one request—they had been told there should be no alcohol in their room.

The official delegation included Pence's chief of staff, Nick Ayers, who had special interest in the region and had traveled there before. Ayers was on the board of an Atlanta megachurch named Leading the Way, which was headed by Rev. Michael Youssef. Many in his church believed that Bible prophecy required that Jews be called to Jerusalem before the so-called end of days when Christians would be called to heaven and those who have not given themselves to Jesus—Jews, for instance—would die in the final reckoning. Youssef and Ayers had traveled to Egypt in April 2017, just before Ayers formally started working with Pence. (Pence, just months into his vice presidency, seemed to be building a foreign policy approach separate from the president and the State Department.) They had met with members of the Egyptian parliament and inquired about treatment of Egypt's Coptic Christian minority. Ayers had been with Pence when Sisi hosted him in Cairo and had sat next to him across the table from King Abdullah in Jordan.

On the morning after his arrival in Israel, Pence met with Prime Minister Benjamin Netanyahu at his office, where he had more reason to feel at home. Netanyahu lavished praise on Pence and Trump. "Mr. Vice President, I've had the privilege over the years of standing here with hundreds of world leaders and welcome them, all of them to Israel's capital, Jerusalem. This is the first time that I'm standing when both leaders can say those three words, 'Israel's capital, Jerusalem.' I want to thank President Trump and you for that historic statement, which I know you supported and championed. I look forward to discussing with you, as we've just begun, how to further strengthen our remarkable alliance—it's never been stronger—and how to advance peace and security in our region, which is our common aim."[7]

While the vice president conducted his official business, Karen Pence toured the Old City of Jerusalem with little fanfare. She did agree to an unusual on-the-air interview with Calev Ben-David, an anchor at i24, a Jerusalem English-language television channel. The ground rules for the interview, done at the King David Hotel, were that Ben-David would not ask political questions. Accordingly, he asked Karen how she defined her role as the vice president's wife, and she responded in a form and substance that channeled her husband.

"Well, first of all, it's a privilege, and it's great to be here in Israel, one of my favorite places in the world," she said, smiling and shaking her head back and forth as her husband frequently did when he answered reporters' questions. "I think the role of the Second Lady is, well, first of all to support the administration," she said. "I talked with First Lady Melania Trump, and we talked about what my role should be, and she strongly encouraged me to choose an initiative near and dear to my own heart. Art therapy [in education] is my main focus."[8]

After the interview, Karen Pence joined her husband for the main event of his trip, the speech at the Knesset. Like so much in Israel, even the hall was a reminder of the unresolved status of a country where many basic disagreements remained unresolved. The most visible decoration was a Galilee limestone inlaid sculpture titled *Pray for the Peace of Jerusalem*, possibly the most photographed art in Israel. It was the work of famed artist Dani Karavan, who had petitioned to have it removed when the Netanyahu government said it would cut some official funding to artists who do not perform or present their works in the contested—some said illegal—Jewish settlements in Arab areas. "The wall in the Knesset, sometimes I am ashamed that I did it," Karavan said. "I have asked many times that they move it or cover it up with a rug until the Knesset embodies the spirit of the country's Declaration of Independence."[9]

When the time came for him to speak, Pence entered and took a seat next to the speaker of the Knesset, Yuli-Yoel Edelstein, who spoke first in Hebrew, then in English. "It's my true honor to invite the vice president of the United States, Mr. Michael Pence, to deliver his address." Pence stepped over to the lectern to a standing ovation by most and began to read from a teleprompter: "Members of the Knesset, Justices of the Supreme Court, citizens of Israel."

Before Pence could continue, the thirteen Arab-Israeli parliamentarians who had been seated during the welcome now stood and unfolded signs that bore a picture of the Dome of the Rock, with an inscription in Arabic and English: "Jerusalem is the Capital of Palestine." Security guards moved in; a melee ensued. The guards grabbed the posters and hustled the Arab members of parliament out of the Knesset. Netanyahu and other parliamentarians clapped rhythmically, supporting their expulsion.

While the protest occurred, Pence stood silently, his hands stiffly at his side, mouth set in a vaguely pained expression. He waited, his gaze shifting mechanically back and forth. Finally, Edelstein spoke in Hebrew, calling for order and observance of protocol, then turned to Pence: "Mr. Vice President, I apologize."

Pence, who had probably been forewarned about the protest, resumed speaking: "It is deeply humbling for me to stand before this vibrant democracy." He stopped as the remaining Knesset members responded with another round of applause.[10]

While he spoke in a calm and measured voice, the vice president did not say anything to soothe Palestinian concerns. He said the date for moving to Jerusalem had been shifted a year earlier than originally announced, since, after all, "Jerusalem is Israel's capital. And as such, President Trump has directed the State Department to immediately begin preparations to move the United States Embassy from Tel Aviv to Jerusalem. In the weeks ahead, our administration will advance its plan to open the United States Embassy in Jerusalem, and that United States Embassy will open before the end of next year."

"Our president made his decision, in his words, 'in the best interests of the United States,' but he also made it clear that we believe that his decision is in the best interests of peace. By finally recognizing Jerusalem as Israel's capital, the United States has chosen fact over fiction. And fact is the only true foundation for a just and lasting peace."

The quiet in the hall was often broken by applause. However, Netanyahu and his allies were silent as Pence said, "President Trump reaffirmed that, if both sides agree, the United States of America will support a two-state solution." However, they did respond positively when Pence said Trump was prepared to abandon the six-nation Iran nuclear deal, which Obama had negotiated to control against Iran creating nuclear weapons.

The Iran deal had been supported throughout Europe and by a

number of Republicans in Congress. Former Israeli prime minister Ehud Barak, for one, warned against Trump decertifying the agreement. However, Netanyahu hated the deal and was pleased to hear Pence describe it as "a disaster," and promise that "the United States of America will no longer certify this ill-conceived agreement."

Although most of what Pence had to say related to current issues and was readily understood by the Israelis, some of his allusions to history and scripture were more opaque. The speech had been laced with references to the Old Testament and several mentions of Abraham as prophet of the Jews, Christians, and Muslims alike. Evangelical Christians often go overboard in their discussion of faith among the Founding Fathers of the United States—Washington, Adams, Jefferson, and Ben Franklin were not particularly religious—so it was natural for Pence to speak of America's founders' respect for the Bible and for Judaism.

"Our founders," said Pence, "turned to the wisdom of the Hebrew Bible for direction, guidance, and inspiration. America's first president, George Washington, wrote with favor to 'the children of the stock of Abraham.' Our second president, John Adams, declared that the Jews, in his words, 'have done more to civilize man than any other nation.'"

To his listeners, including some tuning in via a live transmission on the internet, Pence's remarks surely sounded pious but ordinary. However, a New York University scholar, Joshua Blachorsky, was taken with the fact that Pence used the word *faith* fourteen times. Faith, in isolation, did not express the essence of Jewish religious life, and Blachorsky wondered if Pence's audience understood what he meant. Then Pence said, "It was here, in Jerusalem, on Mount Moriah, that Abraham offered his son, Isaac, and was credited with righteousness for his faith in God." Blachorsky repeated those last words to himself—"was credited with righteousness for his faith in God"—and thought, "That isn't right. The line is adapted from a key phrase in Genesis 15:6, central to Christian doctrine. The accepted text does not use the word 'faith.' Instead, it references 'righteousness.'"

The Christian concept of serving God by having faith alone—without needing to follow the commandments laid down in the Old Testament—was not consistent with what the Old Testament says and what Jews know.

However, it is central to the Christian view of Jesus and the Resurrection, and it is oft repeated by end-of-days evangelicals. To a biblical scholar, it sounded like Pence was making a sneaky attempt to pass off Christian Right theology to a roomful of Jews. One thing was certain: this was not the kind of question that would have been raised had Trump been giving a speech to the Knesset. Trump had created his own controversy in his first week in office by failing to mention the Jews in a statement for International Holocaust Remembrance Day.

Did Pence purposely preach Christian theology to a Jewish audience? "I think that's the $64,000 question," said Blachorsky weeks later. "Is he such a Christian man that he can't speak without dropping some theology in there and that his theology will be good Christian superstitious theology? I would love to ask him. If it was unintentional, someone needs to fire his speechwriter. There should have been no way that—if he didn't mean to say this—that it got into his speech. This is supersessionist theology: Christianity has superseded Judaism in terms of who shall inherit the earth."[11]

Blachorsky posted an analysis of Pence's biblical references on his Facebook page. Amit Gvaryahu at Hebrew University caught Blachorsky's post, and the two scholars spoke about it. Gvaryahu found Pence's stealthy mention of Christian theology to be outrageous and penned an opinion piece for the newspaper *Haaretz*, which published it several days after Pence's departure. LUCKY, read the headline, THE JEWS DIDN'T UNDERSTAND WHAT MIKE PENCE WAS REALLY SAYING.

Gvaryahu wrote: "It takes a special kind of chutzpah to stand in front of a Jewish audience and explain their own tradition to them using language and texts that historically have rendered actual Jews pathologically redundant to the world, and still today cast us as a tool for the salvation of Christians."[12]

The two doctoral students talked further about their analysis of the speech and wondered whether other speeches by Pence in other settings could have the same right-wing Christian dogma. One hint came a few days later, on January 27, recognized as International Holocaust Remembrance Day. Trump was Twitter-silent about the day, but Pence issued his own tweet:

A few days ago, Karen & I paid our respects at Yad Vashem to honor the 6 million Jewish martyrs of the Holocaust who 3 years after walking beneath the shadow of death, rose up from the ashes to resurrect themselves to reclaim a Jewish future.

The language was distinctly Christian. For Jews, the six million who died in the Holocaust were seen as Nazi *murder victims,* not "martyrs." In fact, martyrdom is a Christian and Muslim conceit, and Jews are not encouraged to purposely sacrifice themselves. Likewise, the term rising "up from the ashes" suggested a kind of resurrection not associated with the Jewish experience of World War II. (Given the millions of Jews who were murdered in Nazi gas chambers and crematoria, the word choice was also extremely insensitive.) To use such a term suggested that Pence regarded the Jews as either Christians in waiting, who needed to be converted, or tools for the fulfillment of prophecy. Either way, they were not spiritual equals.

Although Bible scholars and political critics would have found trouble in Pence's performances, his mission to the Middle East was hailed as a success at the White House, where staffers counted twenty-nine interruptions for applause during Pence's speech at the Knesset, just less than one per minute. Pence had also been careful to mention Trump frequently and in the most glowing terms. (This performance served him so well that when the embassy was opened, ahead of schedule, Pence's name was emblazoned on the commemorative plaque, right below the president's name.)

Back in Washington, Pence attended the president's State of the Union speech, where he applauded vigorously and stood when his fellow Republicans stood. Trump later said that Democrats who did not cheer him were "un-American and like death . . . treasonous." The next morning, Pence was on the road again, this time to West Virginia—a conservative state with a Democratic senator named Joe Manchin—praising the president's performance and his accomplishments. He took aim at Manchin, who had actually tried to work with Trump, for voting against a Republican tax overhaul, among other things. "It's not just the tax cuts,"

Pence said. "Folks, Joe is just going to keep voting against West Virginia. But West Virginia needs to let him know."[13]

Manchin was angered by Pence's attack and said, "The vice president's comments are exactly why Washington sucks." This tone, crude and angry, had come to be the norm in much of American politics. Of course, observers have forever moaned about the coarse quality of public debate, with each generation suggesting things were worse than ever before. However, with the advent of Trump, the trend toward divisiveness had gotten measurably worse. In his demeanor, Pence suggested he was working against this trend, but in his rhetoric and positions, he was amplifying it.[14]

Soon after the State of the Union address, Mike and Karen Pence boarded Air Force Two again, this time for a mission to Asia. The first stop would be in Japan, where officials were worried about North Korea's nuclear capabilities. Then it would be on to South Korea—the site of the Winter Olympics and where Trump's bellicose rhetoric toward North Korea was causing deep concern about nuclear war. North Korea's Kim Jong-un had scored a victory against Trump by suddenly announcing that North Korea would participate in the Olympics and sending his sister Kim Yo-jong to attend the games. This move was taken by the nervous South Koreans as a signal from Kim that he was someone they could deal with.

The South Koreans, seeking to soothe tensions with North Korea even more, arranged for Mike and Karen Pence to sit near Kim's sister at the opening ceremonies for the Winter Olympics. Instead of smiling, shaking hands, or merely nodding in recognition, the Pences sat expressionless and were the only ones in the official grandstand who remained seated when the unified Korean athletes passed in review. Later, they ducked attendance at a reception where Pence might have met members of the North Korean delegation; South Korean officials sought détente, but Pence's posture did nothing to soften Trump's frightful, hair-trigger threats of war.

Pence was caught off guard during the Asian trip when reporters got close enough to seek his reaction to the resignation of White House aide Rob Porter, who was forced to resign after two former wives said that he had abused them. Some in the White House—not Trump, of course—

were admitting the case had been mishandled, and Trump's chief of staff, John Kelly, was the focus of criticism because he had known of the allegations for months. When asked about the controversy, he said, "We'll comment on any issues affecting the White House staff when we get back to Washington." In response to follow-up questions, Pence added, "You know it's a great honor for me to serve as vice president." He continued in this vein until he was able to escape reporters without offering an actual answer.[15]

The vice president's performance was so wooden that someone on his staff called for a do-over. Pence soon submitted to an interview in South Korea with Lester Holt of NBC. In this sit-down, he said he hadn't known about the charges that Porter had abused his two former wives, although the prior investigation of those allegations had blocked Porter's ability to obtain a permanent security clearance.

As head of the presidential transition team, Pence should have known about allegations of abuse if Porter had been vetted at all or certainly when there was a problem on security clearance. Pence denied it all, just as he had in dealing with prior notice about Michael Flynn or about a security clearance for Flynn's son. "The time that [Porter] resigned is when I first became aware of the allegations of domestic abuse. And there's no tolerance in this White House and no place in America for domestic abuse." This statement raised a larger question about just what was tolerated in the White House, where stories of erratic behavior emerged daily from unnamed inside sources and Trump ranted incessantly about witch hunts and against officials of his government. Pence never addressed such issues.

In South Korea, Pence also faced a lingering problem that had arisen even before his visit to the Olympics when prominent U.S. figure skater Adam Rippon, the first U.S. Olympic skater who openly acknowledged he was gay, criticized him. Rippon said to a reporter for *USA Today* he would not meet with Pence at the games. "You mean Mike Pence, the same Mike Pence that funded gay conversion therapy?" he said. "I'm not buying it." Rippon was referencing Pence's 2000 campaign literature, which had suggested that the government fund groups offering the discredited practice. "I would absolutely not go out of my way to meet somebody who

I felt has gone out of their way to not only show that they aren't a friend of a gay person but that they think that they're sick," Rippon said. "I wouldn't go out of my way to meet somebody like that."

For Pence, who was doing all he could to avoid embarrassment and controversy, Rippon's statement presented a conundrum. At first, he tried the Trump method, which involved attacking the press for spreading a story that he claimed was inaccurate. Since both the journalist and Rippon confirmed the report, this did not work. Next, Pence tried to negotiate a meeting with Rippon. This too failed, as Rippon didn't want to be distracted from the competition. Finally, he used the president's favorite means of communication—social media—to say to Rippon, "I want you to know we are FOR YOU. Don't let fake news distract you. I am proud of you and ALL OF OUR GREAT athletes and my only hope for you and all of #TeamUSA is to bring home the gold. Go get 'em!"

Watching from afar, President Trump apparently decided that his team was losing the public relations war and sent his daughter Ivanka to attend the closing ceremonies. Rippon would wear a bronze medal around his neck and go home to appear on national TV shows where he was regarded as an icon of the gay community; the first to compete and win a medal after coming out. Upon his return, Pence would get high marks from his supporters and, having benefited from Ivanka Trump's last-minute participation, retained the president's confidence. However, the president would not let Pence forget who was in charge.

In April 2018, Trump acted to curtail Pence's foreign policy ambitions when the vice president attempted to add Jon Lerner, a longtime aide to Nikki Haley, to serve concurrently as Haley's and his own national security advisor. A pollster with no national security experience, Lerner, forty-nine, was credited as being a major player in Haley's gubernatorial career in South Carolina, as he had been for Mark Sanford in his two races for governor in that state. More to the point, Lerner had been one of the so-called Never Trumpers, a group of Republicans who opposed Trump's election as president on grounds that he was temperamentally unfit for the office he sought. In a rare Sunday night announcement, the White House informed reporters that Lerner had withdrawn his name from consideration. Lerner stayed on as Haley's aide at the United Nations, apparently acceptable to Trump as long as he stayed away from the White House.

The dustup over Lerner came as the Trump administration waited for the Senate to confirm Mike Pompeo to replace Rex Tillerson, who had been fired as secretary of state when Trump decided he was not loyal enough. Pence's outreach to Lerner suggested he might be seeking a foreign policy alliance with Haley at a moment when Trump was so preoccupied with scandal that foreign affairs policy seemed to be adrift. It also pointed to the possibility that Pence and Haley might be fashioning themselves into a potential dream team to seek the White House should Trump decline to run for reelection in 2020.

Trump had given Pence wide berth in government appointments, and the vice president had established a number of former colleagues and personal choices in the cabinet and throughout the government. However, none had been so tied to the Never Trump cause as Lerner, and the embattled Trump had moved quickly against his addition to the Pence office. Given the president's tendency toward paranoia—a trait he had embraced in one of his books—he surely wondered if behind his public show of humility, Pence harbored dangerous ambitions.

13

NOT SO HUMBLED

He said to them, "Go into all the world and preach the gospel
to all creation."

—Mark 15:16

During his first eighteen months in office, Mike Pence developed a certain routine. Missions abroad and to the political hinterlands were balanced by periods of rest at the vice president's residence. A sprawling Queen Anne–style house constructed in 1893 for the superintendent of the United States Naval Observatory in northwest Washington, the elegant home was a refuge unapproachable by tourists but still protected by the Secret Service. The agents assigned to the Pences found them generally agreeable, although Mrs. Pence could be quite demanding and didn't seem to bother with learning their names. She didn't like the restrictions that came with her husband's office. When an aide's wife forgot her identification and was barred from attending a pool party at the observatory, Mrs. Pence let her displeasure be known.

With the exception of the occasional venting of frustrations, both Pences showed a remarkable ability to soldier on, despite Donald Trump's erratic and emotional behavior. Trump was sensitive to being upstaged and fearful of threats to his own power, but he also needed Mike Pence.

It was the vice president who had vouched for Trump with GOP donors and with conservative Christians, and they had been essential to Trump's election. As the 2018 midterms approached, he needed the vice president's help in the effort to stave off a Democratic Party surge. A president's party almost always loses seats in the first election following the president's assumption of power. Things looked even worse for Trump as his approval ratings hovered near historic lows and scores of Republicans, including House Speaker Paul Ryan, declared they wouldn't run for reelection. Worse still, if the Democrats took control of either the House or the Senate, they could launch investigations of Trump that could paralyze his presidency and might even force him out of office.

Pence was such an effective surrogate for Trump that he was dispatched on a dizzying schedule of events where he would speak on the president's behalf and raise money for the Republican Party and its candidates. Along the way, he promoted his own deeply conservative social agenda, which was colored with much more religious conviction than Trump ever showed. In speech after speech, Pence said that he and like-minded people were under assault and that Donald Trump, no matter what else he said or did, was a reliable ally.

"From the very first day of this administration, President Trump has been keeping his word to stand without apology for the sanctity of human life," Pence said in Nashville at a meeting of the antiabortion Susan B. Anthony List and Life Issues Institute. He hailed cuts to funding for the UN Population Fund, which promoted contraception, and new scrutiny of Planned Parenthood, which provided abortions and contraception. And he warned that such measures were always in danger as long as Democrats and Democratic-appointed judges were around.

"The truth is that the opposition is always looking for ways to undo our achievements, and notably in the category of the progress that we've made in the cause of life," Pence said that day in Nashville. The goal was no less than overturning *Roe v. Wade*, the 1973 Supreme Court ruling that made abortion legal. "I truly do believe, if all of us do all that we can, that we will once again, in our time, restore the sanctity of life to the center of American law." With Republicans in office, Pence also reminded wavering voters that more judges in the mold of Neil Gorsuch, who has been described as one of the most right-wing Supreme Court justices in U.S. history, would be appointed to the federal bench. (Gorsuch was able to join the court because Senate Majority Leader Mitch McConnell had blocked Merrick Garland, President Obama's choice to replace Antonin Scalia in 2016.) "This president has been busy appointing strict constructionists to our federal courts at every level," Pence said. "These are men and women that will uphold the God-given liberties enshrined in our Constitution."

The rhetoric was the same wherever the vice president went, even if he did vary his greeting. In Ohio, he saluted the Buckeyes. On February 2, 2018, in a visit to Pittsburgh, he declared, "It is great to be back in the Keystone State!" His visit there was part of the all-out effort to push Rick Saccone over the top in a special election for Congress. "I want you to go tell your friends and neighbors why this election matters," Pence said, tying his opponent Conor Lamb to Democrats, who they wanted to paint as out of touch with the Republican version of the common man.

"I believe with all of my heart that all the media in the world, all the advertising, all the commercials, all the mail pieces that might fill up your mailbox are not to be compared to the power and the impact that you can have with someone who knows you and respects you. The conversation across a backyard fence, the grocery store, outside your place of worship, nothing is more powerful than friends talking to friends, neighbors talking to neighbors. I want you to go tell your neighbors and friends why this election matters. It matters not just for this district and not just for this great state but the opportunity we have in this election to elect someone to Washington, D.C., who's going to stand with President Donald Trump and keep America growing."

Pence was a master of homespun style who always seemed like he was addressing a friendly, if fictitious, America of the past where divorce was shocking, doors were never locked, and everyone prayed together on Sundays. In western Pennsylvania, Pence was joined by a troupe of Trump's current real-life version of *The Apprentice* cast—Ivanka Trump, Donald Trump Jr., and Kellyanne Conway—who were desperate to see Saccone elected as a sign of the president's strength. Trump himself visited twice—and Republican supporters spent an estimated $10 million in the effort.

In the end, all the effort wasn't enough. In a district where Trump had defeated Hillary Clinton by twenty points, newcomer Democrat Conor Lamb eked out the victory by just six hundred votes. Pence nevertheless gained from the experience and continued traveling the country, trying to evoke an America that is a series of local tribes—like the Hoosiers, who in his distorted view have special qualities and care for their fellow Hoosiers like no one else. This ultimately fed a divisive narrative of Us and Them that easily translated to politics: Barack Obama, Nancy Pelosi (the prime Republican target of 2018), and the liberals are not like Us.

In politically vital New Hampshire, on March 22, 2018, Pence declared in Manchester, "It is great to be back in the Granite State"—applause—"being able to join all of you hardworking men and women. . . . And it's my great privilege today to bring warm greetings from a man that New Hampshire put on the path to the White House, a man who three months ago today signed historic tax cuts to put America first. I bring greetings from President Donald Trump, a great friend of New Hampshire."

Pence went on to repeat "Granite State" six more times before finishing his pitch and departing for Atlanta, where it was "great to be back in the Peach State. I bring greetings from the forty-fifth president of the United States of America, President Donald Trump."

Each time, in a speech that took him a half hour to deliver, Pence pressed on local issues; coal in Pennsylvania, jobs in New Hampshire. Where he couldn't identify a local issue to stress, Pence praised the president and the Grand Old Party. He was an effective salesman speaking in the style of the midwestern radio host he had once been. Despite the caution of Charles Dickens, who wrote that humility is a quality best identified by the beholder, Pence repeatedly said he was a humble man who by the grace of God had made it further than he could have imagined. He had gotten this far, however, through a blend of methodical self-promotion, the investment of millions of dollars provided by his right-wing supporters, and luck. Pence, like Dickens's Uriah Heep, protestations of humility to the contrary, "aspired" deeply.

While saying he was humbled at every turn, Pence also praised a number of mentors before whom his humility was even greater. Pence said

Rush Limbaugh, a right-wing radio bigot, was his mentor on the airwaves, though he warned that he was only a decaffeinated version of the boisterous opioid abuser; Dick Armey was another, the fellow Tea Party member who served for a while as House majority leader while Pence was in Congress; Charles Colson, White House counsel under Richard Nixon and Watergate felon who found God while serving time in prison; James Dobson, the gay-bashing evangelical Trump supporter who founded the right-wing Christian organization Focus on the Family; Paul Weyrich, another right-wing commentator closely connected to dominionism— governance under Christian biblical law; and Larry P. Arnn, the president of Hillsdale College in Michigan, which rejected U.S. standards for affirmative action and who once publicly referred to minorities as "dark ones."

Pence's aspirations were supported by two secretive, intermingled political action committees, America First Policies and the Great America Committee. America First Policies was created to boost the reelection of Trump, and was formed one week after the inauguration. The staff included Brad Parscale, whom Trump's son-in-law, Jared Kushner, had brought into the Trump orbit in 2016. Parscale had worked closely with the data mining efforts of Cambridge Analytica, which had used eighty-five million pilfered Facebook profiles to aid Trump's social media effort. Founded by top Trump advisor Steve Bannon and bankrolled by billionaire Robert Mercer, Cambridge Analytica was being investigated by British authorities for links with Russian military intelligence. America First Policies was cofounded by Rick Gates, the former assistant to Trump's second presidential campaign manager, Paul Manafort. Both men were indicted by special counsel Robert Mueller in his Russia probe. Gates pled guilty to two counts—lying to investigators and for conspiracy against the United States—and began to cooperate in Mueller's probe.

From the beginning of the Russia controversy, the vice president's team tried to separate him from it, telling anyone who would listen that the only ones who might have had contact with the foreign operatives were denizens of Trump Tower in New York. When it became clear that Mueller could make trouble for Trump, the vice president formed his own political action committee—Great America Committee—and began raising money and employing operatives, including former Trump campaign chief Corey Lewandowski and Nick Ayers. Lewandowski had become notorious for physically bullying a female reporter during the 2016 campaign. Ayers had been chairman of the Pence for Vice President campaign. *Time* magazine had recognized him as one of the most powerful young people in politics. He had been a key consultant to the 2016 election campaign of Missouri governor Eric Greitens, the former Navy SEAL who was indicted in February 2018 on a felony charge stemming from allegations of sexual misconduct and invasion of privacy. Greitens resigned as governor on June 1, 2018.

Although America First Policies was devoted to Trump's reelection in 2020, its structure and message—lower taxes, border security, and the fight against abortion rights—would work just as well for Pence, come what may. Behind Pence's greetings from the president to every crowd brought together in the Americas First Policies traveling road show, Pence was working to enhance his own political brand. Quiet and patient, Pence would do everything he could to fulfill God's plan, perhaps even including the presidency. He would be helped by the longtime allies sprinkled across the administration and installed in political action committees. And he could count on a well-funded and growing Christian nationalist movement.

Dedicated to the pursuit of power under the rubric of religious freedom, the Christian nationalists backed candidates for local, state, and national office and pushed legislation like Pence's Religious Freedom Restoration Act, which would enable discrimination. This movement was led by organizers who made no secret of their aims. David Barton of the group WallBuilders openly promoted the idea that America is a country that should be controlled by conservative Christians for their benefit. A ministry called Integrity Leadership, founded by an evangelist called Buddy Pilgrim, advertised that Christian "dominion in earthly realms of authority (business & politics) is a biblical mandate." A third group, United in Purpose, founded by convicted embezzler Bill Dallas, was devoted to using social media data to deliver votes for candidates like Mike Pence.

Looking forward, the vice president could count on Dallas, Pilgrim, Barton, and many others to augment the usual Republican machinery with everything from money to motivated volunteers who would approach politics as a crusade.

In the meantime, however, Pence was attracting attention as an emblem of intolerance. In early 2018, in his hometown of Columbus, a high school senior named Erin Bailey organized the city's first-ever gay pride festival. Initially planned to occupy just one block in the center of the city, the venue was expanded to accommodate triple the number of vendors than were expected. Although the weather was cloudy and cool, attendance exceeded two thousand as drag performers were cheered by enthusiastic crowds and rainbow flags were draped like capes over young shoulders. One city official told *The Indianapolis Star,* "This is what we do: We welcome everyone to Columbus."[1]

EPILOGUE

THE MAN WHO WOULD BE PRESIDENT

And there will be signs in sun and moon and stars, and on the earth distress of nations in perplexity because of the roaring of the sea and the waves.

—*Luke 21:25*

Mike Pence and his supporters and aides took as an article of faith that the glorious day would come: eventually he would be president of the United States. Pence, a man of supreme faith, never expressed doubt about this destiny. However, others might say that Pence's ascension to the presidency would be the culmination of a perfect storm of improbable events. Who could imagine that a failing governor chosen as the running mate of Donald J. Trump, a man whose candidacy was improbable to the point of mockery, would eventually assume the presidency? In fact, tens of millions could envision such a turn of history, and they had voted for the Trump-Pence ticket in hopes that it would arrive.

In many ways, said former Indiana senator Richard Lugar, Pence's role may have enhanced the survival of the Trump presidency. Certainly, said Lugar, Pence's "loyalty to the president may lead him to make many statements that are dubious." But that was not necessarily a problem.

Members of the religious Right don't "necessarily forgive the president or absolve him for whatever his deeds may be that are really counter to the good religious spirit," said Lugar. "Mike Pence makes up for it. So, the combination of the two makes the president in a stronger situation, even given the criticism of his personal conduct."

Sooner or later, Pence's evangelical supporters—along with Never Trumpers and Republican-or-bust believers—would say that everything justified the wait. The troublesome Donald J. Trump, that imperfect vessel, had been a means to an end. The investigations into the Russia scandal and other matters, which produced indictments and guilty pleas of Trump allies, could provoke Trump's resignation or even impeachment. If, somehow, Donald Trump survived his first term and were reelected, Pence could wait. He was a young man with patience, the patience of Job.

Whenever the blessed day came, Pence would stand at the ceremony he once predicted for the interns in his congressional office. He would again swear "to preserve, protect, and defend the Constitution of the United States. . . . so help me God." In *his* presidential inaugural speech, there would be no bleak talk of wastelands and suffering. He would say as he always did that he was *humbled, very humbled,* and beyond that, he would give thanks for God's providence.

For most of his life Pence had believed he was guided by God's plan. He believed that the Lord intended for him to halt the erosion of religious conviction in the United States. And though he avoided stating it himself, many of his evangelical friends believed Pence's ultimate purpose was to establish a a government based on biblical law. This was what they called Christian Dominionism.

Pence's election to the presidency would cap a remarkable turnaround. He and the religious Right had long seen themselves as victims in a culture war. This is what Pence meant when he said, "Despite the fact that we live in a time when traditional values and even religious convictions are increasingly marginalized by a secular popular culture—a time when it's become acceptable, even fashionable, to malign religious belief—in this time, I believe with all my heart that faith in America is rising, as well." In context, America had been under attack by the forces of nonbelievers. A Pence presidency would repel those attacks.

At the top of Pence's concerns was the destruction of the 1973

Supreme Court decision in *Roe v. Wade*. Pence and the religious Right were one or at most two Supreme Court appointments away from that hallmark victory. "For all the progress since 1973," Pence said, referring to the year of the *Roe v. Wade* decision, "I just know in my heart of hearts that this will be the generation that restores life in America." Looking at the justices of the court, the actuarial tables were in his favor. The two key members under watch were both octogenarians—Ruth Bader Ginsburg, a solid Democratic progressive, and Anthony Kennedy, the middle-of-the-road Republican swing vote. When Kennedy resigned suddenly as of July 2018, Pence's office ran the search for a new justice and the vice president interviewed the candidates. Trump was pledged to choose a conservative ready to overturn *Roe* and push for a hard right turn on the court.

The transition of power from the Trump administration to the presidency of Mike Pence would be a streamlined affair because Pence had seeded his own people throughout the executive branch. Their purpose would be to fulfill the libertarian dreams of those who funded the rise of Mike Pence from his early days in Indiana politics. High on their agenda would be tax cuts, slashed business regulations, the decimation of environmental protections and exploitation of the natural resources—oil, gas, minerals, timber, et cetera—on public lands. Although the Kochs and others would cringe at the idea of restrictions on personal freedoms, they would accept some of the Christian Right's moral regulation if they got the economic policies they wanted. As long as Pence followed the agenda they had trained him to pursue he could have his holy empire on the hill.

Pence would have no problem reconciling the two elements of his base—religious zealots and tax-cutting, anti-government minimalists. His greater problem would be to govern a nation that rejected much of his agenda. Polls showed that most Americans supported abortion rights, preferred environmental regulation, favored preserving Social Security and Medicare, and liked many of the parts of the health care system that the government controlled. Pence's old friend in Congress, lame-duck House Speaker Paul Ryan, had failed in his efforts to destroy Obamacare and privatize Social Security. Would Pence have any more success?

Much as he yearned to act, the Pence presidential dream and agenda would have to wait because, as of summer 2018, his presidency had not arrived. It was not, however, a truly remote fantasy. As the Christian Right's favorite son, Pence had made the difference in the 2016 election. Millions had voted for the Republicans, believing that God was sending a signal as He put Pence on the ticket. Pence's presence had also reassured GOP donors, including the Koch brothers, who had been reluctant to rally behind the erratic Trump. Pence had also brought to Trump a vast network of Christian Right political activists who had been pulling the party in their direction for decades and were more than ready to assume key positions. The Trump administration was filled with Pence people because, bluntly speaking, Trump *didn't have any people of his own*. With high places occupied by his friends, Pence had thus functioned for years as a kind of shadow president, making the machinery work as Trump was consumed by special counsel Robert Mueller's investigation of his 2016 campaign ties to foreign interests and various crimes detected in the probe.

The chaos that was Trump's hallmark had been a challenge for Pence from the moment he joined the campaign. In this case he had been forced to contort his words to make it seem that he was essential to the team, but unaware of Don Jr.'s meetings with the Russians, of Manafort's unsavory business with the Ukraine, of Flynn's Turkish engagement and bluster, of Erik Prince's long support for Pence and Prince's connection to the Russian scandal. Had Pence survived the Russia affair? Would the public overlook it—and would the media forget? And there was always the double trouble of pardons—for a former president and his men. After the resignation of Richard Nixon in 1974, Gerald Ford had declared "our long national nightmare is over"; the pardoning of Nixon did not play well—Ford lost the 1976 election to Jimmy Carter, a liberal Democrat and an evangelical.

Amid the turmoil, Pence would continue to declare that faith in the United States was on the rise. It was a play on words—faith, he meant to say, the practice and declaration of religion at the center of American life, was at the heart of Pence's political career and his arrival at the White House. But he also spoke of faith as trust in America. Where did that reside? Throughout a trajectory that took him from Congress to the governorship of Indiana and to the White House, Pence was taken with suspicion, even by fellow Republicans and non–politically minded evangelicals. Many were disappointed with his appeasement of all Trumpian designs—sex scandals, lies almost beyond counting, money laundering, and brutishness. Pence had done nothing. His team would labor to reconstruct a narrative in which he would be the sober, moderate leader a president is expected to be. There were doubts.

When Trump flouted the separation of powers, called Mueller's investigation a witch hunt, and used shameless surrogates in Congress to attack the justice system, Pence assented with his silence. Asked about the porn star Stormy Daniels and the $130,000 payment she received from Trump's lawyer weeks before the election, Pence said it was a "private matter" and he knew nothing about it. When an aide expressed concern about how far one could go to cover Trump's deceptions, he had the impression that Pence's focus was on doing anything he could to support the president.

The vice president's view, that the ends justify the means, confused close advisors who considered themselves to be the kind of Christians who were honest and truthful. They were troubled when, for example, Pence ignored the scripture that commands "the foreigner residing among you must be treated as your native-born," in order to support Trump's attacks on immigrants. But since the Bible is a self-contradicting text, Pence could select competing passages to defend himself. In extreme circumstances, Christians are permitted so-called righteous lies. And since his brand of Christianity made each believer his or her own authority, Pence was free to practice self-justification ad nauseum. Conveniently, his righteous lies also secured his place in Trump's universe, in which, as White House factotum Kellyanne Conway explained, distortions are merely "alternative facts." With alternative facts and righteous lies, it was easy to justify loyalty to a president who repeatedly attacked the notion of shared reality in order to divide the country into patriotic supporters and traitorous enemies. As Trump would eventually explain, in reference to politics, "everybody plays games."[1]

No one in American politics would have been better suited to the task of serving Trump (especially his ego) while protecting himself than Pence. Reflexively obsequious to the point of self-abasement, Pence seemed to enjoy praising the president in public settings and, when he didn't speak, beaming with admiration when in the top man's presence. However, Pence also had a preternatural ability to absent himself in key moments of peril.

Pence had also devoted himself to retail politicking, crisscrossing the country on behalf of fellow Republicans. In the process, he quietly accumulated political chits and filled the coffers of his own political action committee. Then, in 2018, as Trump attacked judicial officials who investigated him and suffered one scandal after another, Pence moved out of his shadow. First in Israel and then in South Korea, he appeared to be acting as a kind of replacement president, giving speeches and lending his presence to landmark events.

Remarkably, the many crises created by Trump, from staff turmoil in the executive branch to scandals involving mistreating women, played to Pence's advantage. Trump's failures were the failures of an immoral man whose sexual infidelities, lies, and distortions had marked him as a sinner. The contrasting public personas, as Pence raised his profile, couldn't have been starker. This was especially true when it came to religion and politics. At various points in his life, Trump had been a Democrat, an independent, and a Republican. His Christianity had been of a pasted-on type, fixed to his candidacy like wallpaper and just as thin. Throughout his life, Trump had been the most boorish and least subtle man in every room. A lifelong conservative, Republican Pence had been the politest person in every setting, and his approach was always careful and guarded. When added to his frequent evocations of God, his policy stands confirmed his status as the leading voice of political Christianity.[2]

In May 2018 Pence delivered a commencement address at conservative Christian Hillsdale College in Michigan. He used the occasion to proclaim "a new era of opportunity and optimism" for Christian Right believers. He credited "President Trump and our entire administration" with "advancing the very principles that you learned here in the halls at Hillsdale College—the principles that have always been the source of America's greatness and strength."

Pence's decision to appear at Hillsdale was, in itself, a signal to his political base. The alma mater of his allies Erik Prince and Betsy DeVos, Hillsdale was a Christian school that famously had opted out of all forms of federal aid, including programs that underwrite loans, rather than submit to regulations. This decision was announced by the school's trustees, who said they would, "with the help of God, resist, by all legal means, any encroachments on its independence."

In 2013, Larry Arnn, the president of the college, sparked a controversy when he complained that after he took office in 2000, federal authorities suggested the school did not have, as he termed it, enough "dark ones" in its student body. The university apologized for the remarks of the president, who had, himself, taken office in a moment of intense scandal. His predecessor, George Roche III, had resigned after his daughter-in-law announced she had had a nineteen-year affair with him and then committed suicide. In his letter of resignation, Roche said, "We have proved that integrity, values and courage can still triumph in a corrupt world. Hillsdale College is a monument to those beliefs."

Although some in the university community considered him, as one professor put it, "a phony and a fraud," Roche's legacy would include a huge endowment and Hillsdale's place, in the Christian Right subculture, as a citadel of belief and animosity toward government. It was, in short, the ideal setting for a Mike Pence speech.[3]

An amalgam of Christian Right fearfulness about social change and casual misstatement of fact, Pence's Hillsdale address offered few accurate assessments of American life. His most glaring misrepresentation was the centerpiece claim that faith is on the rise. In fact, as measured by church attendance and religious affiliation, it had been in decline since Pence entered Congress in 2001. At the same time, the percentage of Americans with no religious affiliation had almost doubled.[4] Though Pence's loyalty to facts was not much stronger than Donald Trump's, his manner and his tendency to avoid the spotlight meant that he generally got away with his various distortions. At the same time, Pence's team, even those who came to him from within Trump's orbit, was so much less dysfunctional and more disciplined that it seemed capable of performing the normal functions of government. On the political side, he could count on two former Trump operatives, Brad Parscale and Corey Lewandowski, to maintain his legitimacy with the most extreme elements of the base without alienating too many moderates.

For the most part, the various advisors and Pence himself had managed to keep him clear of the scandals that rocked their White House. It was not always possible. More than once, Pence and his staff came up with public excuses that kept the vice president at a distance from the controversy, as if everyone else had been aware but protecting him from knowing the obvious. Frequently, though, he was caught in a plausible-denial trap when Trump made some off-the-cuff remark that showed him saying the opposite. And there were people close to him, Lewandowski, Parscale, and Prince among them, who might be drawn into the Mueller investigation at any time. Not since he paid for the congressional campaign ad featuring a shadowy oil "sheik" had Pence been so close to a problem involving men in traditional garb from the Persian Gulf region.

In the middle of the maelstrom, Pence stayed focused on the agendas set by the two camps of his political base—and never expressed any concern about reconciling them. Whenever possible, Pence preferred to avoid conflict and surprises. He was so wary of journalists that as vice president he almost never submitted to extended interviews, even with the hyperpartisan, conservative Fox News. Instead, with the pleasant demeanor of a neighbor speaking over a backyard fence, an image he sometimes employed, Pence used staged events to communicate his humility and agreeableness.

This approach might have worked superficially, reassuring casual observers, but those who knew Pence remained alarmed by his unblinking loyalty to Trump. Indeed, as time passed, the president showed himself to be consistently callous and cruel in ways Pence had never been. This prompted obvious questions. How could a person of good character do nothing as Trump sowed conspiracy theories and divided the country? Were he alive, Pence's role model Ronald Reagan would ask this question. In fact, in June 2018, Reagan's daughter Patti Davis said that her father would be "appalled and heartbroken" by Trump and "horrified at where we've come to."[5]

In foreign affairs, Pence tried hard to mirror Trump but it was often a struggle because the president was so mercurial. Trump's engagement with the regime of Kim Jong-un in North Korea was a case in point. Although Trump sought a summit in order to deal with Kim's growing nuclear weapons capability, he also insulted him routinely. When national security advisor John Bolton mused about Kim going the way of Libyan dictator Muammar Gaddafi, who was eventually killed after giving up his nuclear ambition, Pence chimed in with support for the comparison. An influential but junior official in the North Korean foreign ministry responded by calling Pence "a political dummy."

After the summit was convened, Pence caused problems when he seemed to contradict Trump's promise to cease military exercises with South Korea. Senate Republicans reported he had told them that at least "some exercises . . . will continue." Pence's spokesman, Jarrod Agen, quickly issued a corrective on Twitter that further muddied the story. "The Vice President did NOT say that military exercises will continue with South Korea." The denial didn't work. A Colorado Republican senator, Cory Gardner, said he knew what he had heard: "VP was very clear: regular readiness training and training exchanges will continue [and] went on to say while this readiness training and exchanges will occur, war games will not."[6]

In the end Pence might have been jumping ahead of White House guidance by telling the truth. In late June, South Korea and the United States did call off scheduled military exercises, as a result of the Kim-Trump summit.

The apparent North Korea misstep came after Trump and Pence had so alienated the world community, including traditional partners like Canada and France, that only Israel, governed by Prime Minister Benjamin Netanyahu and his right-wing coalition, could be counted as an ever-loyal ally. Pence played a role in this process, abandoning the Koch brothers and his other free-trade friends to back Trump's "America first" isolationism, which included imposing tariffs on many trading partners. In Europe, diplomats feared the end of an American-led alliance that had lasted since World War II. In Asia, an emboldened China no longer faced a powerful U.S. check on its ambition to overtake the United States as the world's largest economy. Christine Lagarde, the managing director of the International Monetary Fund, joked darkly about the fact at a meeting in 2017 in Washington at which she barely hid her disdain for Donald Trump. In a decade, she said, the fund's annual meetings "might be held in Chinese at its revamped headquarters—in Beijing. If one used dream binoculars," Lagarde said, "we might not be sitting in Washington, D.C. We'll do it in our Beijing head office."[7]

The threats of trade wars and the apparent decline in America's global leadership seemed to have no effect on the support Christian evangelicals showed for Trump and Pence. These voters were intently focused on domestic affairs, cultural issues, and spreading the Gospel. They believed their agenda was being fulfilled. This is what Mike Pence meant when he said, often, that "faith in America is rising again" and, as a consequence, the country was on the rise.

The rising would be accompanied by an aggressive government campaign against sinners both at home and abroad. This was the mission advocated by Rev. Ralph Drollinger, the leader of the Trump cabinet's weekly prayer meetings, which Mike Pence attended with regularity. Drollinger, who imagines himself to be a prophet, became a trusted advisor to Trump when, in 2016, he urged him to establish a "benevolent dictatorship." Since then, the prophet said, "Of all the Bible studies I've written on policy, Trump's enacting everything I've written."[8]

As Drollinger explained to a German newspaper in 2017, the U.S. government's "God-given responsibility" and "primary calling is to moralize a fallen world through the use of force." At home, this calling suggests a religious police state worthy of Margaret Atwood's *The Handmaid's Tale*. Abroad, said Drollinger, this vision would find America "bearing the sword" as an "avenger who brings on wrath" upon anyone who "practices evil." Islam is a particular problem in Drollinger's view because, he believes, it "has historically spread through the sword and seeks nothing less than world conquest for Allah." Should the United States confront Islam militarily, Drollinger said, "leadership should never enter into it with 'Low Testosterone.' It is an all or nothing commitment of the totality of the nation in its decisive quest for all out victory as quickly as possible!"[9]

In addition to Pence, Drollinger's prayer sessions, which sometimes occurred at the White House, were often attended by Mike Pompeo, who was Trump's first director of the Central Intelligence Agency and then served as secretary of state. In 2015, Pompeo publicly embraced Drollinger as a fellow believer and echoed his talk about America facing off against the evil in the world. Quoting from Pence's favorite book of the Bible,

Jeremiah, he said, "Are they ashamed of their detestable conduct? No, they have no shame at all, so they will fall among the fallen, they will be brought down when they are punished."[10]

If Pence wanted to appoint new members of the court, he would have to survive any scandal that affected the Trump administration. He would also have to continue to manage his own image. For the modestly informed, he offered a mild exterior that made it hard to believe he would outlaw all abortions, which was something a majority opposed. Libertarians simply chose to ignore the abortion issue because they liked what Pence said about cutting taxes and government funding for almost everything other than defense spending. So it was that Pence could represent, simultaneously, the symbols of the cross and the dollar sign.

In campaigns, on the radio, in Congress, and in the White House, Pence carried the two emblems of his beliefs while walking a political tightrope. The traits that permitted him to do this had been noticed long ago by the Club for Growth and other big-money backers. Chief among them was Pence's ability to present himself as a pleasant, even harmless person worthy of the public trust. As a legislator, he had done so little that the public could see that this image was rarely disturbed. As governor, he revealed more of his true self, but since he was isolated in a midwestern state that rarely received much notice from the national press, few outside of Indiana were aware of his missteps and failures. Returning to Washington as Donald Trump's second, he was once again able to act behind the scenes, barely revealing himself even though he had created a shadow administration as loyal to him as it was to the president.

For the most part Pence managed to keep his balance. An exception arose in June 2018, when he addressed the annual meeting of the Southern Baptist Convention in Dallas. The largest conservative Christian denomination in the country, the SBC's members were generally aligned with the Trump/Pence administration, but their faith retained its historic resistance to abject politicking. Pence irritated many when he addressed the gathering as if it were a campaign rally crowd. After listing what he regarded as the Trump team's many accomplishments, Pence said, "With Donald Trump in the White House and God's help, we will make America safe again, we will make America prosperous again, and to borrow a phrase, we will make America great again." In response, an editor for *Christianity Today* took to social media to say, "I seem to remember other politicians (I'm thinking folks like Huckabee, or even Obama) get more into sermonizing/messaging, or reflecting on their own faith?" Newly elected convention president J. D. Greear said, "Commissioned missionaries, not political platforms, are what we do."[11]

One of the youngest people ever elected SBC president, Greear represented a strand of evangelicalism that appealed to those less devoted to conservative politics. In these circles, the Trump/Pence administration's resistance to climate science and harsh treatment of immigrants struck sour notes and Pence's convention speech could be seen as a step too far.

Besides creating a humanitarian tragedy, Trump's "zero-tolerance" policy on the border was a major public relations miscue. The heartrending images and sounds of babies and toddlers separated from their parents provoked outrage at home and around the world. Pence, the descendant of immigrants who fled violence and economic hardship in Europe a century earlier, stood by the president and said nothing about the crisis that Trump had provoked. Former Republican congressman Joe Scarborough used his MSNBC program *Morning Joe* to ask: "How does Mike Pence, how [does] Karen Pence, how do any of these people continue being associated with a man who is now openly bigoted against everybody who is not white and rich?" Scarborough's guest, *Washington Post* columnist Eugene Robinson, added, "Mike Pence stands there and he puts on a frown and he nods sagely at the most sort of racist vile comments and sentiments coming out of the mouth of the president that he serves so loyally and unquestioningly. I certainly hope people remember. This should leave an indelible stain on Mike Pence and his career and on the others around him."

On the day after the Pence address in Dallas, even a formerly fervent Trump supporter, Franklin Graham, the son of Billy Graham, called the administration's practice of separating parents and children at the border "disgraceful."[12] Many evangelicals were, as was Graham, outraged by images of children placed in cages for safekeeping and reports of a nursing baby being wrested from a mother's arms. On the day Pence's remarks were reported, Cardinal Daniel DiNardo, the president of the

United States Council of Catholic Bishops, was blunt: "Separating babies from their mothers is not the answer and is immoral."

One former staff member saw the immigration story as a litmus test for Pence as a moral leader. He was alarmed when his former boss did not react to a brutish comment by Corey Lewandowski. Appearing on Fox News, Lewandowski mocked a commentator who spoke about a ten-year-old girl with Down syndrome who had been wrenched from her migrant mother in south Texas. "Womp, womp," intoned Lewandowski, as if to say too bad, who cares. Lewandowski, fired from Trump's campaign in 2016 after he knocked a woman reporter to the ground, had recently joined Pence's political action committee.

"Whether or not Pence boots Lewandowski from his super PAC advisory board—or whatever his role is—will say a lot about whether Pence is totally hitching his wagon to Trump or whether he's going to start distancing himself," said the staffer, who himself left precisely because of such concerns. "This 'womp-womp' comment should be more than enough to doom Corey (under normal circumstances)." Pence kept Lewandowski on as part of his team.

For Pence, who had previously called for immigrants to be treated with compassion, lockstep agreement with all of Trump's policies brought him close to being called a hypocrite. Columnist George Will, a conscience of American conservatism, called Pence "a sycophantic poodle." However, from Pence's point of view, if he were to be president one day, he needed the visibility that came with serving as Trump's surrogate—no matter what. Although Donald Trump was regarded as a political neophyte when he ran for president, thanks to his TV shows and a lifelong quest for media attention, he was vastly better known than Mike Pence. More important, little separated the real Donald Trump from the bragging, boorish, and divisive figure seen at rallies and debates. Trump was who he said he was. This was not the case with Pence, whose pious and cautious exterior hid a desire for power equal to Trump's. The main difference was that Pence was truly committed to the authoritarian style of religion Trump had seemed to profess for the purpose of gaining election. With it, he intended to do far more to change the nation and the world than Trump could imagine.

NOTES

1: The Sycophant

1. For Pence's explanation of his identity, see "Mike Pence: I'm a Christian, a conservative, and a Republican—in that order," *Week*, July 20, 2016. For Obama quote, see his remarks on Donald Trump's election, *Washington Post*, November 9, 2016.

2. Pence remarks from his speech at the Family Research Council's Values Voter Summit in 2010.

3. For Pence and Trump, see McKay Coppins, "God's Plan for Mike Pence," *The Atlantic*, January 2018, www.theatlantic.com/magazine/archive/2018/01/gods-plan-for-mike-pence/546569/.

4. For Pence's response to Mueller's appointment see Rebecca Ruiz, "Pence Hires Criminal Defense Lawyer to Aid Him in Investigations," *The New York Times*, June 15, 2017.

5. For cabinet members' remarks, see White House, "Remarks by President Donald Trump, Vice President Mike Pence, and Members of the Cabinet," December 20, 2017, www.whitehouse.gov/briefings-statements/remarks-president-donald-trump-vice-president-mike-pence-members-cabinet/.

6. Matt Lewis, "My Theory on Why Mike Pence Kisses Donald Trump's, Uh, Ring So Fulsomely," *Daily Beast*, December 12, 2017, www.thedailybeast.com/my-theory-on-why-mike-pence-kisses-donald-trumps-uh-ring-so-fulsomely.

7. For Pence and the culture war, see Meghan O'Gieblyn, "Exiled: Mike Pence and the Evangelical Fantasy of Persecution," *Harper's*, May 2018, and Damian Sharkov, "Steve Bannon Wanted Culture War to Change U.S. Politics, Says Whistleblower," *Newsweek*, May 17, 2018.

8. For Calvinism, see Michael Massing, *Fatal Discord: Erasmus, Luther, and the Fight for the Western Mind* (New York: HarperCollins, 2018), i–xi.

9. For American Christians as equivalent of ancient Jews, see O'Gieblyn, "Exiled."

10. Coppins, "God's Plan."

11. For Pruitt record, see Alexander C. Kaufman, "Scott Pruitt Twice Introduced Anti-Abortion Bills Giving Men 'Property Rights' Over Fetuses," *Huffington Post,* May 24, 2018, www.huffingtonpost.com/entry/scott-pruitt-abortion_us_5b06ce55e4b05f0fc845a4aa; Brady Dennis, "Scott Pruitt, Longtime Adversary of EPA, Confirmed to Lead the Agency," *Washington Post,* February 17, 2017; Niina Heikkinen, "Scott Pruitt, Christ Follower," E&E News Climatewire, Friday, July 14, 2017, www.eenews.net/climatewire/2017/07/14/stories/1060057367; Evan Halper, "He Once Said Mothers Do Not Belong in State Office. Now He Leads the Trump Cabinet in Bible Study," *Los Angeles Times*, August 3, 2017, www.latimes.com/politics/la-na-la-pol-trump-cabinet-pastor-20170803-story.html.

12. Dana Milbank, "This Week Proved God Exists, and He Has a Wicked Sense of Humor," *Washington Post,* May 4, 2018, www.washingtonpost.com/opinions/who-says-president-trump-doesnt-have-a-prayer/2018/05/04/013eafc6-4fd4-11e8-af46-b1d6dc0d9bfe_story.html?utm_term=.ab84b6b8712e.

13. For DeVos quote, see Valerie Strauss, "She's a Billionaire Who Said Schools Need Guns to Fight Bears. Here's What You May Not Know About Betsy DeVos," *Washington Post,* February 7, 2017, www.washingtonpost.com/news/answer-sheet/wp/2017/02/07/shes-a-billionaire-who-said-schools-need-guns-to-fight-bears-heres-what-you-may-not-know-about-betsy-devos/?noredirect=on&utm_term=.33c4729881da.

14. For Koch's organizations, see Jane Mayer, *Dark Money* (New York: Doubleday, 2016), 56.

15. For training of politicians and their talents, see Jonathan Rausch and Raymond LaRaja, "Re-Engineering Politicians," Brookings Institution, December 7, 2017, www.brookings.edu/research/re-engineering-politicians-how-activist-groups-choose-our-politicians-long-before-we-vote/.

16. For Pence ideology, see Michael Barbaro and Monica Davey, "Mike Pence: A Conservative Proudly Out of Sync With His Times," *New York Times,* July 15, 2016, www.nytimes.com/2016/07/16/us/politics/mike-pence-history.html.

17. For Christian supremacy, see Jeremy Scahill, "Mike Pence Will Be the Most Powerful Christian Supremacist in U.S. History," *Intercept,* November 15, 2016, https://theintercept.com/2016/11/15/mike-pence-will-be-the-most-powerful-christian-supremacist-in-us-history/.

18. For status threat, see Diana Mutz, "Status Threat, Not Economic Hardship, Explains the 2016 Presidential Vote," *Proceedings of the National Academy of Sciences* (April 2018), https://doi.org/10.1073/pnas .1718155115.

19. For Pence and Arpaio, see Sarah Quinlan, "Vice President Pence Calling Joe Arpaio a 'Tireless Champion' of 'Rule of Law' Ignores Arpaio's Record," RedState, May 1, 2018, www.redstate.com/sarahquinlan/2018/05 /01/vice-president-pence-calling-joe-arpaio-a-tireless-champion-of-rule-of -law-ignores-arpaios-record/; Stephen Lemons, "Joe Arpaio: Tent City a 'Concentration Camp,'" *Phoenix New Times*, August 2, 2010, www .phoenixnewtimes.com/news/joe-arpaio-tent-city-a-concentration-camp -6500984.

2: Model Citizen

1. For "Animal House," see Chris Miller, *The Real Animal House: The Awesomely Depraved Saga of the Fraternity That Inspired the Movie* (New York: Little, Brown, 2006); and McKay Coppins, "God's Plan for Mike Pence," *The Atlantic*, January 2018, www.theatlantic.com/magazine/archive /2018/01/gods-plan-for-mike-pence/546569/.

2. For Pence's legislative record, see "Before Mike Pence was Donald Trump's Running Mate, He Served in Congress for 12 years," Govtrack.us, July 18, 2016, https://govtrackinsider.com/before-mike-pence-was -donald-trumps-running-mate-he-served-in-congress-for-12-years -72b511b95d9.

3. For the German side of the family, see "Descendants of Michael Pence (1738–1799)," Neal's Genealogy Page, May 2016, http://neals genealogy.awardspace.info/pence.htm.

4. For the Irish side of Pence's family, see Michael Farry, *Sligo 1914–1921: A Chronicle of Conflict* (Trim, Ireland: Killoran Press, 1992); John P. Brennan, Bureau of Military History, witness statement, https:// wheresmerrill.files.wordpress.com/2014/05/1918-tubbercurry-volunteers .pdf; Sheryl Gay Stolberg, "'I Am an American Because of Him': The Journey of Pence's Grandfather from Ireland," *The New York Times*, March 16, 2017, www.nytimes.com/2017/03/16/us/politics/mike-pence -immigration-grandfather.html.

5. For events surrounding Cawley's journey to America, see "Irish Rebel Chief Dies After Flight," *The New York Times*, April 11, 1923; and P. J. Drudy, *The Irish in America: Emigration, Assimilation, and Impact* (Cambridge, UK: Cambridge University Press, 1985).

6. "Promise to Unmask Ku Klux in Jersey," *The New York Times*, April 11, 1923; "K. of C. Take Charge of Ku Klux Rally," *The New York Times*, April 15, 1923; for the definitive review of Grant, see Jonathan

Spiro, *Defending the Master Race: Conservation, Eugenics, and the Legacy of Madison Grant* (Lebanon, NH: University Press of New England, 2009).

7. For Chicago social activism, see P. David Finks, "Organization Man Saul Alinsky's Legacy Is Alive, Well, and Living in the Neighborhoods," *Chicago Tribune*, May 26, 1985.

8. For Cawley and Irish roots, see Stolberg, "The Journey of Pence's Grandfather."

9. For home demonstration, see Erin Turner Hogue, "To Create a More Contented Family and Community Life: Home Demonstration Work in Arkansas, 1912–1952" (dissertation, University of Arkansas, Fayetteville, 1980).

10. Mike Pence's talk from "Speech Winner Says Get Involved," *Columbus (IN) Herald*, February 11, 1972.

11. For young Pence's civic activism, see "CYO Weed Mowing Program Announced," *The Republic* (Columbus, IN), October 2, 1975.

12. For KKK in Indiana, see Jordan Fischer, "The History of Hate in Indiana: How the Ku Klux Klan Took Over Indiana's Halls of Power," RTV6 ABC, December 8, 2016, www.theindychannel.com/longform/the -ku-klux-klan-ran-indiana-once-could-it-happen-again.

13. For Cummins, see Charles E. Mitchell Retschler, *The Cathedral Builder* (Bloomington, IN: AuthorHouse, 2014).

14. Harry McCawley, "The Mike Pence Story," *The Republic* (Columbus, IN), July 17, 2016, www.therepublic.com/2016/07/14/the-mike-pence -story-from-a-youth-in-columbus-to-candidate-for-vice-president/.

15. K. Conger, *The Christian Right in Republican State Politics* (New York: Macmillan, 2009).

16. Steve Kukolla, "Penance, Redemption Punctuate Life of Mike," *Indiana Business Journal*, January 31, 1994.

17. For Pence on his conversion and devotion to the Christian mission, see "Hooked - Hooked (Interview with Mike Pence, Vice President of USA)," YouTube video, 43:22, posted by "Church by the Glades," March 19, 2017, www.youtube.com/watch?v=fphvH9NvvkA&feature=youtu.be&t=12m24s.

3: Mudslinger

1. Brian Howey, "The Old Hoosier Stemwinder, It's Nearly Extinct," *Star Press* (Muncie, IN), July 27, 1997.

2. John Schorg, "Riding the 2nd District," *The Republic* (Columbus, IN), July 10, 1988.

3. For early campaign events and funding, see Schorg, "Riding"; for interview, see "Interview with Terry and Mary Kohler," *Philanthropy Roundtable*, July 2014, www.philanthropyroundtable.org/topic/excellence _in_philanthropy/interview_with_terry_and_mary_kohler.

4. For primary victory, see "Pence Takes 2nd District GOP Nomination," *Star Press*, May 1988.

5. For Phil Sharp biography, see Steven V. Roberts, "Working Profile; The Life Of A 'Watergate Baby': Philip R. Sharp," *The New York Times*, May 13, 1986, and authors' interview with Sharp.

6. For Pence campaign argument, see John Schorg, "Pence Hopes to Overcome Outsider Role," *The Republic* (Columbus, IN), September 25, 1988.

7. For Hitler Youth, see Jim Jachimiak, "Even Third-Place Candidates Show Good Sense of Humor," *Daily Journal* (Johnson County, IN), November 14, 1988.

8. For candidate roast, see Brian Francisco, "Heat Turned Up Under Politicians," *Muncie Star,* October 29, 1988; Joan D. LaGuardia, "Congressional Candidates Take the Heat at Sigma Delta Chi Roast," *Muncie Evening Press,* October 29, 1988.

9. For Atwater and Pence's 1990 preparation, see Rick Perlstein, "Exclusive: Lee Atwater's Infamous 1981 Interview on the Southern Strategy," *Nation*, November 13, 2012; "Gravely Ill, Atwater Offers Apology," *New York Times*, January 13, 1991; "Pence Looks, Sounds, Like a '90 Candidate," *Daily Journal* (Franklin, IN), November 9, 1989.

10. *Council for National Policy Membership Directory* (Washington, D.C.: Council for National Policy, 2014), www.splcenter.org/sites/default /files/cnp_redacted_final.pdf.

11. Scott Hall, "Man on a Mission," *Daily Journal* (Johnson County, IN), September 30, 2000.

12. For Lynch and 1986 election, see David McCarty, "AIDS Victims Not in Schools, Says State," *Indianapolis News,* April 2, 1986; "Donald Lynch Hopes to Oust Philip Sharp," *Noblesville Daily Ledger,* September 14, 1986.

13. For Miss Gay USA pageant, see "Miss Gay USA Crowned, Protesters Picket Pageant," *Republic* (Columbus, IN), April 11, 1988.

14. For Christian Right status, see David Dawson, "Religious Right Regroups After Losing Mandate," *Journal & Courier* (Lafayette, IN), November 16, 1988.

15. *New Yorker* writer Jane Mayer revealed the construction of the shadow party in *Dark Money: The Hidden History of the Billionaires Behind the Rise of the Radical Right* (New York: Doubleday, 2016).

16. For equality and gay rights issues, see David Corn, "Remember How Dinesh D'Souza Outed Gay Classmates—and Thought It Was Awesome," *Mother Jones,* January 2014; Rebecca Buckman, "Rethinking the Issues," *Indianapolis Star,* February 7, 1993.

17. For Pence's donors, see Stuart Silverstein, "This Is Why Your Prescriptions Cost So Damn Much," *Mother Jones,* October 21, 2016; for Pence health care donors, see "Rep. Mike Pence—Indiana," OpenSecrets .org, www.opensecrets.org/members-of-congress/summary?cid

=N00003765&cycle=CAREER; Drew Doggett, "Following the Money Behind Mike Pence," Sunlight Foundation, July 25, 2016.

18. For Tom Huston, see *Hearings Before the Select Committee to Study Governmental Operations with Respect to Intelligence Activities, Ninety-Forth Congress, First Session: Huston Plan,* vol. 2 (Washington, D.C.: U.S. Government Printing Office, 1976).

19. For Trump quote, see "Sharp Pence Round 2," *Indianapolis Star,* September 9, 1998.

20. For negative campaigning, see Brian Francisco, "Campaign's Nasty Boys Get in Last Jabs," *Star Press* (Muncie, IN), November 4, 1990; for confession, see Craig Fehrman, "Mike Pence's 'Confessions of a Negative Campaigner,'" CraigFehrman.com, January 6, 2013; Mike Pence, "Confessions of a Negative Campaigner," *Indiana Policy Review* (Summer 1991).

4: Limbaugh Light

1. For a full consideration of think tanks, see Jason Stahl, *Right Moves: The Conservative Think Tank in American Political Culture* (Chapel Hill: University of North Carolina Press, 2016); for supply-side economics, see Noah Smith, "Supply-Siders Still Push What Doesn't Work," August 1, 2017, Bloomberg News, www.bloomberg.com/view/articles/2017 -08-01/supply-siders-still-push-what-doesn-t-work.

2. Ronald Ray, "Military Necessity and Homosexuality," *Indiana Policy Review* (August 1993): 9–12; for *Indiana Policy Review* positions, see Rebecca Buckman, "Rethinking the Issues," *Indianapolis Star,* February 7, 1993, and "Some of the Truths Are Not Self-Evident," *Indianapolis Star,* April 25, 1993.

3. For IPR controversies, see Douglas Kmiec, "The Message in Magic's Disclosure," *Indianapolis Star,* November 26, 1991; "Report: Systemic Corruption in State's Public Colleges," *Logansport Pharos-Tribune,* August 24, 1992; William Styring III, "The Bedrock Reason Why George Bush Is in Trouble," *Star Press* (Muncie, IN), August 16, 1992; "The Pink Newsroom," *Indiana Policy Review* (December 1993).

4. For Solomon, see Kristina Marlow, "DJ Says His Views Distorted," *Indianapolis Star,* August 7, 1993; John Krull, "A Joyful Loss in Solomon," *Indianapolis News,* June 10, 1994; John Griffin, "CEO Says Station Personalities Today 'Really Touch a Nerve Here,'" April 16, 2014, http:// radio-indiana.com/20140416/20-years-ago-this-week-emmis-bought-am1070 /; "Rightist Vexes Fellow Jews," *Jewish Post* (Indianapolis), August 11, 1993.

5. For Pence's early media career, see Brian Francisco, "Talk Radio Suits Former Congressional Candidate," *Star Press* (Muncie, IN) March 7, 1994.

6. For Pence on the radio, see Bryan Corbin, "Pence Happy to Ride

Wagon," *Daily Journal* (Johnson County, IN), April 5, 1991; Judy Chatham, "Pence Still a Positive Force," *Daily Journal* (Franklin, IN), September 26, 1995.

7. For Dickson, see "Family First United People of Many Faiths," *Palladium-Item* (Richmond, IN), May 14, 1996.

8. For Pence opposition to AIDS activist speaker, see Ari Rabin Havt, "Mike Pence Lamented AIDS Activists Speaking at GOP Convention," Right Wing Watch, August 31, 2016, www.rightwingwatch.org /post/mike-pence-lamented-aids-activists-speaking-at-gop-convention -published-anti-gay-articles-in-indiana-journal/.

9. For Hood and Solomon, see Scott Hall, "Man on a Mission," *Daily Journal* (Johnson County, IN), September 30, 2000.

10. For Pence column on impeachment, see Mike Pence, "Why the Impeachment Movement Failed," *Indianapolis Star,* February 18, 1999.

11. For Hilbert and Conseco, see Floyd Norris and Alex Berenson, "Conseco Files for Bankruptcy Protection," *New York Times*, December 18, 2002; "Conseco Announced Bankruptcy," *Guardian*, Dec, 18, 2002; Dann Denny and Sam Stall, "Lifestyle of the Rich and Famous: Steve and Tomisue Hilbert in the '90s," *Indianapolis Monthly,* November 1995.

12. For nouthetic counseling, see Institute for Nouthetic Studies, www.nouthetic.org/.

13. For Karen Pence objections to article on gay teens, see "Express on Homosexuality," *Indianapolis Star,* August 11, 1991; "Being Gay Compounds Teens' Problems," *Indianapolis Star,* July 29, 1991.

14. For school voucher issue, see Thomas B. Edsall, "Indiana's Moral Battle on School Vouchers," *Washington Post,* October 19, 1998.

5: Guns, God, and Money

1. For Pence and campaign funding, see Bryan Corbin, "Pence Hopes Third Time is a Charm," *Daily Journal* (Franklin, IN), April 26, 2000; Joel Achenbach, Scott Higham, and Sari Horwitz, "How NRA's True Believers Converted a Marksmanship Group into a Mighty Gun Lobby," *Washington Post,* January 12, 2013; Walter Hickey, "How the Gun Industry Funnels Tens of Millions of Dollars to the NRA," *Business Insider,* January 16, 2013.

2. For guns and the Christian Right, see Kate Shellnutt, "Packing in the Pews: The Connection Between God and Guns, Ministry Leaders More Likely Than Evangelicals Overall to Favor More Gun Control," *Christianity Today,* November 8, 2017.

3. Brian Francisco, "Pence's Path Traces Back to Muncie Exec," *Journal Gazette,* July 16, 2016.

4. For Club for Growth and its candidates, see John Kamman, "No

Secret: Flake Rolls in Club for Growth Cash," *Arizona Republic*, October 8, 2000; Matt Bai, "Fight Club," *New York Times*, August 10, 2003.

5. For right-wing political foundations, see "Medikill: Doing Unto Others," *Mother Jones*, January/February 1996; Daniel Comiskey, "Making Waves," *Indianapolis Monthly*, December 2, 2011.

6. For neophyte Rock, see Martha Carmichael, "Candidate Cares," *Daily Journal* (Johnson County, IN), October 26, 2000.

7. For Pence's positions, see Rick Yencer, "Republicans Talk Trade, Education," *Star Press* (Muncie, IN), April 19, 2000.

8. For Pence and the Christian Right movement generally, see John Clark, "Teens Grill Pence on Tough Issues," *Republic* (Columbus, IN), September 22, 2000; Frances Fitzgerald, *The Evangelicals: The Struggle to Shape America* (New York: Simon and Schuster, 2017); R. Marie Griffith, *Moral Combat* (New York: Basic Books, 2017); Julie Ingersoll, *Building God's Kingdom: Inside the World of Christian Reconstruction* (New York: Oxford University Press, 2015).

9. For science denialism, see "From Atheist to Creationist: Nuclear Chemist Jay Wile," *Uncommon Descent*, July 9, 2012, https://uncommondescent.com/creationism/from-atheist-to-creationist-nuclear-chemist-jay-wile/; Seth Slabaugh, "Global Warming Debate Continues," *Star Press* (Muncie, IN), November 3, 2000.

10. For Christian Right views on science, see *Frontline*, "Timelines—Full Chronology," www.pbs.org/wgbh/pages/frontline/shows/settlement/timelines/fullindex.html; Lisa Vox, "Why Don't Christian Conservatives Worry About Climate Change? God," *Washington Post*, June 2, 2017, www.washingtonpost.com/posteverything/wp/2017/06/02/why-dont-christian-conservatives-worry-about-climate-change-god/?utm_term=.da0537c5009b.

11. For Tobacco Road ad and the Pences, see Boris Ladwig, "Ad Agency, TV Spots Meet the Law," *Republic* (Columbus, IN), July 20, 2000.

12. For early findings on tobacco and cancer, see Charles Cameron, "Lung Cancer and Smoking: What We Really Know," *Atlantic*, January 1956.

13. For Pence orientation to Washington, see "Rep-elect Mike Pence Is Learning the Basics," *Star Press* (Muncie, IN), November 18, 2000.

6: The Frozen Man

1. For Buchanan, see Patrick J. Buchanan, "The Stealth Amnesty of Mike Pence," *Human Events*, June 13, 2006.

2. For data on Indiana's population, see Jerry Conover, Carol Rogers, and Matt Kinghorn, *Indiana's Latino Population: Demographic and Economic*

Perspectives (Bloomington, IN: Kelley School of Business, 2007), www.ibrc .indiana.edu/briefs/Latinos-Apr07.pdf.

3. For post-abortion syndrome, see Nada L. Stotland, "The Myth of the Abortion Trauma Syndrome," *Journal of the American Medical Association* 268, no. 15 (1992): 2078–2079; Mike Pence, "The Case for Life," *Congressional Record* 149, no. 133 (2003): H8942–H8944.

4. For how Pence's declaration follows the so-called Billy Graham rule, see Emma Green, "How Mike Pence's Marriage Became Fodder for the Culture Wars," *Atlantic,* March 30, 2017, www.theatlantic.com/politics /archive/2017/03/pence-wife-billy-graham-rule/521298/.

5. For campaign spending trends, see Michael Scherer, Pratheek Rebala, and Chris Wilson, "The Incredible Rise In Campaign Spending," *Time,* October 23, 2014, http://time.com/3534117/the-incredible-rise-in -campaign-spending/; Paul Steinhauser and Robert Yoon, "Cost to Win Congressional Election Skyrockets," CNN, July 11, 2013, www.cnn.com /2013/07/11/politics/congress-election-costs/index.html; Steven Levitt, "Using Repeat Challengers to Estimate the Effect of Campaign Spending on Election Outcomes in the U.S. House," *Journal of Political Economy* 102, no. 4 (1994): 777–798.

6. Data on campaign funding from Federal Election Commission filings and Center for Public Integrity Opensecrets.org reports.

7. For McConnell, see John Cheves, "Senator's Pet Issue: Money and the Power It Buys," *Lexington Herald-Leader,* October 15, 2006.

8. For full text, see Mike Pence, "Conservatives: Reset Your Course," *Human Events,* January 23, 2004.

9. For more on Weyrich and voter suppression, see Meteor Blades, "Paul Weyrich Wanted Fewer People to Vote for a Simple Reason: When More Do, Republicans Lose," *Daily Kos,* November 5, 2012.

10. For original, see Eric Heubeck, "The Integration of Theory and Practice: A Program for the New Traditionalist Movement," Free Congress Foundation, 2002, http://web.archive.org/web/20010713152425/www .freecongress.org/centers/conservatism/traditionalist.htm#3d.

11. For marriage equality issue, see "Bush Wants Marriage Reserved for Heterosexuals: 'We Ought to Codify That,'" CNN, October 28, 2003, www .cnn.com/2003/ALLPOLITICS/07/30/bush.gay.marriage/index.html; "5. Homosexuality, Gender and Religion," Pew Research, October 5, 2017, www .people-press.org/2017/10/05/5-homosexuality-gender-and-religion/.

12. For Rove and his father, see Andrew Sullivan, "Karl Rove and His Gay Dad," *Atlantic,* March 17, 2010, www.theatlantic.com/daily-dish /archive/2010/03/karl-rove-and-his-gay-dad/189234/.

13. For more on equality and political figures, see Andrew Sullivan, "Reihan Defends Rove," *Atlantic,* October 7, 2009, www.theatlantic.com

/daily-dish/archive/2009/10/reihan-defends-rove/195700/; Marc Ambinder, "Bush Campaign Chief and Former RNC Chair Ken Mehlman: I'm Gay," *Atlantic,* August 25, 2010, www.theatlantic.com/politics/archive/2010/08/bush-campaign-chief-and-former-rnc-chair-ken-mehlman-im-gay/62065/; Joshua Green, "Karl Rove in a Corner," *Atlantic,* November 2004, www.theatlantic.com/magazine/archive/2004/11/karl-rove-in-a-corner/303537/; Christopher Orr, "Karl Rove, Lifelong Gay-Baiter," *New Republic,* October 7, 2009, https://newrepublic.com/article/70046/karl-rove-lifelong-gay-baiter; "Same-Sex Poll Surprises," *Star Press* (Muncie, IN), January 18, 2004.

14. For fund-raising details, see "Congressional Race Off to Slow Start," *Star Press* (Muncie, IN), February 1, 2004.

15. For family firm bankruptcy, see Rick Yencer, "Pence, Family, Had Ties to Failed Company," *Star Press* (Muncie, IN), October 5, 2006.

16. Keith Roysdon, "Woman's Deportation Delayed," *Star Press* (Muncie, IN), November 23, 2004.

17. For Pence reversal under pressure, see Dana Milbank, "Deep Pockets, Small Government and the Man in the Middle," *Washington Post,* September 27, 2005, www.washingtonpost.com/wp-dyn/content/article/2005/09/26/AR2005092601859.html.

18. For quote, see, Maureen Groppe, "Mike Pence in His Own Words," *Indianapolis Star,* July 14, 2016, www.indystar.com/story/news/politics/2016/07/14/pence-his-own-words/87083676/.

19. For Pence leadership aspirations, see Phil Kerpen, "Mike Pence Is the Leader GOP Needs," *Human Events,* November 15, 2006.

20. For Prince, Blackwater, etc., see "Mr. Prince Goes to Washington: Blackwater Founder Testifies Before Congress," *Democracy Now!,* October 3, 2007; Jeremy Scahill, "Mike Pence Will Be the Most Powerful Christian Supremacist in U.S. History," *Intercept,* November 15, 2016, https://theintercept.com/2016/11/15/mike-pence-will-be-the-most-powerful-christian-supremacist-in-us-history/; James Risen, "Before Shooting In Iraq: A Warning On Blackwater," *New York Times,* June 29, 2014, www.nytimes.com/2014/06/30/us/before-shooting-in-iraq-warning-on-blackwater.html; Matt Apuzzo, "Ex-Blackwater Guards Given Long Terms For Killing Iraqis," *New York Times,* April 13, 2015, www.nytimes.com/2015/04/14/us/ex-blackwater-guards-sentenced-to-prison-in-2007-killings-of-iraqi-civilians.html; Richard Lardner and Anne Flaherty, "Blackwater Chief Defends Firm," Associated Press, October 2, 2007.

21. For fellowship program, see "Syllabus," Kennedy Center for Christian Leadership, https://leadership.statesman.org/syllabus; for Christian Right policies and allies, see Cameron Scott, "Why Christians

Hate Gays, Blackwater USA Is Even Creepier Than You Thought, And You Shouldn't Buy Bolthouse Farms," *Mother Jones,* April 6, 2007.

22. For Israel and the Christian Right, see Julie Ingersoll, "Why Trump's Evangelical Supporters Welcome His Move on Jerusalem," Religion News Service, December 7, 2017, https://religionnews.com/2017 /12/07/why-trumps-evangelical-supporters-welcome-his-move-on -jerusalem/; Diana Butler Bass, "For Many Evangelicals, Jerusalem Is About Prophecy, Not Politics," CNN, December 8, 2017, www.cnn.com /2017/12/08/opinions/jerusalem-israel-evangelicals-end-times-butler-bass -opinion/index.html.

23. For the definitive analysis of the Family, see Jeff Sharlet, *The Family, The Secret Fundamentalism at the Heart of American Power* (New York: Harper 2008); for concentric rings, see page 45; see also Peter J. Boyer, "Frat House for Jesus," *New Yorker,* September 13, 2010, www .newyorker.com/magazine/2010/09/13/frat-house-for-jesus; "The Secret Political Reach of 'the Family,'" NPR, November 24, 2009, www.npr.org /templates/story/story.php?storyId=12074651.

24. For Tea Party, see Kate Zernike, "Tea Partiers Bring Cause to Washington," *New York Times,* September 12, 2010, www.nytimes.com /2010/09/13/us/politics/13protest.html.

7: Higher Ambitions

1. For scuffle, see Douglas Walker, "Republican Registration Worker Calls Attack an 'Attention-Getter,'" *Star Press* (Muncie, IN), April 11, 2008.

2. "Pence Remarks at Values Voter Summit in Washington," Christian News Wire, September 17, 2010, www.christiannewswire.com /news/3800515022.html.

3. Sandhya Somashekhar, "Legislative Proposal Puts Abortion Rights Supporters on Alert," *Washington Post,* February 1, 2011, www .washingtonpost.com/national/bills-foes-see-a-test-for-definition-of-rape /2011/01/31/AB3kBbE_story.html; Jane Mayer, "The Danger of President Pence," *New Yorker,* October 23, 2017, www.newyorker.com/magazine /2017/10/23/the-danger-of-president-pence.

4. For gambling proposals, see David Sirota, "Donald Trump VP Mike Pence Pledged To Limit Gaming, Then Helped Casinos After Campaign Donations," *International Business Times,* October 4, 2016.

5. Jed Lewison, "GOP Congressman Vows Shutdown Unless Planned Parenthood Defunded," *Daily Kos,* April 8, 2011, www.dailykos.com /stories/2011/4/8/964824/.

6. Christina Wilkie, "Mike Pence Holds Top-Secret Dinner with GOP Donors," *Huffington Post,* June 15, 2011, www.huffingtonpost.com

/2011/06/15/mike-pence-holds-top-secr_n_877693.html; R. Emmett Tyrrell Jr., "My Hoosier Connections in Cleveland," *American Spectator*, July 22, 2016.

7. Aaron Blake, "Pence For Governor? Indiana Lt. Gov. Becky Skillman Bows Out," *Washington Post*, December 20, 2010, http://voices .washingtonpost.com/thefix/governors/indiana-lt-gov-becky-skillman .html; Steven Ertelt, "Mike Pence Announces 2012 Campaign for Indiana Governor," LifeNews.com, May 5, 2011, www.lifenews.com /2011/05/05/mike-pence-announces-2012-campaign-for-indiana -governor/.

8. "Pence Truck Tour Kicks Off in Brownsburg," *Flyover* (Hendricks County, IN), October 16, 2012; Dan Carden, "Gregg Pummels Pence in Lively Final Debate," *Northwest Times* (Munster, IN), October 25, 2012, www.nwitimes.com/news/local/govt-and-politics/elections/gregg -pummels-pence-in-lively-final-debate/article_97d1fc02-0399-57c9-ac9d -66c896a9433c.html; "Pence, Gregg & Boneham Talk Trucks, Marijuana, Creationism and More at Third Debate," TheStatehouseFile.com, October 25, 2012, http://thestatehousefile.com/pence-gregg-boneham -talk-trucks-marijuana-creationism-and-more-at-third-debate/7780/.

9. "I'm not painting . . ." www.in.gov/governorhistory/mikepence/2530 .htm.

8: Head Hoosier

1. "A Special Day in the Life of Gov. Mike Pence," *Republic* (Columbus, IN), January 15, 2013.

2. "Inaugural Address of Michael R. Pence," IN.gov, January 14, 2013, www.in.gov/governorhistory/mikepence/2571.htm.

3. Kurt Vonnegut, *Cat's Cradle* (New York: Dell, 1998).

4. For a further look at Medicaid in Indiana, see Jake Harper, "Indiana's Claims About Its Medicaid Experiment Don't All Check Out," NPR, February 24, 2017, www.npr.org/sections/health-shots/2017/02/24 /516704082/indiana-s-claims-about-its-medicaid-program-dont-all-check -out.

5. For a further look at Pence measures in the legislature, see Brandon Smith, "Senators Up Marijuana Penalties to Appease the Governor," Indiana Public Media, March 28, 2013; Chris Sikich, "Americans for Prosperity Says It's Focusing More Attention on State Governments," *Indianapolis Star*, March 7, 2013.

6. Dan Carden, "Pence Claims Tax Cut Victory," *Northwest Times* (Munster, IN), April 29, 2013, www.nwitimes.com/news/local/govt-and -politics/pence-claims-tax-cut-victory/article_9666c555-2344-5966-86f7 -4d732a1f6a59.html.

7. Mary Beth Schneider, "What do Hoosiers Know?," *Indianapolis Star,* April 22, 2013.

8. Ann DeLaney, interview with the authors, January 21, 2018.

9. For Obama's windbreaker, see Andrew Rosenthal, "THING; the Presidential Windbreaker," *New York Times,* October 25, 1992; for Pence's gear, see Katha Pollitt, "Mike Pence Might Be Even Worse for Women Than Donald Trump Is," *Nation,* July 21, 2016, www.thenation.com/article /trumps-vice-presidential-pick-might-be-even-worse-for-women-than-he-is/.

10. For more on Pence and the Koch Brothers, see Kenneth P. Vogel and Maggie Haberman, "Mike Pence's Koch Advantage," *Politico,* August 28, 2014, www.politico.com/story/2014/08/mike-pence-koch-brothers-2016 -election-110408; J. T. Stapleton, "Names in the News: Mike Pence," FollowTheMoney.org, July 21, 2016, www.followthemoney.org/research /institute-reports/names-in-the-news-mike-pence.

11. Chelsea Schneider and Tony Cook, "Indiana Governor's Top Donors Revealed," *Governing,* August 31, 2015, www.governing.com /topics/politics/whos-paying-pences-travel-tab.html.

12. Brian Howey, "For Indiana Republicans It's Tax Cut Showtime," *Northwest Times* (Munster, IN), March 23, 2014.

13. John Krull, interview with the authors, February 5, 2018.

14. Jonathan Chait, "Mike Pence Shoulder Fetish Update," *New York Magazine,* May 14, 2018, http://nymag.com/daily/intelligencer/2018/05 /mike-pence-shoulder-fetish-update.html?ref=gazelle.popsugar.com.

15. David Graham, "*Pravda* on the Plains: Indiana's New Propaganda Machine," *Atlantic,* January 27, 2015, www.theatlantic.com/politics/archive /2015/01/Indiana-Governor-Mike-Pence-to-Start-State-Sponsored-News -Service-Just-IN/384867/.

16. Mark Dynarski, *On Negative Effects of Vouchers* (Washington, D.C.: Brookings Institution, 2016).

17. Mike Pence, "A Word from Gov. Mike Pence on Education," *Nuvo,* November 14, 2013, www.nuvo.net/voices/guest_voices/a-word -from-gov-mike-pence-on-education/article_0d52f2a7-6804-5130-aa3c -b22e0287bd3b.html.

18. Shadee Ashtari, "Right Wing Group's Extreme Anti-Gay History Revealed In New Document," *Huffington Post,* December 5, 2013, www .huffingtonpost.com/2013/12/05/alec-anti-gay-documents_n_4386318 .html.

19. Julie Underwood, "ALEC Exposed: Starving Public Schools," *Nation,* July 12, 2011, www.thenation.com/article/alec-exposed-starving -public-schools/.

20. For more background on ALEC and Pence, see Steven Yaccino, "Tensions Rise as Indiana Schools Chief and Governor Clash Over New

Agency," *New York Times*, December 8, 2013, www.nytimes.com/2013/12 /09/us/politics/tensions-rise-as-indiana-schools-chief-and-governor-clash -over-new-agency.html; Underwood, "ALEC Exposed"; *Report Card on American Education: Ranking State K-12 Performance, Progress and Reform*, 19th ed. (Arlington, VA: American Legislative Exchange Council, 2014); Valerie Strauss, "How Gov. Mike Pence Worked to Undermine the Will of Indiana's Voters," *Washington Post*, July 15, 2016, www.washingtonpost.com /news/answer-sheet/wp/2016/07/15/how-mike-pence-tried-to-undermine -the-will-of-indianas-voters/?utm_term=.a4cd63b280f7; Eric Bradner, "Pence, Daniels say they stand by Bennett's education changes," *Evansville Courier & Press*, November 7, 2012.

21. For data on education in Indiana, see *A Comparison of State-Funded Pre-K Programs* (Bloomington: University of Indiana, 2017), www .in.gov/sboe/files/CEEP-SBOE-IN%20Pre-K-2-17-2017.pdf.

22. For background on the public partnership, see John B. Goodman and Gary W. Loveman, "Does Privatization Serve the Public Interest?," *Harvard Business Review*, November–December 1991, https://hbr.org/1991 /11/does-privatization-serve-the-public-interest; Sergei Guriev and William Megginson, "Privatization: What Have We Learned?," World Bank, https://siteresources.worldbank.org/INTDECABC2006/Resources /gurievmegginson.PDF; Ted Gregory, Patrick M. O'Connell, and Cecilia Reyes, "The Water Drain," *Chicago Tribune*, December 27, 2017, http:// graphics.chicagotribune.com/news/lake-michigan-drinking-water-rates /privatization.html; Phineas Baxandall, Kari Wohlschlegel, and Tony Dutzik, *Private Roads, Public Costs* (New York: U.S. PIRG Education Fund, 2009); Macquarie Investment Group, "Indiana Toll Road," Power-Point presentation, slide 5; Roger Skurski, report prepared for trial testimony May 15, 2006, in *Bonney et al. v. Indiana Finance Authority et al*, St. Joseph County, Indiana Superior Court.

23. "Governor Pence Announces $260 Million Agreement to Lease State Communications Infrastructure," IN.gov, September 6, 2016, https://calendar.in.gov/site/gov/event/governor-pence-announces-260 -million-agreement-to-lease-state-communications-infrastructure/.

24. "Pence's $260 Million Tower Deal Legacy for Indiana Is Terminated," Wireless Estimator, February 9, 2017, http://wirelessestimator .com/articles/2017/pences-260-million-tower-deal-legacy-for-indiana-is -terminated/.

25. For background on I-69, see Mark Alesia and Kaitlin Lange, "Mike Pence's Infrastructure Mess: What Went Wrong with I-69?," *Indianapolis Star*, June 18, 2017.

26. For coverage of the Keith Cooper Case, see Christy Gutowski, "Chicago-area Man Seeks Historic Pardon in Indiana," *Chicago Tribune*,

May 27, 2015, www.chicagotribune.com/news/ct-keith-cooper-pardon
-met-20150527-story.html; Madeline Buckley, "For Wrongfully Convicted Keith Cooper, an 'Uphill Battle' After Pence Letter," *Indianapolis
Star,* September 21, 2016, www.indystar.com/story/news/politics/2016
/09/21/pence-lawyer-keith-cooper-must-exhaust-court-remedies
/90772348/.

27. For news coverage of the needle exchange, see Megan Twohey,
"Mike Pence's Response to H.I.V. Outbreak: Prayer, Then a Change of
Heart," *New York Times,* August 7, 2016. www.nytimes.com/2016/08/08/us
/politics/mike-pence-needle-exchanges-indiana.html; Maureen Hayden,
"Doctors Fear HIV Epidemic Spreading Beyond Scott County," *News and
Tribune,* April 20, 2015, www.newsandtribune.com/news/doctor-fears
-hiv-epidemic-spreading-beyond-scott-county/article_8707dde2-e7ab-11e4
-85a7-efb5734968c0.html.

28. Will Higgins, "Bakery That Refused to Do Cake for Gay Couple
Closes Its Doors," *The Indianapolis Star,* February 27, 2015, www.usatoday
.com/story/money/business/2015/02/27/anti-gay-marriage-bakery-gone
/24133651/.

29. Curt Smith, *Deicide: How Eliminating The Deity is Destroying
America* (n.p.: CreateSpace Independent Publishing Platform, 2016); Tim
Evans, "Backers Mostly Silent," *Indianapolis Star,* March 28, 2015.

30. Hunter Schwarz, "David Letterman Counts Down the Top 10
Guys Indiana Gov. Mike Pence Looks Like," *Washington Post,* April 1,
2015, www.washingtonpost.com/news/the-fix/wp/2015/04/01/david
-letterman-counts-down-the-top-10-guys-indiana-gov-mike-pence-looks
-like/?utm_term=.71e44c21b727.

31. Transcript and video of Pence-Stephanopoulos interview,
March 29, 2015, *This Week,* ABC, https://abcnews.go.com/ThisWeek
/video/gov-mike-pence-religious-freedom-law-29987447.

32. Dave Bangert, "Pence's 'Yes or No' on Discrimination," *Lafayette
Journal & Courier,* March 30, 2015.

33. Tom LoBianco, "Fallout May Be Boon for Pence," *Indianapolis
Star,* March 30, 2015.

34. Fatima Hussein, "Attorney General Plans to Appeal Federal
Judge's Ruling That Blocks Indiana Abortion Law," *Indianapolis Star,*
September 25, 2017.

35. Dave Mosher and Skye Gould, "How Likely Are Foreign Terrorists to Kill Americans? The Odds May Surprise You," *Business Insider,*
January 31, 2017, www.businessinsider.com/death-risk-statistics-terrorism
-disease-accidents-2017-1.

36. Melanie Garunay, "President Obama Offers a Statement on the
Attacks in Paris," White House Obama Presidency Archives, November 13,

2015, https://obamawhitehouse.archives.gov/blog/2015/11/13/watch
-president-obamas-statement-attacks-paris.

37. Tal Kopan, "Donald Trump: Syrian Refugees a 'Trojan Horse,'"
CNN, November 16, 2015, www.cnn.com/2015/11/16/politics/donald
-trump-syrian-refugees/index.html.

38. Natasha Hall, "Refugees Are Already Vigorously Vetted. I
Know Because I Vetted Them," *Washington Post,* February 1, 2017, www
.washingtonpost.com/posteverything/wp/2017/02/01/refugees-are-already
-vigorously-vetted-i-know-because-i-vetted-them/?utm_term=
.179df18cc730.

39. Juliet Eilperin, "Obama Calls Idea of Screening Syrian Refugees
Based on Religion 'Shameful,' Defends White House Strategy," *Washington
Post,* November 16, 2015, www.washingtonpost.com/news/post-politics/wp
/2015/11/16/obama-calls-idea-of-screening-syrian-refugees-based-on
-religion-shameful-defends-white-house-strategy/?utm_term=
.8073a9669e41.

40. Stephanie Wang, "Pence Stops Syrian Refugee Resettlement in
Indiana," *Indianapolis Star,* November 16, 2015.

41. For details on ACLU suit, see "Victory!: U.S. Court of Appeals
Denies Indiana's Effort to Prevent Resettlement of Syrian Refugee Families,"
ACLU, October 3, 2016, www.aclu.org/news/victory-us-court-appeals
-denies-indianas-effort-prevent-resettlement-syrian-refugee-families.

42. "Statement from the Archbishop Joseph W. Tobin Regarding the
Resettlement of a Family of Refugees from Syria," Archdiocese of Indianapolis, December 8, 2015, www.archindy.org/archbishop/syria-2015.html.

43. Patrick Healy and Michael Barbaro, "First Draft," *New York
Times,* December 7, 2015.

44. Avi Selk, "Pence Once Called Trump's Muslim Ban 'Unconstitutional.' He Now Applauds the Ban on Refugees," *Washington Post,* January 28, 2017, www.washingtonpost.com/news/the-fix/wp/2017/01/28
/mike-pence-once-called-trumps-muslim-ban-unconstitutional-he-just
-applauded-the-order/?utm_term=.fcbea3838d0d.

45. Patricia Montemurri, "Can Cardinal Joe, a Native Detroiter, Rise
to Become 1st American Pope?," *Detroit Free Press,* April 1, 2018, www
.freep.com/story/news/2018/04/01/can-cardinal-joe-native-detroiter-rise
-become-1st-american-pope/474176002/.

9: When Trump Calls

1. Nolan D. McCaskill, "8 Times Chris Christie Suggested Donald
Trump Shouldn't Be President," *Politico,* February 26, 2016, www.politico
.com/blogs/2016-gop-primary-live-updates-and-results/2016/02/chris
-christie-endorsement-donald-trump-shouldnt-be-president-219864.

2. "Ted Cruz: I'm Proud to Stand with Gov. Mike Pence!," *Right Scoop,* March 5, 2017, http://therightscoop.com/ted-cruz-im-proud-to-stand-with -gov-mike-pence/.

3. Ian Schwartz, "Pence Endorses Cruz," *Real Clear Politics,* April 29, 2016, www.realclearpolitics.com/video/2016/04/29/pence_endorses_cruz_i _commend_donald_trump_for_being_voice_of_frustration_grateful_for _carrier_stance.html.

4. Isaac Arnsdorf, "Could the Trump VP Vetting Process Go Off the Rails?," *Politico,* July 14, 2016, www.politico.com/story/2016/07/donald -trump-vp-vetting-culvahouse-225363.

5. Chris Cillizza, "Donald Trump Will Make His Mind Up on VP Pick in 'Next Three to Four Days,'" *Washington Post,* July 11, 2016, www .washingtonpost.com/news/the-fix/wp/2016/07/11/donald-trump-will -make-his-mind-up-on-vp-pick-in-next-three-to-four-days/?utm_ term=.f1735d9aee82.

6. "Chris Christie Introduces Donald Trump In Virginia Beach Va 7/11/16," YouTube video, 7:42, posted by "LesGrossman News," June 11, 2016, www.youtube.com/watch?v=vSoNE0HeIhQ.

7. Brian Eason, Chelsea Schneider, Tony Cook, and Jill Disis, "Will Trump Pick Mike Pence for V.P.? 'Who the Hell Knows?' Trump Says," *Indianapolis Star,* July 12, 2016, www.indystar.com/story/news/politics /2016/07/12/live-donald-trump-vp-mike-pence-central-indiana-today /86993012/.

8. John Nichols, "Manafort Monday Turns into a Very Bad Day for Trump—and Mike Pence," *Nation,* October 30, 2016, www.thenation.com /article/manafort-monday-turns-into-a-very-bad-day-for-trump-and-mike -pence/; Jacqueline Alemany, "Donald Trump Offered Chris Christie Vice President Role Before Mike Pence, Sources Say," CBS News, October 30, 2016, www.cbsnews.com/news/donald-trump-offered-chris-christie-vice -president-role-before-mike-pence/.

9. Transcript of Pence statement, CNN, July 14, 2016, http://edition .cnn.com/TRANSCRIPTS/1607/14/es.03.html.

10. "Mike Pence Praises Ted Cruz Backing of Trump at Faith & Freedom Rally (9-24-16)," YouTube video, 44:57, posted by "Live Satellite News," September 24, 2016, www.youtube.com/watch?v=-am0Fhglug8.

11. "Presidential Candidate Donald Trump Vice Presidential Selection Introduction," C-SPAN video, 49:03, July 16, 2016, www.c-span .org/video/?412804-1/donald-trump-announces-governor-mike-pence -running-mate.

12. "Chris Christie Reacts to Losing Vice Presidential Nomination," YouTube video, 0:42, posted by "NJ.com," July 17, 2016, www.youtube.com /watch?v=kwhxzxkUYFg.

13. "Coll: U.S. Needs Diplomacy to Complement Military in Afghanistan," *Rachel Maddow Show*, MSNBC, February 5, 2018, www.msnbc.com/rachel-maddow/watch/coll-u-s-needs-diplomacy-to-complement-military-in-afghanistan-1154504771792?playlist=associated.

14. Tom LoBianco, "Former intel chief says WH worried over re-elect 'narrative,'" CNN, December 2, 2015, www.cnn.com/2015/12/01/politics/michael-flynn-obama-isis/.

15. "Top Trump Adviser Defends Payment for Russian Speaking Engagement," Yahoo News, July 18, 2016, www.yahoo.com/news/trump-supporter-defends-payment-russian-175611942.html?soc_src=mail&soc_trk=ma.

16. Andrew Kaczynski, "Michael Flynn in August: Islamism a 'Vicious Cancer' in Body of all Muslims That 'Has to Be Excised,'" CNN, November 22, 2016, www.cnn.com/2016/11/22/politics/kfile-michael-flynn-august-speech/index.html.

17. Blade Staff, "VP Candidate Pence Gives Campaign Speech in Rossford," *Toledo Blade*, October 7, 2016, www.toledoblade.com/Politics/2016/10/07/Vice-presidential-candidate-Mike-Pence-makes-campaign-appearance-in-Rossford.html.

18. Daniel Victor, "'Access Hollywood' Reminds Trump: 'The Tape Is Very Real,'" *New York Times*, November 28, 2017, www.nytimes.com/2017/11/28/us/politics/donald-trump-tape.html; Ryan Sit, "Mike Pence's Wife Thinks Donald Trump Is 'Reprehensible' And 'Totally Vile,'" *Newsweek*, December 5, 2017, www.newsweek.com/mike-pence-karen-pence-vile-reprehensible-donald-trump-access-hollywood-sexual-735181.

19. Pence interview with "CBS This Morning," October 14, 2016. www.youtube.com/watch?v=mjGN7orhc8c&feature=youtu.be&t=3m49s.

20. Authors' interview with Phil Sharp.

10: Russians, What Russians?

1. John Wagner, "Chris Christie: 'I Wouldn't Let General Flynn in the White House, Let Alone Give Him a Job,'" *Washington Post*, May 22, 2017, www.washingtonpost.com/news/post-politics/wp/2017/05/22/chris-christie-i-wouldnt-let-general-flynn-in-the-white-house-let-alone-give-him-a-job/?utm_term=.07ab442103e7.

2. Eli Watkins, "Chris Christie: 'I Warned Trump About Flynn,'" CNN, May 22, 2017, www.cnn.com/2017/05/22/politics/chris-christie-mike-flynn/index.html.

3. Dan Priest, "Trump Adviser Michael T. Flynn on His Dinner with Putin and Why Russia Today Is Just Like CNN," *Washington Post*, August 15, 2016, www.washingtonpost.com/news/checkpoint/wp/2016/08

/15/trump-adviser-michael-t-flynn-on-his-dinner-with-putin-and-why
-russia-today-is-just-like-cnn/?utm_term=.9fd8c585ed92.

4. Tamara Keith, "Mike Pence Says Trump Never Said That. Well, He Did," NPR, October 5, 2016, www.npr.org/2016/10/05/496691508 /mike-pence-says-trump-never-said-that-well-he-did.

5. Matthew Haag and Maya Salam, "Gunman in 'Pizzagate' Shooting Is Sentenced to 4 Years in Prison," *New York Times*, June 22, 2017, www .nytimes.com/2017/06/22/us/pizzagate-attack-sentence.html.

6. Michael McFaul, "Let's Get the Facts Right on Foreign Involvement in Our Elections," *Washington Post*, December 10, 2016, www .washingtonpost.com/news/global-opinions/wp/2016/12/10/lets-get-the -facts-right-on-foreign-involvement-in-our-elections/?utm_term= .54cf357b2fe1.

7. Russell Berman, "A President Without an Administration," *Atlantic*, January 3, 2017, www.theatlantic.com/politics/archive/2017/01 /trump-transition-cabinet-behind-schedule/511928/.

8. "Statement by the President on Actions in Response to Russian Malicious Cyber Activity and Harassment," White House Obama Presidency Archives, December 29, 2016, https://obamawhitehouse.archives .gov/the-press-office/2016/12/29/statement-president-actions-response -russian-malicious-cyber-activity.

9. Matthew Nussbaum, "Pence Is Half a World Away from D.C. Drama," *Politico*, January 20, 2018, www.politico.com/story/2018/01/20 /government-shutdown-mike-pence-middle-east-353310.

10. Michael S. Schmidt, Sharon LaFraniere, and Scott Shane, "Emails Dispute White House Claims That Flynn Acted Independently on Russia," *New York Times*, December 2, 2017, www.nytimes.com/2017/12/02 /us/russia-mcfarland-flynn-trump-emails.html.

11. James Comey, *A Higher Loyalty: Truth, Lies, and Leadership* (New York: Flatiron Books, 2018).

12. "Statement by the President of Russia," President of Russia website, December 30, 2016, http://en.kremlin.ru/events/president/news/53678.

13. Peter Eisner and Knut Royce, *The Italian Letter: The Forgery That Started the Iraq War* (New York: Rodale, 2014), Kindle edition.

14. Alan He, "Mike Pence Walks a Fine Line on Donald Trump's Tweets Regarding Hacking," CBS News, January 5, 2017, www.cbsnews .com/news/mike-pence-walks-a-fine-line-on-donald-trumps-tweets -regarding-hacking.

15. James Clapper, *Facts and Fears: Hard Truths from a Life in Intelligence* (New York: Viking Press, 2018).

16. Ibid., p. 395. After the fact and once retired from government, however, Clapper said the Russians did have a very particular impact.

17. Tony Cook, Chelsea Schneider, and Kaitlin Lange, "With Pence Gone, Fellow Republicans Undo His Work in Indiana," *Indianapolis Star,* February 9, 2017.

18. David Ignatius, "Why Did Obama Dawdle on Russia's Hacking?," *Washington Post,* January 12, 2017, www.washingtonpost.com/opinions /why-did-obama-dawdle-on-russias-hacking/2017/01/12/75f878a0-d90c -11e6-9a36-1d296534b31e_story.html?utm_term=.cbbb29ec89bd.

19. The U.S. Intelligence Community reported that it had not been tasked and could not assess the success of Russian efforts to undermine the election result. See the intelligence findings *"Assessing Russian Activities and Intentions in Recent US Elections"* (Washington, D.C.: Office of the Director of National Intelligence, 2017), www.dni.gov/files/documents/ICA_2017_01.pdf.

20. Greg Miller, Adam Entous, and Ellen Nakashima, "National Security Adviser Flynn Discussed Sanctions with Russian Ambassador, Despite Denials, Officials Say," *Washington Post,* February 9, 2017, www .washingtonpost.com/world/national-security/national-security-adviser -flynn-discussed-sanctions-with-russian-ambassador-despite-denials -officials-say/2017/02/09/f85b29d6-ee11-11e6-b4ff-ac2cf509efe5_story .html?utm_term=.8a2705a09714.

21. For details on transition funding, see Travis Lewis, GSA, letter to Peter Smith, Center for Public Integrity, January 16, 2018, www.documentcloud .org/documents/4361895-Center-for-Pub-Integrity-Statement.html.

22. The Park County, Wyoming, school district near Yellowstone National Park that DeVos referred to did finally vote in 2018 to allow teachers to carry guns, not against grizzlies, but to protect against human intruders, whether the move was a good idea or not. Mead Gruver, "Wyoming District Allows Armed Staff in Area Cited by DeVos," Associated Press, April 18, 2018, https://apnews.com/cdbdb18dd45994ad2b 8175f47dbc50a32/Wyoming-district-allows-armed-staff-in-area-cited-by DeVos?utm_campaign=SocialFlow&utm_source=Twitter&utm_ medium=APWestRegion.

11: Shadow President

1. Justin Levitt, "A comprehensive investigation of voter imperson-ation finds 31 credible incidents out of one billion ballots cast," *Washington Post,* August 6, 2014. For perspective on Republican voter fraud claims, see Matt Dunlap, "I Was on Trump's Voter Fraud Commission. Its Demise Was Inevitable," *Washington Post,* January 7, 2018, www.washingtonpost .com/opinions/i-was-on-trumps-voter-fraud-commission-its-demise-was -inevitable/2018/01/07/b5c1bec8-f261-11e7-97bf-bba379b809ab_story .html?utm_term=.768de6c837af; "PA GOP leader admits Voter ID is for Democratic vote suppression," *Rachel Maddow Show,* MSNBC, July 18,

2013, www.msnbc.com/rachel-maddow-show/watch/pa-gop-leader-admits
-voter-id-is-for-democratic-vote-suppression-37641795643.

2. On the Indiana Voter Registration project, Craig Veroga, interview
with the authors, May 31, 2018; Vanessa Williams, "Indiana Voter
Registration Group, Employees Charged with Falsifying Applications,"
Washington Post, June 9, 2017, www.washingtonpost.com/news/post-nation
/wp/2017/06/09/indiana-voter-registration-group-employees-charged-with
-falsifying-applications/.

3. Christopher Ingraham, "Federal Judge Upholds Fine Against Kris
Kobach for 'Pattern' of 'Misleading the Court' in Voter-ID Cases,"
Washington Post, July 26, 2017, www.washingtonpost.com/news/wonk/wp
/2017/07/26/federal-judge-upholds-fine-against-kris-kobach-for-pattern-of
-misleading-the-court-in-voter-id-cases/.

4. Pam Fessler, "Trump's Voting Commission Embroiled in New
Controversy Ahead of Next Meeting," NPR, September 12, 2017, www
.npr.org/2017/09/12/550253168/trump-s-voting-commission-embroiled-in
-new-controversy-ahead-of-next-meeting.

5. Philip Bump, "There Have Been Just Four Documented Cases of
Voter Fraud in the 2016 Election," *Washington Post,* December 1, 2016,
www.washingtonpost.com/news/the-fix/wp/2016/12/01/0-000002-percent
-of-all-the-ballots-cast-in-the-2016-election-were-fraudulent/.

6. "Full Transcript of VP Mike Pence's Historic Speech to March for
Life," *LifeSite,* January 27, 2017, www.lifesitenews.com/news/vp-mike-pence
-full-transcript-2017-march-for-life-address.

7. Nick Visser, "Mike Pence's Press Secretary Won't Say If His Boss
Met with Russians," *Huffington Post,* July 13, 2017, www.huffingtonpost.com
/entry/mike-pence-marc-lotter-fox-news-no-answer_us
_5966f931e4b0a8d46d12100b.

8. Joel K. Goldstein, "Why Pence's One-Sided Bromance Is Dangerous," December 23, 2017, CNN, www.cnn.com/2017/12/22/opinions
/vice-president-sycophant-pence-trump-goldstein-opinion/index.html.

9. Kathryn Watson, "Pence Statement: Accusations Against Roy
Moore 'Very Disturbing,'" CBS News, November 9, 2017, www.cbsnews
.com/news/mike-pence-roy-moore-allegations-disqualify-anyone-from
-office/.

12: Good Cop / Crazy Cop

1. For Pence's remarks on Israel, see "Remarks by the Vice President
at In Defense of Christian Solidarity Dinner," White House, October 25,
2017, www.whitehouse.gov/briefings-statements/remarks-vice-president
-defense-christians-solidarity-dinner/.

2. Dennis C. Sasso, "Indiana Jews Have Long Been Repelled by Mike

Pence's anti-LGBTQ, Anti-Immigrant, Anti-Choice Stances," *Haaretz,* August 6, 2016, www.haaretz.com/world-news/indiana-jews-know-pence-s-restrictive-stances-all-too-well-1.5419617.

3. Gabriel Sherman, "Hollinger Hell: Jerusalem Post Suit Filed Here," *Observer,* September 19, 2005, http://observer.com/2005/09/hollinger-hell-ijerusalem-posti-suit-filed-here/. Following his dismissal, Rose filed a defamation suit that was later dismissed. Ben Sales, "Four things to know about Bret Stephens, the latest Jewish Grey Lady columnist," https://jewishchronicle.timesofisrael.com/four-things-to-know-about-bret-stephens-the-latest-jewish-grey-lady-columnist/. Rose has defended his tenure during the time the paper faced financial difficulties, claiming, "That paper wouldn't exist today if we hadn't done something." Daniel S. Comiskey, "Making Waves," *Indianapolis Monthly,* Dec. 2, 2011, www.indianapolismonthly.com/features/making-waves/

4. Jeff Mason, "Pence Tells Egypt's Sisi That U.S. Would Back Two-State Solution," Reuters, January 20, 2018, www.reuters.com/article/us-usa-egypt/pence-tells-egypts-sisi-that-u-s-would-back-two-state-solution-idUSKBN1F90YG.

5. Udi Shaham and Tovah Lazaroff, "Pence Arrives After Saying U.S. Won't Let Iran Dominate Mideast," *Jerusalem Post,* January 21, 2018, www.jpost.com/Israel-News/US-Vice-President-Pence-arrives-in-Israel-in-third-stop-of-Middle-East-visit-539378.

6. Ibid.

7. Amir Tibon, "VP Pence to Speak at Knesset, Visit Western Wall During Upcoming Visit to Israel," *Haaretz,* January 22, 2018, www.haaretz.com/israel-news/pence-to-meet-netanyahu-speak-at-knesset-amid-palestinian-anger-1.5750103.

8. "Karen Pence to i24NEWS: 'It's Moving to Be in Israel, Where Jesus Walked,'" i24News, January 22, 2018, www.i24news.tv/en/news/international/americas/165788-180122-karen-pence-to-i24news-it-s-moving-to-be-in-israel-where-jesus-walked.

9. Shany Littman, "Citing 'Dictatorship,' Israeli Artist Wants His Work Removed from the Knesset," *Haaretz,* June 15, 2016, www.haaretz.com/israel-news/israeli-artist-wants-his-work-removed-from-the-knesset-1.5396610.

10. For Pence's full speech in the Knesset, see "Vice President Pence Address to the Israeli Knesset," C-SPAN video, 32:06, January 22, 2018, www.c-span.org/video/?440058-1/vice-president-pence-addresses-israeli-knesset.

11. Joshua Blachovsky, interview with the authors, February 8, 2018.

12. Amit Gvaryahu, "Lucky the Jews Didn't Understand What Mike

Pence Was Really Saying," *Haaretz,* January 27, 2018, www.haaretz.com /misc/writers/1.5764783.

13. Michael Virtanen, "Pence Touts Tax Cuts, Slams Manchin in West Virginia," *US News,* January 31, 2018, www.usnews.com/news /politics/articles/2018-01-31/pence-touts-tax-cuts-slams-manchin-in-west -virginia.

14. "The Partisan Divide on Political Values Grows Even Wider," October 5, 2017, Pew Research, www.people-press.org/2017/10/05/the -partisan-divide-on-political-values-grows-even-wider/.

15. Brandon Carter, "Pence Declines to Answer on Why He Seems 'Out of the Loop' on Major News," Hill, February 8, 2018, http://thehill .com/homenews/administration/373017-pence-declines-to-answer -question-on-why-he-seems-out-of-the-loop-on.

13: Not So Humbled

1. Will Higgins, "In Pence's Hometown of Columbus, a Gay Pride Festival Draws a Larger Than Expected Crowd," *Indianapolis Star,* April 14, 2018.

Epilogue: The Man Who Would Be President

1. For crowd size and games, see Eric Bradner, "Conway: Trump White House Offered 'Alternative Facts' on Crowd Size," CNN, January 23, 2017, www.cnn.com/2017/01/22/politics/kellyanne-conway-alternative -facts/index.html; Catherine Lucey, Zeke Miller, and Matthew Penning-ton, "Korea Summit After All? Trump Says 'Everybody Plays Games,'" *Dallas News,* May 25, 2018.

2. For Christian nationalism, see Julie J. Ingersoll, *Building God's Kingdom: Inside the World of Christian Reconstruction* (New York: Oxford University Press, 2015).

3. Rebecca Klein, "Hillsdale College President Larry Arnn Under Fire," *Huffington Post,* August 1, 2013, www.huffingtonpost.com/2013/08 /01/larry-arnn-dark-ones-hillsdale_n_3691839.html; Jonathan Ellis, "Sex, Lies and Suicide," Salon.com, January 19, 2000, www.salon.com/2000/01 /19/hillsdale/.

4. Glen Kessler, "Pence's Claim That 'Religion in America Isn't Receding. It's Just the Opposite,'" *Washington Post,* May 15, 2018, www .washingtonpost.com/news/fact-checker/wp/2018/05/15/pences-claim-that -religion-in-america-isnt-receding-its-just-the-opposite/.

5. Laura Italiano, "Reagan's Daughter: My Dad Would Be 'Appalled' by Trump Presidency," *New York Post,* June 4, 2018, https://nypost.com /2018/06/04/reagans-daughter-my-dad-would-be-appalled-by-trump -presidency/.

6. Burgess Everett, "Pence tries to soothe GOP over South Korea military exercises," June 12, 2018, *Politico,* www.politico.com/story/2018 /06/12/pence-korea-military-exercises-642046.

7. "IMF could be based in Beijing in a decade," Lagarde, Reuters, July 24, 2017. www.reuters.com/article/us-imf-china-lagarde/imf-could-be -based-in-beijing-in-a-decade-lagarde-idUSKBN1A922L.

8. Nina Burleigh, "Does God Believe in Trump? White Evangelicals Are Sticking with Their 'Prince of Lies,'" *Newsweek,* October 5, 2017, www .newsweek.com/2017/10/13/donald-trump-white-evangelicals-support-god -677587.html.

9. Von Lucas Wiegelmann, "Meet the Preacher Who Teaches the Bible to the U.S. Cabinet," *Welt Am Sonntag,* October 29, 2017, www.welt .de/kultur/article170140247/Meet-the-preacher-who-teaches-the-Bible-to -the-US-Cabinet.html; Ralph Drollinger, "The ISIS Threat: The Bible on When War is Justifiable—Part 1," *Capitol Ministries* (blog), July 6, 2015, https://capmin.org/the-isis-threat-the-bible-on-when-war-is-justifiable/; Ralph Drollinger, "How Would You Rate Level of Spiritual Discern- ment?," *Capitol Ministries* (blog), March 24, 2014, https://capmin.org /how-would-you-rate-your-level-of-spiritual-discernment/; Ralph Drollinger, "Institutions: Are You a Tritutionalist or a Pentetutionalist?" *Capitol Ministries* (blog), October 30, 2017, https://capmin.org/are-you-a -tritutionalist-or-a-pentetutionalist.

10. "Summit Church God and Country Rally 2015," YouTube Video, 42:37, filmed June 28, 2015, posted by "Summit Church," July 8, 2015, www.youtube.com/watch?v=sO0opXYM52w.

11. For Southern Baptist Convention speech and immigration, see *Christianity Today* editor's quote, https://twitter.com/kateshellnutt/status /1006943339369959434. Tom Gjelten, "Pence Speech Riles Some As Southern Baptist Moderates Gain Strength," NPR.com June 14, 2018 www.npr.org/2018/06/14/619806451/pence-speech-riles-some-as-southern -baptists-moderates-gain-strength.

12. Joe Marusak, "Franklin Graham rips separating kids and parents at border: 'It's disgraceful.'" *Charlotte Observer,* June 14, 2018.

INDEX